Historic Michigan

Travel Guide
7th Edition

Edited by
Larry J. Wagenaar
and Nancy Feldbush

AN OFFICIAL PUBLICATION OF THE

SPONSORED BY

meijer

The Historical Society of Michigan
Lansing

Published by
The Historical Society of Michigan
5815 Executive Drive
Lansing, MI 48911
hsmichigan.org

Manufactured and printed in the United States of America.

ISBN 978-1-880311-13-4

Contents

Introduction **5**

Acknowledgments. **7**

Western **9**

Central **45**

Eastern **79**

Northern. **137**

Upper Peninsula **163**

Index. **193**

About HSM **205**

Introduction

Michigan's history is closer than it appears!

The Great Lakes State's diverse history is waiting to be explored, and with a *Historic Michigan Travel Guide* in hand, you'll be sure not to miss anything. From the Music House Museum's rare 1922 Theofiel Mortier Dance Organ and Michigan's first lighthouse, the Fort Gratiot Light Station, to the Gilmore Car Museum's varied exhibits and more than 2,000 artifacts at the Ziibiwing Center of Anishinabe Culture & Lifeways, this guide will show you exactly what's unique about our state.

This travel guide features 525 historical museums, sites, and attractions that allow you to experience the state's rich cultural and heritage resources like never before. To really make your trips complete, we added historic inns to this addition. Many entries also include exterior photos to make finding your way even easier, and some show interior images to offer a sneak peek of what you'll find when you arrive.

The *Historic Michigan Travel Guide* is divided by regions. Within each section, sites are listed alphabetically by the city or town name. You may also search for sites and cities using the index in the back of the book. Each entry consists of a detailed listing that provides the pertinent information needed to visit. All our organizations were given the opportunity to refresh their information so that you would have the most up-to-date details to plan your trips. If we did not get a response from a member, we revised the data using websites and other sources. However, we recommend contacting the sites ahead of your visit to avoid any unpleasant surprises.

Each of the following destinations is operated by a member organization of the Historical Society of Michigan, which is a requirement to be included in this publication. The sites also need to have a physical location open to the general public and be considered a "tourist attraction" of historical interest. If your local institution or one you visit is not included, it likely means we are unaware of it or it is not an HSM member.

We hope using this book will take you on new journeys and help you gain a deeper understanding of the Great Lakes State's colorful past.

Acknowledgments

The 7th edition of the *Historic Michigan Travel Guide* could not have come together without the help of our sponsor, staff members, and Board of Trustees. Likewise, we greatly appreciate the hundreds of member organizations that submitted information to the Historical Society of Michigan for inclusion.

I would like to thank my co-editor, Nancy Feldbush, for all the hard work and many hours she put into developing this guide, which serves to promote cultural and heritage tourism in Michigan.

We built on the work of the past three editions to create this new volume, and many improvements were made to the design to make this the best *Historic Michigan Travel Guide* yet. We added photos of buildings or interiors and included QR codes, which can be scanned with a smartphone and will link you to the sites' web presence.

We bolded the headings to make finding information easier and created tabs on the edge of the pages so you will always know which section you're looking at. Plus, this 7th edition has 50 more sites than the 6th edition—including some historical inns!

I would also like to thank Meijer for serving as our sponsor. That help made it possible to do the extensive work of collecting the necessary data and writing, editing, typesetting, and publishing this guide. In addition, Meijer has provided distribution in all of its Michigan stores to make this new edition of the *Historic Michigan Travel Guide* widely available.

A special word of thanks goes to our database team—Amy Bradfield, Todd McBride, and Andie McBride—for dedicating much of their time to researching and compiling the information for this publication. The following staff members also played a part in completing this guide: Christopher Blaker, Chong-Anna Canfora, James Hall, Andrea Lorion, Jordan Stoddard, and Mary Toshach. In addition, I appreciate Melissa Kiesewetter's eagle eye in proofreading this publication.

And a special thanks goes out to Tim Allen for sharing his thoughts about exploring Michigan for the back cover.

All of these efforts have combined to create our best *Historic Michigan Travel Guide* ever. Enjoy!

Larry J. Wagenaar
Executive Director, Historical Society of Michigan
Publisher, HSM Magazines

ADA

Averill Historical Museum of Ada

Location: 7144 Headley St., Ada, MI 49301 **Contact Info:** (616) 676-9346 • adahistoricalsociety@gmail.com • www.adahistoricalsociety.org **Hours:** Fri-Sat 1-4 p.m. Closed Jan-Feb. Also by appointment. **Admission:** Donations accepted. **Accessibility:** Free on-site and street parking. Wheelchair accessible. Tour guides available. Museum store.

Site Info: The Averill Historical Museum of Ada is located in a turn-of-the-century farmhouse and adjacent barn. The museum features exhibits on farmhouse life, the railroad, area schools, and businesses. It also houses a collection of historic Ada photographs. The gift shop features Ada-themed items.

ALLEGAN

Allegan Old Jail Museum

Location: 113 Walnut St., Allegan, MI 49010 **Contact Info:** (269) 673-8292 • oldjailmuseum06@yahoo.com • www.alleganoldjail.com **Hours:** Sat 10 a.m.-4 p.m. Also by appointment. **Admission:** Donations accepted. **Accessibility:** Free on-site and street parking. Not wheelchair accessible. Tour guide available. Museum store.

Site Info: In 1963, the Allegan County Historical Society acquired the former jail, built in 1906, and converted it into the Old Jail Museum with period rooms and displays. Exhibits contain items from the pioneer days up to 1950 and include artifacts from the War of 1812, Civil War, Spanish American War, World War I, and World War II.

John C. Pahl Historical Village

Location: 150 Allegan County Fair Grounds, Allegan, MI 49010 **Contact Info:** (269) 673-8292 • oldjailmuseum06@yahoo.com • www.alleganoldjail.com **Hours:** 2nd full week in Sep (during Allegan County Fair); Also during Michigan Fiber Festival (Aug). **Admission:** Fair gate fee. **Accessibility:** On-site and street parking for a fee. Wheelchair accessible. Self guided. Museum store.

Site Info: The John C. Pahl Historical Village hosts several historical buildings, which were relocated from throughout the county. The buildings include the Jewett School, a one-room schoolhouse that holds classes during the week of the fair; a working blacksmith shop; and an authentically restored 1924 Chesapeake & Ohio wooden caboose.

ALLENDALE
Allendale Historical Museum Complex
Location: 11080 68th Ave., Allendale, MI 49401
Contact Info: (616) 895-9777 • www.facebook.com/AllendaleHistoricalSociety **Hours:** Mar-Nov: 1st Mon monthly 7-9 p.m. **Admission:** $2/individual donation. **Accessibility:** Free parking. Partially wheelchair accessible; main floor only. Tour guides available by appointment only.

 Site Info: The Allendale Historical Society's Museum Complex contains the recently revamped Carriage House Museum and the Knowlton House Museum, both of which depict the history and cultural heritage of Allendale Township and the surrounding area. The Retro Museum, which represents life in the 1940s through 1960s, is also available. The complex is adjacent to the township park.

ALTO
Bowne Township Historical Museum and Bowne Center School

 **Location:** 8240 Alden Nash Ave., Alto, MI 49302 **Contact Info:** (616) 868-6424 • srjohnson4@charter.net • www.bownetwp.org **Hours:** Jun-Sep: 1st Sun monthly 2-4 p.m. Also by appointment. **Admission:** Donations accepted. **Accessibility:** Free on-site parking. Partially wheelchair accessible. Self-guided.

 Site Info: The Bowne Township Historical Museum is home to many historical items that reflect the past history of Bowne Center and Bowne Township. Visitors will see artifacts from the mid-1800s through the 1900s from home to business to military. The Bowne Center School House is filled with old desks, books, and other school artifacts and historical information. The school is located on the southeast corner of 84th Avenue and Alden Nash Road.

BALDWIN
Shrine of the Pines
Location: 8962 S. M37, Baldwin, MI 49304 **Contact Info:** (231) 745-7892 • www.facebook.com/shrineofthepines **Hours:** Mid-May to mid-Oct: Mon-Sat 10 a.m.-6 p.m., Sun 1:30-6 p.m. **Admission:** $5/adult, $4/senior, $2.50/children (6-17), $12.50/family, children under 6 free. **Accessibility:** Tour guide available. Museum store.

Site Info: The Shrine of the Pines is a museum in a hunting lodge that displays furniture made from pine stumps by Raymond W. Overholzer. Overholzer fashioned beds, chairs, chandeliers, and a dining room table made from a 700-pound stump—without using metal fasteners. He finished the projects using broken glass as handmade sandpaper and raw deer hide.

BELMONT

Hyser Rivers Museum

Location: 6440 West River Rd., Belmont, MI 49306 **Contact Info:** (616) 784-7264 • plainfieldhistory@gmail.com • www. facebook.com/Hyser-Rivers-Museum-217048081783452 **Hours:** Apr-Dec: 1st Sun monthly 2-4:30 p.m. Also by appointment. **Admission:** Free. **Accessibility:** Free on-site parking. Partially wheelchair accessible. Tour guide available.

 Site Info: The Hyser Museum is located in the 1852 Greek Revival home of Dr. William Hyser, a pioneer surgeon and Civil War captain. It was moved to its present site in 1976 and opened as a museum in 1984. It displays family living quarters and township artifacts and is one of the last remaining structures of the original Plainfield Village.

BENTON HARBOR

Mary's City of David

Location: 1158 E. Britain Ave., Benton Harbor, MI 49023 **Contact Info:** (269) 925-1601 • info@maryscityofdavid.org • www.maryscityofdavid.org **Hours:** Memorial Day-Labor Day: Sat-Sun 1-5 p.m. **Admission:** $1/individual for museum admission, $4/individual for guided tour at 1:30 p.m. **Accessibility:** Free on-site parking. Wheelchair accessible. Tour guide available Sundays; call ahead for Saturday availability. Museum store.

 Site Info: Mary's City of David, listed on the National Register of Historic Places in 2009, offers a museum and tour. The organization spans 110 years in Michigan and is America's third-oldest practicing Christian community. The site includes 81 structures, 11 of which are available for viewing.

BERRIEN SPRINGS

History Center at Courthouse Square

Location: 313 N. Cass St., Berrien Springs, MI 49103 **Contact Info:** (269) 471-1202 • bcha@berrienhistory.org • www.berrienhistory.org **Hours:** Jan-Mar: Mon-Fri 10 a.m.-5 p.m.; Apr-Dec: Mon-Sat 10 a.m.-5 p.m.

Closed major holidays. **Admission:** Free. Fees for special events.
Accessibility: Free on-site parking. Partially wheelchair
accessible. Self-guided. Museum store.

 Site Info: The History Center is located at historic
Courthouse Square in Berrien Springs and is the
Midwest's oldest-surviving county government
complex. Visitors to the site can self-tour the 1839
Berrien County Courthouse, an 1830 log house, an
1870 sheriff's residence and jail plaza, and a working forge. The
center also holds extensive archival collections accessible to the
public. Tours and programs are available for schools and
community groups.

BLOOMINGDALE

Bloomingdale Depot Museum
Location: 110 N. Van Buren St., Bloomingdale,
MI 49026 **Contact Info:** (269) 521-7880 • www.
bloomingdaleareahistoricalassoc.org **Hours:** Memorial Day-Oct:
Sat 10 a.m.-4 p.m., Sun 1:30-4:30 p.m. Also by appointment.
Admission: Donations accepted. **Accessibility:** On-site
parking. Wheelchair accessible. Tour guides available.

 Site Info: The Bloomingdale Area Historical
Association maintains the village museum on the
Kal Haven Trail, which features photos and
newspaper clippings dating back to the early 1900s
and medical artifacts from the Civil War period.
Also present is a train caboose filled with train memorabilia,
which includes a duplicate of a toy train presented to President
Ronald Reagan by a local company.

BYRON CENTER

Byron Area Historical Museum
Location: 2506 Prescott St. SW, Byron Center, MI 49315
Contact Info: (616) 878-0888 • byronmuseum@sbcglobal.net
• www.commoncorners.com/kent/kent_byron_bchs.htm **Hours:**
Tue 9 a.m.-2 p.m. Also by appointment. **Admission:** Free.
Accessibility: Free on-site parking. Wheelchair accessible. Tour
guide available by appointment.

 Site Info: Byron Area Historical Museum is located
in the historic 1876 Town Hall, a two-story white
brick building in the center of Byron Township.
The museum features multiple exhibits. The main
floor includes the old post office, a doctor's office,
and a store. Displays on farming reflect the rich rural history of all
36 square miles of the township. A collection of pictures, quilts,
and farm implements are also available in the museum.

CALEDONIA

Caledonia Historical Museum
Location: 6260 92nd St. SE, Caledonia, MI 49316
Contact Info: www.angelfire.com/mi/CaledoniaHistory •

(616) 260-0052 **Hours:** By appointment. **Admission:** Free. **Accessibility:** On-site parking. Wheelchair accessible. Tour guides available by appointment.

 Site Info: The Caledonia Historical Museum focuses on local area history and is home to 1,500 photos, microfilm of early newspapers, early county histories, a genealogy database of family names, and other items.

CANNONSBURG

Cannon Township Historical Museum

 **Location:** 8045 Cannonsburg Rd., Cannonsburg, MI 49317 **Contact Info:** (616) 874-6865 **Hours:** May-Sep: Sun 2-4 p.m. Also by appointment. **Admission:** Free. **Accessibility:** Free nearby parking. Wheelchair accessible. Self-guided.

Site Info: The museum houses Cannon Township artifacts, including school and family photographs. Visitors can also view machinery, furniture, and household goods. There is also a local genealogy collection.

CASSOPOLIS

Cass County Pioneer Log Cabin Museum

 **Location:** 400 South Broadway, Cassopolis, MI 49031 **Contact Info:** (269) 445-3759 • mpioneer1@aol.com • www.facebook.com/pioneerlogcabinmuseum **Hours:** Memorial Day-Labor Day: Fri-Sun 12-4:30 p.m. **Admission:** Donations accepted. **Accessibility:** Free on-site parking. Not wheelchair accessible. Tour guide available.

 Site Info: The pioneer log cabin was built in 1923 from logs donated by decedents of early pioneers. The museum contains old tools, dollhouses, a bird collection, household items, a Civil War collection, and many other items related to the early history of Cass County. It is located in Shoestring Park, which overlooks Stone Lake.

Edward Lowe Information and Legacy Center

Location: 58220 Decatur Rd., Cassopolis, MI 49031 **Contact Info:** (800) 232-5693 • info@lowe.org • www.edwardlowe.org **Hours:** Mon-Fri 8 a.m.-5 p.m. **Admission:** Free. **Accessibility:** Free on-site parking. Wheelchair accessible. Self-guided. Tours held Wed (Apr-Oct) at 2 p.m.; call for reservations.

 Site Info: The Edward Lowe Information and Legacy Center was founded by Edward Lowe, who invented Kitty Litter in 1947. The information center features an exhibit of Lowe's business ventures and the Edward Lowe Foundation and includes videos, print materials, a live web feed, and photos and artifacts dating back to the 1940s. The historical collections department maintains an archival collection of materials about Edward and Darlene Lowe and their foundation.

CEDAR SPRINGS

Cedar Springs Museum

Location: 60 Cedar St., Cedar Springs, MI 49319 **Contact Info:** (616) 696-3335 • cedarspringsmuseum@gmail.com • www.cedarspringsmuseum.org **Hours:** Wed 10 a.m.-5 p.m. Also by appointment. **Admission:** Free. **Accessibility:** Wheelchair accessible. Self-guided. Museum store.

Site Info: The Cedar Springs Museum features an old general store and displays on Native Americans, lumbering, farming, and railroads. The Payne School was moved to Morley Park in 1971 and has since been restored as a one-room school. A stump puller, used to remove stumps in the area so land could be farmed, is also featured.

CLARKSVILLE

Farmall Acres Farm Museum

Location: 170 McCormick St., Clarksville, MI 48815 **Contact Info:** (616) 868-6639 • ihgranny@sbcglobal.net **Hours:** May-Aug: 2nd and 4th Sun 1-5 p.m. **Admission:** $5/individual donation. Children 13 and under free. **Accessibility:** Free on-site parking. Wheelchair accessible. Tour guide available.

Site Info: Farmall Acres Farm Museum features Farmall tractors; Cub Cadet lawn mowers; 17 show boxes filled with various types of memorabilia; farm equipment on steel wheels; and displays of saws, hooks, scales, and other tools. Additionally, exhibits that celebrate the life and workings of the American farmer are included.

COLOMA

North Berrien Historical Society and Museum

Location: 300 Coloma Ave., Coloma, MI 49038 **Contact Info:** (269) 468-3330 • info@northberrienhistory.org • www.northberrienhistory.org **Hours:** May-Sep: Tue-Sat 10 a.m.-4 p.m.; Oct-Apr: Tue-Fri 10 a.m.-4 p.m. Also by appointment. **Admission:** Free. **Accessibility:** Free on-site parking. Wheelchair accessible. Self-guided. Call for groups.

Site Info: North Berrien Historical Society opened its museum in 1992. The museum focuses on the local history of northern Berrien County and includes five buildings used for exhibits and programs. The main gallery features Native Americans, lake resorts, rural schools, Lake Michigan shipwrecks, daily life, and businesses, such as the Watervliet Paper Mill. The Nichols-Beverly Barn presents lumbering and agricultural history with the permanent exhibit "Moving From Forest to Fruit Belt."

COLON

Community Historical Museum of Colon

Location: 219 N. Blackstone Ave., Colon, MI 49040 **Contact Info:** (269) 432-3804 • www.colonmi.com/historical.html **Hours:** Jun-Aug: Tue, Thu 2-4:30 p.m. Also by appointment. **Admission:** Donations accepted. **Accessibility:** Parking available in the Methodist Church parking lot. Wheelchair accessible. Tour guide available.

Site Info: The Community Historical Museum of Colon features area artifacts pertaining to medicine, education, Native Americans, pioneers, a general store, toys, military, and more. Since Colon is the "Magic Capital of the World," the museum features a magic collection and a print shop. Also on-site is the Farrard/Hoekzema Annex.

COMSTOCK PARK

Alpine Township Historical Museum

Location: 2408 Seven Mile Rd. NW, Comstock Park, MI 49321 **Contact Info:** (616) 784-1262 • b.alt@alpinetwp.org • www.alpinetwp.org **Hours:** By appointment. **Admission:** Free. **Accessibility:** Public parking. Wheelchair accessible. Free tour guides available.

Site Info: The Alpine Township Historical Museum is located in the 1860 township hall, which was restored in 1987 and is now listed in the State Register of Historic Places. Collections include photo galleries of early settlers, 12 one-room schools, and more than 300 township veterans. Visitors can also view furniture and artifacts of pioneer families and an extensive file of township family histories and obituaries.

COOPERSVILLE

Coopersville Area Historical Society Museum

Location: 363 Main St., Coopersville, MI 49404 **Contact Info:** (616) 997-7240 • historicalsoc@allcom.net • www.coopersvillemuseum.com **Hours:** Tue 2-5:30 p.m., Wed 10 a.m.-2 p.m., Fri 1-4 p.m., Sat 10 a.m.-4 p.m. **Admission:** Donations accepted. **Accessibility:** Free on-site and street parking. Wheelchair accessible. Call for tours. Museum store.

Site Info: The museum's main red-brick building, which was built in 1902 as a depot and substation for one of West Michigan's electric interurban railways, houses extensive railroad displays, along with early business, household, and military exhibits. The museum also houses memorabilia on Coopersville rock-and-roll star Del Shannon. The early settlers building commemorates early settlement of the area with a sawmill, model railroad, tools, logging items, and schoolroom.

DOUGLAS

Old School House History Center and Garden

Location: 130 Center St., Douglas, MI 49406 **Contact Info:** (269) 857-5751 • info@sdhistoricalsociety.org • www. sdhistoricalsociety.org **Hours:** Archives: Daily Mon 1-4 p.m. Exhibits: See website. Garden and Boathouse: Apr-Oct: 10 a.m.-4 p.m. **Admission:** Free. Donations accepted. **Accessibility:** Free on-site parking. Not wheelchair accessible. Self-guided. Museum store.

Site Info: The Old School House History Center is the Saugatuck-Douglas Historical Society's main presentation site. It is also home to the society's extensive archives and collections. The grounds of the Old School House History Center contain the back-in-time garden, with several learning stations and pathways. The Francis Surf Boat exhibit is open from April to October within the garden and showcases the only restored surf boat of its type from the U.S. Lifesaving Service.

DOWAGIAC

Dowagiac Area History Museum

Location: 201 E. Division St., Dowagiac, MI 49047 **Contact Info:** (269) 783-2560 • museum@dowagiac. org • www.dowagiacmuseum.info **Hours:** Tue-Fri 10 a.m.-5 p.m., Sat 10 a.m.-2 p.m. **Admission:** Free. **Accessibility:** Free on-site parking. Wheelchair accessible. Self-guided.

Site Info: Located near historic downtown Dowagiac, the Dowagiac Area History Museum features 6,000 square feet of history in an updated facility. Highlights include exhibits on the Round Oak Stove Company, Heddon fishing tackle, the "First Spaceman" Captain Iven C. Kincheloe, the Underground Railroad, and other local history. A temporary exhibit gallery rotates displays several times per year.

Heddon Museum

Location: 414 West St., Dowagiac, MI 49047 **Contact Info:** (269) 782-4068 • heddonmuseum@lyonsindustries.com • www.heddonmuseum.org **Hours:** Tue 6:30-8:30 p.m., last Sun monthly 1:30-4 p.m. Also by appointment. **Admission:** Free. Donations accepted. **Accessibility:** Free on-site and street parking. Wheelchair accessible. Tour guides available.

Site Info: The museum is located in the former Heddon manufacturing facilities in Dowagiac. On display are more than 140 reels, 150 Heddon rods, and 1,000 Heddon lures, including an original James Heddon frog, one of the most sought after of all collector lures. Other highlights include the Heddon truck, a Heddon boat, and a second room showing some classic cars and car-related memorabilia. Museum exhibits tell the history of the area and the sport of fishing.

EAST GRAND RAPIDS

East Grand Rapids History Room

Location: 746 Lakeside Drive SE, East Grand Rapids, MI 49506 **Contact Info:** (616) 241-2092 • egrhistoryroom@gmail.com • www. eastgrandrapidshistoryroom.weebly. com **Hours:** Mon-Thu 9:30 a.m.-8 p.m., Fri 9:30 a.m.-6 p.m., Sat 9:30 a.m.-5 p.m., Sun 1-5 p.m. Closed Sun Memorial Day-Labor Day. **Admission:** Free. **Accessibility:** Free on-site parking. Wheelchair accessible. Self-guided.

Site Info: Visitors to the East Grand Rapids' Local History Room housed inside the East Grand Rapids Library will learn about the community's past. The museum holds treasures from the bygone days, including pictures and information on the Ramona Amusement Park and Poisson Family excursion steamboats. Items of local importance are obtained via auctions, estate sales, antique dealers, and private donations. Come explore the history of West Michigan's resort area in days past.

EDWARDSBURG

Edwardsburg Area Historical Museum

Location: 26818 Main St., Edwardsburg, MI 49112 **Contact Info:** edwardsburgmuseum@frontier. com • www.facebook.com/ Edwardsburg-Area-Historical-Museum-106608379400372 **Hours:** May-Dec: Tue-Sat 1-4 p.m., Sat 11 a.m.-2 p.m. **Admission:** $2/individual donation. **Accessibility:**

Free street parking. Wheelchair accessible. Tour guides available.

Site Info: The museum is located in an old house that was once a hotel. Visitors can view a collection of historical photographs and documents from businesses, organizations, railroads, farms, lakes, churches, and schools. A collection of household goods depict life of early settlers.

GALESBURG

Galesburg Historical Museum

Location: 190 E. Michigan Ave., Galesburg, MI 49053
Contact Info: (269) 665-7839 • www.galesburgcity.org **Hours:**
Wed 4:30-6:30 p.m., Sat 10 a.m.-2 p.m. **Admission:** Donations accepted. **Accessibility:** On-site parking. Wheelchair accessible. Self-guided. Call (269) 665-9953 for tours.

Site Info: The museum's exhibits include an 1860s linear four-room house—kitchen, parlor, dining room, and bedroom. Other collections include photos, early business history, military memorabilia, railroad and interurban history, small appliances, General William Rufus Shafter history, and more.

GRAND HAVEN

Depot Museum of Transportation

Location: 1 North Harbor Drive, Grand Haven, MI 49417
Contact Info: (616) 842-0700 • sradtke@tri-citiesmuseum.
org • www.tri-citiesmuseum.org **Hours:** Summer: Tue-Fri 10
a.m-8 p.m., Sat-Sun 12-8 p.m.; Sep-Oct: Tue-Fri 10 a.m.-5 p.m.,
Sat-Sun 12-5 p.m.; Nov-Apr: by appointment. **Admission:**
Free. Donations accepted. **Accessibility:** Free street and on-site parking. Wheelchair accessible. Self-guided.

Site Info: Located in a restored 1870 Detroit &
Milwaukee Depot, the Depot Museum of
Transportation showcases the history of railroading,
automobiles, and maritime history of the Great
Lakes region.

Tri-Cities Historical Museum

Location: 1 North Harbor Dr., Grand
Haven, MI 49417 **Contact Info:** (616)
842-0700 • sradtke@tri-citiesmuseum.
org • www.tri-citiesmuseum.org **Hours:**
Summer: Tue-Fri 10 a.m-8 p.m.,
Sat-Sun 12-8 p.m.; Sep-Oct: Tue-Fri 10
a.m.-5 p.m., Sat-Sun 12-5 p.m.;
Nov-Apr: by appointment. **Admission:** Free. Donations
accepted. **Accessibility:** Free street and on-site parking.
Wheelchair accessible. Self-guided.

Site Info: The museum is located in the renovated
Akeley Building in Grand Haven's historic
downtown. Exhibits include an authentic Native-
American Wicciup; the 1920s Ekkens Store; a

re-created Bastian and Blessing soda fountain; and displays relating to local and state geology, fur trading, lumbering, pioneers, farming, industry, banking, business, building, and general living.

GRAND RAPIDS

Gerald R. Ford Presidential Museum

Location: 303 Pearl St. NW, Grand Rapids, MI 49504 **Contact Info:** (616) 254-0400 • ford.museum@nara. gov • www.fordlibrarymuseum.gov **Hours:** Mon-Sat 9 a.m.-5 p.m., Sun 12-5 p.m. Closed major holidays. **Admission:** $8/adult, $7/senior and military, $6/college student, $4/child (6-18). **Accessibility:** Free on-site parking. Wheelchair accessible. Self-guided. Call for groups. Museum store.

Site Info: The permanent exhibits are the core of the museum's program. They allow visitors to participate in history, not just view it, while reviewing the highlights of the lives of President and Mrs. Ford. In addition to the permanent exhibits, a succession of temporary exhibits draws upon the rich holdings of the entire presidential libraries system, the Smithsonian Institution, the National Archives, and others.

Grand Rapids Public Museum

Location: 272 Pearl St. NW, Grand Rapids, MI 49504 **Contact Info:** (616) 929-1700 • info@grmuseum.org • www.grmuseum.org **Hours:** Mon-Sat 9 a.m.-5 p.m., Sun 12-5 p.m. Closed major holidays. **Admission:** $11/adult, $10/senior, $6/children (3-17), children 2 and under free. **Accessibility:** Parking ramp across the street. Wheelchair accessible. Self-guided. Museum store.

Site Info: Founded in 1854, the Grand Rapids Public Museum is Michigan's oldest and third-largest museum. Permanent exhibits include streets of old Grand Rapids, collecting A to Z, Anishinabek: People of this place, habitats, Furniture City, and new comers. Check the website to view changing exhibits. There are additional charges for special shows and exhibits.

Heritage Hill Historic District

Location: 126 College Ave. SE, Grand Rapids, MI 49503 **Contact Info:** (616) 459-8950 • heritage@heritagehillweb. org • www.heritagehillweb.org **Hours:** Mon-Thu 9 a.m.-5 p.m. **Admission:** Free. **Accessibility:** Limited free on-site parking. Not wheelchair accessible. Self-guided.

Site Info: Take a self-guided walking tour of the Heritage Hill Historic District, which highlights examples of most American architecture from the 19th and 20th centuries. The neighborhood is close to downtown, medical institutions, and universities. Many of the early leaders of Grand Rapids, including lumber barons, teachers, judges, and legislators, lived in the Heritage Hill neighborhood. A self-guided walking tour brochure is available on the website under the "tours" tab.

Michigan Masonic Museum & Library

Location: 233 E. Fulton St., Suite. 10, Grand Rapids, MI 49503 **Contact Info:** (616) 459-9336 • dhughes@ mmcfonline.org • www.masonichistory. org **Hours:** Tue, Wed, Fri, Sat: 10 a.m.-6 p.m., Thu 12-8 p.m. **Admission:** Free. **Accessibility:** Free on site parking. Wheelchair accessible. Tour guide available. Call for groups.

Site Info: Housed in the lower level of the historic Grand Rapids Masonic Center Building, which was constructed in 1915, and located between the Heritage Hill Historic District and the popular Heartside District, the Michigan Masonic Museum & Library offers visitors an interesting glimpse into the world's oldest and largest fraternity. Investigate the displays of Masonic memorabilia, artifacts, and regalia, or browse the large collection of Masonic-related books in the lending library to learn more about this honorable organization.

Temple Emanuel of Grand Rapids Archives

Location: 1715 E. Fulton, Grand Rapids, MI 49503 **Contact Info:** (616) 459-5976 • archives@templeemanuelgr.org • www. templeemanuelgr.org **Hours:** Tue-Fri 9 a.m.-5 p.m. Weekends by appointment. **Admission:** Free. **Accessibility:** Free on-site parking. Wheelchair accessible. Call for tours.

Site Info: The Temple Emanuel of Grand Rapids Archives was established in 1873. Visitors will discover a hall of glass cases containing important documents and artifacts. The front of the building has two large display cases containing other documents. The present temple was designed by Eric Mendelsohn and built between 1952 and 1953, and it has the Tiffany window from the original building built in 1881.

GRANDVILLE

Grandville Museum

Location: 3195 Wilson Ave. SW, Grandville, MI 49418 **Contact Info:** (616) 531-3030 • grandvilleHC@ hotmail.com • www.facebook.com/ GrandvilleHistoricalCommission **Hours:** 1st Wed monthly 1-4 p.m. Also

2nd Mon monthly in the evening. Also by appointment.
Admission: Free. **Accessibility:** Free on-site parking.
Wheelchair accessible. Tour guide available.

 Site Info: The museum is in the lower level of the city hall. It consists of two large rooms filled with local memorabilia, including a large photo collection of area residents, residences, and community-related events. Visitors can also view newspaper and obituary files.

No. 10 Schoolhouse

 **Location:** Heritage Park on Canal Avenue (Near 44th Street), Grandville, MI 49418 **Contact Info:** (616) 531-3030 • grandvilleHC@hotmail.com • www.facebook.com/GrandvilleHistoricalCommission **Hours:** By appointment. **Admission:** Free. **Accessibility:** Free on-site parking. Wheelchair accessible. Tour guide available.

 Site Info: The No. 10 Schoolhouse has original desks, pictures of students, old books, chalk boards, clothing to try on, teacher quarters, and bell. Visitors will experience what school was like in 1887.

GREENVILLE

Oakfield Museum

 Location: 11009 Podunk Rd. NE, Greenville, MI 48838 **Contact Info:** (616) 874-6271 • jagager@aol.com • www.commoncorners.com/kent/kent_oakfield_museum.htm **Hours:** Jun-Sep: 2nd and 4th Sun 2-4 p.m. **Admission:** Donations accepted. **Accessibility:** Free on-site parking. Partially wheelchair accessible; main floor only. Tour guide available.

 **Site Info:** The museum showcases school, church, Gleaner, and community history, along with commercial, agricultural, and residential ways of life. The archives are available for genealogical research. Other exhibits include the Harvard Store, the Podunk Mill, an 1898 dishwasher, and other home and farming items.

HART

Chadwick-Munger House

 **Location:** 114 Dryden St., Hart, MI 49420 **Contact Info:** (231) 873-2600 • info@oceanahistory.org • www.oceanahistory.org **Hours:** Wed 10 a.m.-4 p.m. Also by appointment. **Admission:** Free. **Accessibility:** Free

on-site and street parking. Partially wheelchair accessible. Tour guide available.

Site Info: The Chadwick-Munger House is the headquarters of the Oceana County Historical & Genealogical Society. It contains county newspapers, postcards of the area, historical background on the area's settlers, and genealogical history of many of the county residents.

Hart Historic District

Location: 570 E. Lincoln, Hart, MI 49420 **Contact Info:** (231) 873-2488 • ggoldberg@ci.hart.mi.us • www.ci.hart. mi.us **Hours:** Jul-Aug: Wed-Sat 1-4 p.m. Also by appointment. **Admission:** $5/adult, $2/child, $10/family. Call for group pricing. **Accessibility:** Free on-site parking. Partially wheelchair accessible. Tour guide available. Call for groups.

Site Info: The Hart Historic District is managed jointly by the Hart Historic District Commission and the Heritage Preservation Group. Attractions include a Native-American log cabin, railroad depot, Randall School, Sackrider Church, log house, Native-American artifacts, miniature piano collection, antique animated dolls, antique pipe organ, wildlife collections, and more. See the website for a complete list of the historic buildings.

HARTFORD

Van Buren County Historical Museum

Location: 58471 Red Arrow Highway, Hartford, MI 49057 **Contact Info:** (269) 621-2188 **Hours:** Jun-Sep: Wed, Fri-Sat 12-5 p.m. **Admission:** $5/adult, $1/children (0-12). **Accessibility:** On-site parking. Wheelchair accessible. Tour guide available; private tours by appointment.

Site Info: The Van Buren County Historical Museum is housed in a former county poorhouse that was built circa 1884. The building features three floors of historical items and exhibits, including a one-room school, general store, music room, old-fashioned kitchen, turn-of-the-century parlor, old dentist office, and military room. There is also a replica log cabin and blacksmith works on the grounds.

HASTINGS

Historic Charlton Park

Location: 2545 S. Charlton Park Rd., Hastings, MI 49058 **Contact Info:** (269) 945-3775 • info@charltonpark. org • www.charltonpark.org **Hours:** May-Nov: Mon-Sun 8 a.m.-9 p.m.; Nov-May: Mon-Sun 8 a.m.-5 p.m. **Admission:** Free. Fees for special events. **Accessibility:** Free on-site parking. Partially wheelchair accessible. Tour guide available; $4/individual. Call for guided tours. Museum store.

Site Info: Situated on 300 acres along the Thornapple Lake, Historic Charlton Park offers many options for outdoor enthusiasts, history lovers, and family adventurers. Explore more than 30,000 artifacts that represent life at the turn of the century. The artifact collection includes agricultural equipment, vocational tools, furniture, textiles, housewares, firearms, communication devices, and archival documents.

HICKORY CORNERS

Gilmore Car Museum

Location: 6865 Hickory Rd., Hickory Corners, MI 49060 **Contact Info:** (269) 671-5089 • jfollis@gilmorecarmuseum.org • www.gilmorecarmuseum.org **Hours:** Mon-Fri 9 a.m.-5 p.m., Sat-Sun 9 a.m.-6 p.m. **Admission:** $13/adult, $10/child (7-17), children under 6, school tours, and active military free. **Accessibility:** Free on-site parking. Wheelchair accessible. Self-guided. Museum store.

Site Info: The 90-acre Gilmore Car Museum campus is home to nearly 400 incredible vehicles and seven independent auto museums—all for one price. The site contains several historic buildings, including four vintage car dealerships, a 1930s gas station, a small-town train depot, and an authentic 1940s diner that serves lunch. A vast collection of auto original artwork and advertising that dates from the 1890s to present is also available.

Midwest Miniatures Museum

Location: 6855 W. Hickory Rd., Hickory Corners, MI 49060 **Contact Info:** (269) 671-4404 • midwestminiaturesmuseum@gmail.com • www.midwestminiaturesmuseum.com **Hours:** May-Oct: Mon-Fri 11 a.m.-5 p.m., Sat-Sun 11 a.m.-6 p.m. **Admission:** Donations accepted.

Site Info: The Midwest Miniatures Museum includes dozens of historic, miniature rooms and houses that seem to be awaiting their occupants' return. All are painstakingly created by artisans in 1:12 scale. The tables and chairs are made of the finest wood and covered with the finest fabrics. The place settings are real crystal, silver, and hand-painted china. Some of the rooms even have light fixtures that brighten the displays.

HOLLAND

Cappon House & Settler's House

Location: 228 W. 9th Street, Holland, MI 49423 **Contact Info:** (616) 796-3329 • www.hollandmuseum.org **Hours:**

May-Sep: Sat-Sun 12-4 p.m. **Admission:** $5. Children 6 and under free. **Accessibility:** Free street parking. Not wheelchair accessible. Tour guide available.

Site Info: The Italianate Cappon House was built by Holland's first mayor and tannery owner, Isaac Cappon, after the fire of 1871. Used by the family until 1980, the building has since been restored and furnished with Grand Rapids furniture. One of the few buildings to survive the Holland fire, the Settler's House was built in 1867 by Irish Canadian shipbuilder Thomas Morrissey. Highlights include period furnishings.

Holland Museum

Location: 31 W. 10th Street, Holland, MI 49423 **Contact Info:** (616) 796-3329 • hollandmuseum@ hollandmuseum.org • www. hollandmuseum.org **Hours:** Wed-Sat 11 a.m.-4 p.m., Sun 12-4 p.m. **Admission:** $7/adult, $6/senior, $4/ student, children 6 and under free. **Accessibility:** Free street parking. Wheelchair accessible. Tour guide available.

Site Info: The Holland Museum features cultural attractions from the "old country," including Dutch paintings and decorative arts and exhibits from the Netherlands Pavilion of the 1939 New York World's Fair. The museum also depicts local history, including Lake Michigan maritime and agricultural history. Artifacts in the collections include local history items from the start of "Holland Kolonies" to locally produced furniture and automotive and boatbuilding components.

Joint Archives of Holland

Location: Theil Research Center, 9 E. 10th St., Holland, MI 49423 **Contact Info:** (616) 395-7798 • archives@hope.edu • www.jointarchives.org **Hours:** Mon-Fri 8 a.m.-12 p.m. and 1-5 p.m. **Admission:** Free. **Accessibility:** Free street parking. Wheelchair accessible. Tour guide available by appointment.

Site Info: Resources at the Theil Research Center include the archival collections of Hope College, Western Theological Seminary, area governmental units, and other contractual members of the Joint Archives of Holland. It serves as a history research center for students, faculty, and staff of Hope College; contractual members; and the general public. Other collections include Reformed Church records, 19th-century Midwest Dutch immigration, West Michigan history, maritime and pleasure craft industry history, and the Pere Marquette Historical Society collection.

Olive Township Historical Society & Museum

Location: 11768 Polk St, Holland, MI 49424 **Contact Info:** (616) 399-6939 • jaarsmab@yahoo.com • www.olivetownship. com/oths.html **Hours:** By appointment. **Admission:** Donations accepted. **Accessibility:** Parking lot. Wheelchair accessible. Tour guide available.

Site Info: Organized in 2004, the society operates a museum in the former township hall and Olive Center School. Exhibits highlight local and regional artifacts, including the Pioneer school, a military display, and the church room.

Windmill Island Gardens

Location: 1 Lincoln Ave., Holland, MI 49423 **Contact Info:** (616) 355-1030 • windmill@cityofholland.com • www. windmillisland.org **Hours:** Apr-Oct: Daily 9:30 a.m.-6 p.m. Extended hours during Tulip Time (early May). **Admission:** $9/adult, $5/children(5-15). **Accessibility:** Free on-site parking. Partially wheelchair accessible. Tour guide available. Museum store.

Site Info: The 36-acre Windmill Island Gardens commemorate Holland's Dutch heritage with DeZwaan (The Swan) windmill, built in 1761. It was the last to leave the Netherlands, in 1964. Costumed guides provide a tour of the windmill. There is also a "Story of DeZwaan" movie, an Amsterdam street organ, an antique children's carousel, a miniature Little Netherlands, and more.

LODGING IN HOLLAND

Bonnie's Parsonage 1908 Bed & Breakfast

Location: 6 E. 24th St., Holland, MI 49423 **Contact Info:** (616) 396-1316 • www.bonniesparsonage.com **Property Info:** Bed & Breakfast. Seasonal: May-Oct. Privately owned; no public tours; pre-booking required. Free on-site parking. Not wheelchair accessible. Food available on-site. **Price:** $130-$150.

Site Info: This historic Dutch parsonage was built in 1908 by the first congregation of the Prospect Park Christian Reformed Church in Holland. The inside integrity of the parsonage is still intact, and the dark oak woodwork has never been painted. Nine ministers and their families lived in the parsonage. Bonnie Verwys has shared the parsonage and its history since 1984.

JENISON

Jenison Museum

Location: 28 Port Sheldon Dr., Jenison, MI 49428 **Contact Info:** (616) 457-4398 • info@jenisonhistory. org • www.jenisonhistory.org **Hours:** Mar-Dec: Tue 10 a.m.-12 p.m.; Mar-Oct: 3rd Sat 2-4 p.m.; Dec: 1st Sat

1-4 p.m. Also by appointment. **Admission:** Donations accepted.
Accessibility: Free on-site parking. Not wheelchair accessible.
Self-guided. Museum store.

 Site Info: The Jenison Historical Association
oversees and cares for a turn-of-the-century house
that is decorated with period-appropriate
furnishings and features several displays regarding
the history of the Jenison area. Exhibits include
"then and now," which compares Jenison of the past with its
present, as well as a display about the interurban railroad that ran
through Jenison.

KALAMAZOO

Kalamazoo Valley Museum

 **Location:** 230 North Rose St.,
Kalamazoo, MI 49007 **Contact Info:**
(269) 373-7990 • museumstaff@kvcc.
edu • www.kalamazoomuseum.org
Hours: Mon-Sat 9 a.m.-5 p.m., Sun 1-5
p.m. Closed major holidays.
Admission: Free. **Accessibility:** Street
parking available for a fee. Wheelchair accessible. Self-guided.

 Site Info: Attractions at the Kalamazoo Valley
Museum include an interactive science gallery, a
new history gallery, a planetarium, the Challenger
Learning Center, a children's landscape preschool
area, and national traveling exhibits. Also featured
are 56,000 objects made or used in Southwest Michigan, along
with samples of materials from other times and places. The
museum offers a regional history collection and more than 20,000
images for researchers.

KENTWOOD

Heritage Room at the Richard L. Root Branch Library

Location: 4950 Breton SE, Kentwood, MI 49518 **Contact
Info:** (616) 554-0709 • golderl@ci.kentwood.mi.us • www.
ci.kentwood.mi.us/committees/historical **Hours:** Mon-Thu: 9:30
a.m.-8 p.m. **Accessibility:** Free on-site parking. Wheelchair
accessible. Self-guided.

 Site Info: The Kentwood Historic Preservation
Commission shares its history at the Richard L.
Root Branch Library, from Kentwood's beginnings
as Paris Township to today. Collections relate to
the city's beginnings as a farming community
through becoming a first-tier suburb and employment center in
the Grand Rapids area. Collections include artifacts,
photographs, documents, and oral histories. The museum offers
this history through educational programs, exhibits, displays, and
other special events.

LOWELL

Lowell Area Historical Museum

Location: 325 West Main St., Lowell, MI 49331 **Contact Info:** (616) 897-7688 • history@lowellmuseum.org • www.lowellmuseum.org **Hours:** Tue, Thu, Sat, Sun 1-4 p.m. **Admission:** $3/adult, $1.50/student. **Accessibility:** Free on-site parking. Wheelchair accessible. Tour guide available. Museum store.

Site Info: The Lowell Area Historical Museum preserves Lowell area history. It is housed in the Graham Building, which was built in 1873 and used as a residential duplex. Today, the building features Victorian rooms, early Lowell history, businesses and industries, and the Lowell Showboat. It is listed in the National Register of Historic Places.

LUDINGTON

Big Sable Point Lighthouse

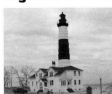

Location: 8800 West M-116, Ludington, MI 49431 **Contact Info:** (231) 845-7417 • splkadirector@gmail.com • www.splka.org **Hours:** Early May-Oct: Daily 10 a.m.-5 p.m. **Admission:** $5/adult, $2/child (12 and under). **Accessibility:** On-site parking for a fee. Not wheelchair accessible. Self-guided. Museum store.

Site Info: The Big Sable Point Lighthouse features its original keepers' quarters, which is attached to the tower. The quarters provide housing for the lighthouse's summer volunteers, a gift shop, and a video room for visitors. Several different displays highlighting the history of the lighthouse are available for guests to enjoy. Visitors can also climb the 130 steps to the watchtower room, walk out on the catwalk, and witness spectacular views of the Ludington State Park and Lake Michigan.

Historic White Pine Village

Location: 1687 South Lakeshore Dr., Ludington, MI 49431 **Contact Info:** (231) 425-3825 • rick@mchshistory.org • www.masoncountyhistoricalsociety.com **Hours:** Mon-Sat 10 a.m.-5 p.m. **Admission:** $9/adult, $6/children, $25/family. **Accessibility:** Free on-site parking. Partially wheelchair accessible. Self-guided. Museum store.

Site Info: Historic White Pine Village is an exciting interactive, historical, and educational experience in a beautiful and serene setting overlooking Lake Michigan just south of Ludington. Visitors can tour 30 buildings and sites displaying items from Mason County's past. Classic cars, beautiful flowers and gardens, Fresnel lenses from local lighthouses, and a beautiful chapel can all be experienced while touring the village.

Ludington North Breakwater Light

Location: North Pier in Downtown Ludington, Ludington, MI 49431 **Contact Info:** (231) 845-7417 • splkadirector@gmail.com • www.splka. org **Hours:** Late May-early Sep: Daily 10 a.m.-5 p.m. **Admission:** $5/adult, $2/child (12 and under).

Accessibility: Free on-site parking. Not wheelchair accessible. Self-guided. Museum store.

Site Info: The lighthouse house is located on the north breakwater pier at the end of Main Street in Ludington. The structure is made of steel plates in the shape of a four-sided pyramidal tower with four round porthole windows on each of its three decks. Each level has interesting items and pictures for visitors to explore as they make their way to the lantern room. At the top, guests are treated to a view of Ludington harbor.

Port of Ludington Maritime Museum

Location: 107 Lakeshore Dr., Ludington, MI 49431 **Contact Info:** (231) 425-3825 • rick@ mchshistory.org • www. masoncountyhistoricalsociety.com **Hours:** Mon-Sat 10 a.m.-5 p.m. **Admission:** $9/adult, $6/children, $25/family. **Accessibility:** Free on-site parking. Wheelchair accessible. Self-guided. Museum store.

Site Info: This site is scheduled to open May 2017. Situated in the former 1934 United States Coast Guard station at Ludington, a landmark of the city's waterfront for more than three-quarters of a century, the Port of Ludington Maritime Museum entertains, enlightens, and instructs. Through a variety of diverse, family-friendly, interactive exhibits, the museum provides visitors with a captivating look at the rich maritime heritage of Ludington and the greater West Michigan region.

S.S. Badger

Location: 701 Maritime Drive, Ludington, MI 49431 **Contact Info:** (231) 843-1509 • tbrown@ ssbadger.com • www.ssbadger.com **Hours:** May-Oct. **Admission:** Travel fare prices listed on website. **Accessibility:** Free on-site parking. Wheelchair accessible. Self-guided.

Site Info: The ferry, which is listed on the National Register of Historic Places, has a room with displays detailing maritime history. Built in 1952, the S.S. Badger offers passengers and vehicles cross-lake service between Ludington, Michigan, and Manitowoc, Wisconsin.

LODGING IN LUDINGTON

Cartier Mansion

Location: 409 E. Ludington Ave., Ludington, MI 49431 **Contact Info:** (231) 843-0101 • info@cartiermansion. com • www.cartiermansion.com **Property Info:** Bed & Breakfast. Open year-round. Privately owned; no public tours; pre-booking required. Free on-site parking. Not wheelchair accessible. Gift shop.

Site Info: Construction of the Cartier Mansion began in 1903. Almost everything in the mansion is original-the floors, the woodwork, and even some wall coverings. There are five fireplaces, each decorated with imported tiles from Italy. The outside brick on both the main house and carriage house was brought from France. The tile and bricks were shipped into the harbor of Ludington. Listed on the National Register of Historic Places.

The Inn at Ludington

Location: 701 E Ludington Ave., Ludington, MI 49431-2224 **Contact Info:** (231) 845-7055 • innkeeper@inn-ludington. com • www.inn-ludington.com **Property Info:** Bed & Breakfast. Open year-round. Privately owned; no public tours; pre-booking required. Free on-site parking. Food available on-site. **Price:** $154-$321.

Site Info: The structure was built in 1889 as the home of Dr. Latimer, an investor and the owner of Latimer Drugs. Later, it was the childhood home of Baseball Hall of Famer Larry McPhail. In the 1920s, it was bought by the Stark family, owners of the Stark Gold Watchcase Factory. There are seven themed rooms for guests to enjoy. All rooms include private baths, cable TV, air conditioning, and free broadband wireless Internet access. Listed on the State Register of Historic Places.

MEARS

Little Sable Point Lighthouse

Location: 287 North Lighthouse Dr., Mears, MI 49436 **Contact Info:** (231) 845-7417 • splkadirector@gmail.com • www.splka.org **Hours:** Late May-late Sep: Daily 10 a.m.-5 p.m. **Admission:** $5/adult, $2/child (12 and under). **Accessibility:** On-site parking for a fee. Wheelchair accessible. Self-guided. Museum store.

Site Info: The lighthouse sits on the beach in the Silver Lake State Park. Guests can climb the 139 stairs to the top of the lighthouse. The catwalk windows and roof reveal a beacon for mariners. The original Fresnel lens that was installed in 1874 still remains in the tower. Little Sable has an ADA-complaint walkway from the parking area through the dunes for easy access to the light.

Oceana Historical Park & Museum

Location: 5809 Fox Rd., Mears, MI 49436 **Contact Info:** (231) 873-2600 • info@oceanahistory.org • www.oceanahistory.org **Hours:** Jun-Aug: Sat-Sun 1-4 p.m. **Admission:** Free. **Accessibility:** Free on-site and street parking. Wheelchair accessible. Tour guide available. Call for special tours.

Site Info: The Oceana Historical Park & Museum contains a transportation museum; a special exhibit building; the home of Swift Lathers, who was editor of "The Mears Newz"; a tool museum; an early mission church; an early 20th-century Lake Michigan cottage; and a trapper's cabin.

Old Town Hall

Location: 5698 Fox Rd., Mears, MI 49436 **Contact Info:** (231) 873-2600 • info@oceanahistory.org • www.oceanahistory.org **Hours:** Jun-Aug: Sat-Sun 1-4 p.m. **Admission:** Free. **Accessibility:** Free on-site and street parking. Wheelchair accessible. Tour guide available. Call for special tours.

Site Info: The Old Town Hall depicts a replica "country schoolroom." Visitors can see what life was like in a one-room schoolhouse and explore other special exhibits that are changed annually.

MONTAGUE

Montague Museum

Location: 8717 Meade Street, Montague, MI 49437 **Contact Info:** (231) 894-9267 • www.cityofmontague.org/museum.html **Hours:** Memorial Day-Labor Day: Sat-Sun 1-5 p.m. Also by appointment. **Admission:** Free. **Accessibility:** Free on-site parking. Not wheelchair accessible. Tour guide available.

Site Info: The Montague Museum shares state and local history through exhibits about local industry, military, music, and Native-American history. Displays include the Lumber Era on White River and White Lake, local farming tools and pictures, military guns and clothing, and Admiral Byrd's South Pole Explorations. Exhibits on Nancy Ann Fleming, Miss America

1961; local art; photo collections; fire and police equipment; and the post office are also featured.

MUSKEGON

Fire Barn Museum

Location: 510 W. Clay Ave, Muskegon, MI 49440 **Contact Info:** (231) 722-0278 • info@lakeshoremuseum.org • www.lakeshoremuseum.org **Hours:** May-Oct: Thu, Fri, Sat, Mon: 10 a.m.-4 p.m., Sun 1-4 p.m. **Admission:** Free. **Accessibility:** Free street parking. Partially wheelchair accessible. Self-guided.

Site Info: The Fire Barn tells the history of fire fighting in the Muskegon area with artifacts including alarms and call boxes, hose carts, ladders, and a 1928 American LaFrance Pumper Truck. The second floor includes the recreated living quarters of early fire fighters. Photographs of some of the area's most devastating fires are displayed.

Hackley & Hume Historic Site

Location: 484 W. Webster Ave, Muskegon, MI 49440 **Contact Info:** (231) 722-0278 • info@lakeshoremuseum.org • www.lakeshoremuseum.org **Hours:** May-Oct: Thu, Fri, Sat, Mon: 10 a.m.-4 p.m., Sun 1-4 p.m. **Admission:** Free.

Accessibility: Free street parking. Not wheelchair accessible. Tour guide available; call ahead to schedule a group tour. Museum store.

Site Info: The site features two of the finest examples of Victorian Era architecture in the Midwest. The restored homes of Muskegon's most well-known lumber barons were built in the late 1800s. The homes feature exquisite wood carvings, stained-glass windows, and period furnishings. Tours include the lower and upper floors of each house.

Lakeshore Museum Center

Location: 430 W. Clay Ave., Muskegon, MI 49440 **Contact Info:** (231) 722-0278 • info@lakeshoremuseum.org • www.lakeshoremuseum.org **Hours:** Mon-Fri 9:30 a.m.-4:30 p.m., Sat-Sun 12-4 p.m. **Admission:** Free.

Accessibility: Free on-site and street parking. Wheelchair accessible. Self-guided. Museum store.

Site Info: A tour of the Lakeshore Museum Center offers visitors an opportunity to explore 400 million years of Michigan in the making, view animal habitats, and see a life-size mastodon in the "coming to the lakes" gallery. Hands-on opportunities abound in the science center with a simulated tornado, magnet table, 30 science-themed drawers full of activities, and much more. Three additional sites of the Lakeshore Museum Center are within walking distance.

Muskegon Heritage Museum

Location: 561 W. Western Ave., Muskegon, MI 49440 **Contact Info:** (231) 722-1363 • info@ muskegonheritage.org • www. muskegonheritage.org **Hours:** Mid-May to mid-Oct: Thu-Sat 11 a.m.-4 p.m. Also by appointment. **Admission:** $4/ adult, $2/student, children 5 and under free, MHA members free. Group rates available. **Accessibility:** Free street parking. Partially wheelchair accessible. Tour guide available.

Site Info: Exhibits focus on more than 75 companies that made Muskegon an industrial capital. Some exhibits are changed or modified during the year. There is a working spring winding machine, a Brunswick automatic pinsetter, and a Corliss Valve Steam Engine from the 1890s that operates 11 machine tools, via large leather belts, as well as three ceiling fans. A walking tour brochure is available for historic homes in the surrounding Heritage Village area.

Muskegon Museum of Art

Location: 296 W. Webster Ave, Muskegon, MI 49440 **Contact Info:** (231) 720-2571 • mcurran@mpsk12.net • www.muskegonartmuseum.org **Hours:** Tue, Wed, Fri, Sat 11 a.m.-5 p.m., Thu 11 a.m.-8 p.m., Sun 12-5 p.m. **Admission:** $8/adult, $5/student w/ID, children 17 and under free. **Accessibility:** Free on-site and street parking. Wheelchair accessible. Self-guided. Museum store.

Site Info: The Muskegon Museum of Art was established in 1912 and is known for its historic building and fine permanent collection that includes works by major American and European artists, African-American artists, and studio glass artists. The museum offers a diverse schedule of changing exhibits and programs.

Scolnik House of the Depression Era

Location: 430 W. Clay Ave., Muskegon, MI 49440 **Contact Info:** (231) 722-0278 • info@lakeshoremuseum.org • www. lakeshoremuseum.org **Hours:** May-Oct: Thu-Mon 10 a.m.-4 p.m., Sun 1-4 p.m. **Admission:** Free. **Accessibility:** Free street parking. Not wheelchair accessible. Self-guided.

Site Info: This site tells the story of common families living in Muskegon during the Great Depression. The house features period furnishings, wallpaper, and flooring. Guides stationed on each floor of the house provide basic information and answer visitors' questions. The home is named for Herman and Ida Scolnik, who raised their family during the Depression.

USS LST 393 Veterans Museum

Location: 506 Mart St., Muskegon, MI 49440 **Contact Info:** (231) 730-1477 • info@lst393.org • www.lst393.org **Hours:** May-early Oct: Daily 10 a.m.-5 p.m. **Admission:** $8/adult, $5/ student. **Accessibility:** Free on-site parking. Partially wheelchair accessible. Tour guides available. Call for groups. Museum store.

Site Info: Visit a restored WWII USS LST 393—a 350-foot landing ship tank—and view artifacts from 20th- and 21st-century wars and services. The museum honors all veterans from all branches of the American armed forces and provides educational programs for students and the general public.

USS Silversides Submarine Museum

Location: 1346 Bluff St., Muskegon, MI 49441 **Contact Info:** (231) 755-1230 • contactus@ silversidesmuseum.org • www. silversidesmuseum.org **Hours:** Jun-Aug: Daily 10 a.m.-5:30 p.m.; Sep-May: Sun-Thu 10 a.m.-4 p.m., Fri-Sat 10 a.m.-4 p.m. **Admission:** $15/adult, $12.50/senior, $10.50/ children (5-18). WWII Veterans, active duty, and children 4 and under are free. **Accessibility:** Free on-site parking. Wheelchair accessible. Tour guide available. Museum store.

Site Info: The USS Silversides Submarine Museum honors men and women of the United States military, preserves military history, and provides experiences that educate the public about past and present military history and technology. Self-guided tours of the museum allow visitors to see what it was like to serve aboard the World War II submarine USS Silversides. Guests can visit the deck topside as well as the major internal compartments below deck.

LODGING IN MUSKEGON

Port City Victorian Inn Bed and Breakfast

Location: 1259 Lakeshore Dr., Muskegon, MI 49441 **Contact Info:** (231) 759-0205 • pcvicinn@comcast. net • www.portcityinn.com **Property Info:** Bed & Breakfast. Seasonal: May-Oct. Privately owned; no public tours; pre-booking required. Free on-site and street parking. Not wheelchair accessible. Food available on-site. **Price:** $165-$235.

Site Info: This Queen Anne Victorian mansion was built by Alexander Rodgers in 1877. The five-bedroom home sits on the bluffs of Muskegon Lake just minutes from Lake Michigan's sand beaches and the downtown business district. Soon after his arrival from Scotland in 1858, Mr. Rodgers built his first company and invented many tools for use in the lumber mill and logging industries. In 1874, Mr. Rodgers started one of the first sawmills on Muskegon Lake.

NEWAYGO

Newaygo County Museum and Heritage Center

Location: 12 Quarterline Rd, Newaygo, MI 49337 **Contact Info:** (866) 901-7489 • museum@newaygocountyhistory.org • www.newaygocountyhistory.org **Hours:** May-Sep: Wed-Sun 11 a.m.-4 p.m. **Admission:** Free. Donations accepted. **Accessibility:** Free on-site parking. Wheelchair accessible. Self-guided. Museum store.

Site Info: The Newaygo County Museum and Heritage Center is home to exhibits designed and constructed by local talent to share the unique story of the area, its people, and the changes that have taken place during the last 150 years. Some of the attractions include Native American, logging, farming, and businesses, including a Fremont's Gerber Baby Food exhibit. Period rooms and a military tribute room are also included in the gallery.

NILES

Chapin Home

Location: 508 E. Main St., Niles, MI 49120 **Contact Info:** (269) 683-4702 • nileshistory@nilesmi.org • www.nileshistorycenter.org **Hours:** Late Apr-Early May: Fri-Sat 11:30 a.m.-1:30 p.m. **Admission:** $5/person, children 9 and under free. **Accessibility:** Free on-site and street parking. Partially wheelchair accessible. Tour guide available.

Site Info: Henry and Ruby Chapin constructed their home in 1882. Donated to the city of Niles in 1933, it served as the city hall and a hospital. Ornate stained-glass windows, beveled mirrors, impressive brass chandeliers, beautiful hand-carved woodwork, and nine fireplaces will transport you back to the ornate Aesthetic Movement of the 1880s.

Fort St. Joseph Museum

Location: 508 East Main St., Niles, MI 49120 **Contact Info:** (269) 845-4054 • nileshistory@nilesmi.org • www.nileshistorycenter.org **Hours:** Wed-Fri 10 a.m.-4 p.m., Sat 10 a.m.-3 p.m. **Admission:** Free. **Accessibility:** Free on-site and street parking. Partially wheelchair accessible. Tour guide available. Museum store.

Site Info: The Fort St. Joseph Museum is located in the former carriage house of the Victorian period Chapin Home and features exhibits that tell the story of Niles from the prehistoric period to the 1691 founding of Fort St. Joseph to the modern businesses and industrial era. Special artifacts highlighted throughout the exhibits include discoveries made through the Fort St. Joseph Archaeological Project, Ice Age fossils, pictographs drawn by Chief Sitting Bull, railroad memorabilia, and more.

OTSEGO

Otsego Area Historical Museum

Location: 218 N. Farmer, Otsego, MI 49078 **Contact Info:** (269) 692-3775 • oahs@otsegohistory.org • www.otsegohistory. org **Hours:** Sat 10 a.m.-2 p.m. Also by appointment. **Admission:** Free. **Accessibility:** Free parking. Wheelchair accessible.

Site Info: The museum highlights the pioneer history of Michigan and the papermaking industry of Otsego, which had seven operational mills in the 20th century, plus other artifacts related to Otsego's history.

PENTWATER

Pentwater Historical Museum

Location: 327 S. Handcock St., Pentwater, MI 49449 **Contact Info:** (231) 869-8631 • info@ pentwaterhistoricalsociety.org • www. pentwaterhistoricalsociety.org **Hours:** Jun-Aug: Tue-Sat 1-4 p.m.; Sep-Oct: Thu-Sat 1-4 p.m. **Admission:** Donations accepted. **Accessibility:** Free on-site parking. Wheelchair accessible. Self-guided.

Site Info: The Pentwater Historical Museum showcases the diverse history of the greater Pentwater area, which was part of the late 19th century's brick-making, furniture-making, and lumbering industries. It also has displays on the area's maritime history. A map for a self-guided walking tour leads visitors to many older homes and buildings as well as the historical interpretive panels located through the village.

ROCKFORD

Algoma Township Historical Society Displays

Location: 10531 Algoma Ave., Rockford, MI 49341
Contact Info: (616) 866-1583 • planning@algomatwp.org
• www.algomatwp.org **Hours:** Mon-Fri 8:30 a.m.-4:30 p.m.
Admission: Free. **Accessibility:** Free on-site parking. Partially wheelchair accessible. Self-guided.

 Site Info: The Algoma Township Historical Society's display cabinets are located in the Algoma Township Hall building for the public to view. Items are exchanged in and out for a fresh display.

Rockford Area Historical Museum

 **Location:** 21 S. Monroe St., Rockford, MI 49341 **Contact Info:** (616) 866-2235 • rockfordmuseum@gmail.com • www.rockfordmuseum.org **Hours:** Tue, Wed, Fri, Sun 1-4 p.m., Thu 10 a.m.-4 p.m., Sat 12-4 p.m. **Admission:** Free. **Accessibility:** Free on-site parking. Wheelchair accessible. Tour guide available. Tour groups by appointment. Museum store.

 **Site Info:** The Rockford Area Historical Society has operated the Rockford Area Historical Museum since 1975. Exhibits focus on the development of the Rockford area as a logging community and its evolution into a dynamic small city. Other exhibits tell the story of Rockford's business community, schools, and connection to America's military history and agriculture.

SAUGATUCK

Saugatuck-Douglas Museum

Location: 735 Park St., Saugatuck, MI 49453 **Contact Info:** (269) 857-5751 • info@sdhistoricalsociety.org • www.sdhistoricalsociety.org **Hours:** Memorial Day-Labor Day: Daily 12-4 p.m.; Sep-Oct: Sat-Sun 12-4 p.m. **Admission:** Free. Donations accepted. **Accessibility:** Free on-site parking. Wheelchair accessible. Self-guided. Museum store.

 Site Info: Discover the unique history of Saugatuck, Douglas, Lake Kalamazoo, and the surrounding lakeshore area of West Michigan at the Saugatuck-Douglas Museum. The museum's exhibit called WATER uncovers the changing and challenging story of the relationship between local inhabitants and the resource that makes the area special. Additional exhibits discuss local landmarks through maps and the history of the Saugatuck Pump House, in which the museum is housed.

SOUTH HAVEN

Hartman School

Location: 355 Hubbard St., South Haven, MI 49090 **Contact Info:** (269) 637-6424 • info@historyofsouthhaven.org • www.historyofsouthhaven.org **Hours:** Tue-Wed 9 a.m.-3 p.m. **Admission:** Free. **Accessibility:** Free street parking. Wheelchair accessible. Tour guide available. Museum store.

Site Info: Formed in 2002 to preserve and promote the understanding of South Haven history, the Hartman School building includes exhibits and archives maintained by the Historical Association of South Haven.

Liberty Hyde Bailey Museum

Location: 903 South Bailey Ave, South Haven, MI 49090 **Contact Info:** (269) 637-3251 • info@libertyhydebailey.org • www.libertyhydebailey.org **Hours:** May-Sep: Tue-Sat 9 a.m.-4 p.m. **Admission:** Free. **Accessibility:** Free on-site parking. Wheelchair accessible. Self-guided.

Site Info: The museum presents the story of the Bailey family's life, loves, and adventures. It is situated in the childhood home of the Father of Modern Horticulture, Dr. Liberty Hyde Bailey Jr. Built in 1858 by Liberty Hyde Bailey Sr., the museum is set in a park featuring themed gardens demonstrating aspects of Dr. Bailey's books and research. The grounds include a nature path through the woods and shady picnic areas.

Michigan Flywheelers Museum

Location: 06285 68th St., South Haven, MI 49090 **Contact Info:** (269) 639-2010 • michiganflywheelers@yahoo.com • www.michiganflywheelers.org **Hours:** May-Sep: Wed, Sat-Sun 10 a.m.-3 p.m. or by appointment. **Admission:** Donations accepted. Admission charged during special events. **Accessibility:** Free on-site parking. Wheelchair accessible. Tour guide available. Museum store.

Site Info: Take a step back in time and experience farming history at the Michigan Flywheelers Museum. Located minutes from the shore of beautiful Lake Michigan, the museum showcases an unique collection of antique farm machinery, a 1920s replica "old towne" filled with places such as "over the hill forge," "peaceful knoll church," a log cabin, and the farm history building, as well as a working sawmill, a shingle mill, and a 130-year-old post and beam barn.

Michigan Maritime Museum

Location: 260 Dyckman Avenue, South Haven, MI 49090 **Contact Info:** (269) 637-8078 • info@michiganmaritimemuseum.org • www.michiganmaritimemuseum.org **Hours:** May-Dec: Mon-Sun 10 a.m.-5 p.m. **Admission:** $8/adult, $7/senior, $5/children (5-15). **Accessibility:** Free on-site and street parking. Partially wheelchair accessible. Self-guided. Museum store.

Site Info: Five separate buildings offer a variety of engaging opportunities for the museum visitor, including permanent and changing exhibits on Michigan maritime history. A center for teaching boatbuilding and related maritime skills and a regionally renowned research library are also available. Waterfront festivals and events are complemented by the hustle and bustle of a modern harbor and vast sandy beaches in one of West Michigan's most picturesque shoreline communities.

SPRING LAKE

The Dewitt School House

Location: Taft Street & 180th Avenue, Spring Lake, MI 49456 **Contact Info:** (616) 842-0700 • sradtke@tri-citiesmuseum.org • www.tri-citiesmuseum.org **Hours:** Apr-Jun: by appointment. **Admission:** Free. Donations accepted. **Accessibility:** Free street and on-site parking. Not wheelchair accessible. Tour guide available; call ahead to schedule a group or private tour.

Site Info: The Dewitt School House presents a classroom program for children to allow them to experience what school was like more than 100 years ago. Located in Spring Lake Township, the museum offers a five-hour program highlighting the curriculum used in 1895.

ST. JOSEPH

Priscilla U. Byrns Heritage Center

Location: 601 Main St., St. Joseph, MI 49085 **Contact Info:** (269) 983-1191 • charseneau@theheritagemcc.org • www.theheritagemcc.org **Hours:** Tue-Sat 10 a.m.-4 p.m., Memorial Day-Labor Day: Sun 12-4 p.m. **Admission:** Free. **Accessibility:** Free on-site parking. Wheelchair accessible. Self-guided. Tours available. Museum store.

Site Info: The heritage center houses the area's history, artifacts, archival collections, and a research library in a historic building along Main Street. Carefully preserved and beautifully appointed, it presents the area's stories in spacious exhibit halls and creates new memories in elegant banquet facilities.

Silver Beach Carousel

Location: 333 Broad Street, St. Joseph, MI 49085 **Contact Info:** (269) 982-8500 • info@silverbeachcarousel.com • www.silverbeachcarousel.com **Hours:** Sep-May: Thu 4-8:30 p.m., Fri-Sat 11 a.m.-5 p.m., Sun 12-5 p.m.; Jun-Aug: Mon-Sat 10 a.m.-10 p.m., Sun 12-10 p.m. **Admission:** 1 token per ride: 1 token - $2, 3 tokens - $5, 7 tokens - $10, 15 tokens - $20. **Accessibility:** Free on-site and street parking. Wheelchair accessible. Museum store.

Site Info: Pick your favorite of the 48 unique carousel figures, and ride beneath 1,000 twinkling lights as the organ's music happily soars and dips with the gears. Each figure is beautifully hand-carved and hand-painted by the artisans at The Carousel Works. Visitors can learn about local history by viewing the historic photographs around the top of the carousel.

STURGIS

Sturgis Museum

Location: Jefferson & Chicago St., Sturgis, MI 49091 **Contact Info:** (269) 625-6071 • sturgismuseum@gmail.com • www.sturgismuseum.org **Hours:** Mon-Fri 8:30 a.m.-4:30 p.m. **Admission:** Donations accepted. **Accessibility:** Free on-site parking. Wheelchair accessible.

Site Info: The museum is housed in an 1895 Tudor Revival brick depot, which was moved to its current location in 2014. It features 1,500 area items, including a motor home built from a Spartan bus. Spartan buses were built in Sturgis from 1947 to 1949 and sold both in the United States and overseas.

THREE RIVERS

Sue Silliman House & Blacksmith Shop

Location: 116 South Main St., Three Rivers, MI 49093 **Contact Info:** (269) 435-4795 • rjduddshank@gmail.com • www.michigandar.com/silliman_house.htm **Hours:** By appointment. **Admission:** Free. **Accessibility:** Free on-site and street parking. Not wheelchair accessible. Tour guide available.

Site Info: The Abiel Fellows Chapter of the Daughters of the American Revolution is housed in the Sue Silliman House & Blacksmith Shop, an 1876 home originally used as a factory. Three forges once operated in the lower level, which were reconstructed and are used for demonstrations at special events. A gallery upstairs showcases the history of the area, including the

Sheffield Car Company, Kellogg Farms, Tannery and Three Rivers Furs, and a prehistoric artifact collection.

LODGING IN THREE RIVERS

Voyager's Inn Bed & Breakfast

Location: 210 East St., Three Rivers, MI 49093 **Contact Info:** (269) 279-9260 • reservations@voyagers-inn.com • www.voyagers-inn.com **Property Info:** Bed & Breakfast. Open year-round. Privately owned; no public tours; pre-booking required. Free on-site parking. Not wheelchair accessible. Food available on-site. **Price:** $95-$105.

Site Info: Voyageur's Inn displays the Victorian Era's beauty and fine craftsmanship, including hardwood floors, elegant pocket doors, and crown moldings. Rich, dark blue tile surrounds the fireplace in the main parlor, and a grand staircase leads to the second floor. There are three unique guest rooms, each with a private bath. The architect was D.S. Hopkins of Grand Rapids, and the home was built, circa 1898, for General F.H. Case, of the Michigan National Guard.

VANDALIA

Bonine House

Location: 18970 M-60, Vandalia, MI 49095 **Contact Info:** (269) 646-0401 • info@urscc.org • www.urscc.org **Hours:** Jun-Sep: Mon-Sat 1-4 p.m. **Admission:** Free. Donations accepted. **Accessibility:** Free on-site parking. Wheelchair accessible. Tour guide available. Tour groups by appointment. Museum Store.

Site Info: The Bonine House is a Second Empire Victorian home of Quaker abolitionists James E. and Sarah B. Bonine. The home and the adjoining carriage house were used to shelter freedom-seekers escaping slavery between 1850 and 1860. The Bonine House also played a vital role in establishing "Ramptown," a community for freed African Americans.

VICKSBURG

Vicksburg Historic Village

Location: 300 N. Richardson St., Vicksburg, MI 49097 **Contact Info:** (269) 649-1733 • info@vicksburghistory.org • www.vicksburghistory.org **Hours:** May-Dec: Sat 10 a.m.-3 p.m. **Admission:** Free. **Accessibility:** Free on-site parking. Partially wheelchair accessible. Tour guide available; call ahead to schedule a group or private tour.

Site Info: The Vicksburg Historic Village, located on a multi-acre site in the village of Vicksburg, has 11 structures. On display or in storage are some 20,000 artifacts dating from Native-American habitation to the 1930s Depression Era. Buildings include the 1904 brick depot, restored to its original condition and serving as a museum; a railroad express building; a village garage, depicting the history of transportation; and a blacksmith shop.

WHITE PIGEON

U.S. Land Office Museum

Location: 113 West Chicago Rd., White Pigeon, MI 49099 **Contact Info:** (269) 483-7122 • mstarmann@yahoo.com • www.hstarmann.wix.com/sjchs **Hours:** By appointment. **Admission:** Donations accepted. **Accessibility:** Free on-site and street parking. Partially wheelchair accessible. Tour guide available. Museum store.

Site Info: The U.S. Land Office Museum is in an original post-and-beam building. The building houses items collected by the pioneers and many original maps, sharing the history of White Pigeon and the surrounding area.

Wahbememe Memorial Park

Location: U.S. 12 and 131, White Pigeon, MI 49099 **Contact Info:** (269) 483-7122 • mstarmann@yahoo.com • www.hstarmann.wix.com/sjchs **Hours:** Dawn to dusk. **Admission:** Free. **Accessibility:** Free on-site parking. Wheelchair accessible. Self-guided.

Site Info: Markers on the site tell the story of Chief Wahbememe's life and the placing of the stone marker on the site by a local women's club in the early 1900s. The site is listed on the National Register of Historic Places.

WHITEHALL

Michigan's Heritage Park

Location: 8637 North Durham Rd., Whitehall, MI 49461 **Contact Info:** (231) 722-0278 • info@lakeshoremuseum.org • www.lakeshoremuseum.org **Hours:** May & Oct: Mon-Fri 10 a.m.-4 p.m.; Jun-Sep: Thu-Mon 10 a.m.-4 p.m., Sun 1-4 p.m. **Admission:** $10/adult, $8/senior, $5/child (2-12). **Accessibility:** Free on-site parking. Self-guided. Museum store.

Site Info: Learn about 10,000 years of Michigan history as they walk along a paved trail through the woods at the park. Costumed interpreters are stationed along the trail at stops, which include a Native-American wigwam village, fur trader's post, Civil War camp, and 1900s farmhouse. Visitors will have an opportunity to participate in a variety of historic activities, such as grinding corn and spinning wool.

White River Light Station and Museum

Location: 6199 Murray Rd., Whitehall, MI 49461 **Contact Info:** (231) 845-7417 • splkadirector@gmail.com • www.splka.org **Hours:** Late May-Oct: Tue-Sun 10 a.m.-5 p.m. **Admission:** $5/adult, $2/child (12 and under). **Accessibility:** Free on-site parking. Not wheelchair accessible. Self-guided. Museum store.

Site Info: The White River Light Station was built in 1875. The beautiful brick building reverberates with character and stories of prominent residents, such as the first keeper. The light station was decommissioned in 1960 and opened its doors as a museum in 1970. Visitors can climb to the top of the tower or wander around the museum and grounds. Don't miss viewing the original Fresnel lens in the museum.

LODGING IN WHITEHALL

Lewis House Bed & Breakfast

Location: 324 South Mears Ave., Whitehall, MI 49461 **Contact Info:** (844) 854-6424 • debi@thelewishousemi.com • www.thelewishousemi.com **Property Info:** Bed & Breakfast. Open year-round. Privately owned; no public tours; pre-booking required. Free on-site parking. Not wheelchair accessible. Food available on-site. **Price:** $155-$225.

Site Info: The Lewis House is a two-story structure with Gothic and Italianate influences. The house was originally built in 1878 by John C. Lewis, a prominent lumber barren and banker in Whitehall. Today, the Lewis House has returned to its architectural beauty and features. Listed on the National Register of Historic Places.

White Swan Inn Bed & Breakfast

Location: 303 S. Mears Ave., Whitehall, MI 49461 **Contact Info:** (231) 894-5169 • stay@whiteswaninn.com • www.whiteswaninn.com **Property Info:** Bed & Breakfast. Open year-round. Privately owned; no public tours; pre-booking required. Free on-site parking. Not wheelchair accessible. Food available on-site. Gift shop. **Price:** $119-$189.

Site Info: This structure was built circa 1884 as a private home for the Covell family of the Staples-Covell Mill in Whitehall. White Swan Inn maintains the original woodwork, spacious rooms, decorative inlaid floors, and a walnut staircase, along with a screened porch for summer enjoyment. Four guest rooms with private en suite baths and generous-size common areas create a relaxing environment to enjoy while exploring all the historic wonders located around the Whitehall/Montague area.

ZEELAND

Dekker-Huis and Zeeland Museum

Location: 37 E. Main St., Zeeland, MI 49464 **Contact Info:** (616) 772-4079 • zeelandmuseum@charter.net • www.zeelandhistory.org **Hours:** Mar-Oct: Thu 10 a.m.-5 p.m.; Year-round: Sat 10 a.m.-2 p.m. Business hours by appointment. **Admission:** Free. Donations accepted. **Accessibility:** Free street parking. Partially wheelchair. Tour guide available. Museum store.

Site Info: Exhibits cover Dutch immigration, the first Zeeland bank, farming, local veterans, and much more. The structure was built in 1876 by Dirk Dekker, one of Zeeland's prominent early residents and businessmen, and it was restored to its original Victorian-Era style in 1979. The museum features numerous local history displays including a pioneer room, the Zeeland State Bank, Huizenga Grocery Store, Main Street, a veterans memorial room, and the furniture and clock-making industries.

New Groningen Schoolhouse

Location: 10537 Paw Paw Dr., Zeeland, MI 49464 **Contact Info:** (616) 212-3076 • newgschoolhouse@gmail.com • www.zeelandhistory.org **Hours:** By appointment. **Admission:** Free. Donations accepted. **Accessibility:** Free on-site parking. Wheelchair accessible. Self-guided.

Site Info: The New Groningen Schoolhouse dates back to 1881, when it served as a rural school for children in the Zeeland/Holland area. The New Groningen Schoolhouse, restored and opened in 2011, includes an early 1900s classroom complete with desks, maps, schoolbooks and a 40-seat meeting room available for rental.

ALBION

Gardner House Museum

Location: 509 S. Superior St., Albion, MI 49224 **Contact Info:** (517) 629-5100 • info@albionhistoricalsociety.org • www.albionhistoricalsociety.org **Hours:** Mother's Day-Sep: Sat-Sun 2-4 p.m. Also by appointment. **Admission:** Donations accepted. **Accessibility:** Free street parking. Partially wheelchair accessible; first floor only. Tour guides available.

Site Info: The Gardner House Museum features period furniture and three floors. In the basement, visit a neighborhood grocery store and kitchen. The first floor is filled with antique furniture, decorations, musical instruments, and pictures. On the second floor, visitors will find antique beds and clothing in the Victorian bedroom and bathroom. The second floor also features clothes worn between 1870 and 1970 and a World War II exhibit showcasing 400 photos and memorabilia.

CENTRAL

LODGING IN ALBION

Palmer House Inn Bed & Breakfast

Location: 108 W Erie St., Albion, MI 49224 **Contact Info:** (517) 629-0001 • palmerhouseinnbnb@gmail.com • www.palmerhouseinnbnb.com/ **Property Info:** Bed & Breakfast. Open year-round. Privately owned; no public tours; pre-booking required. Free on-site parking. Not wheelchair accessible. **Price:** $100-$150.

Site Info: This elegant three-story Queen Anne Victorian home, circa 1885, is situated within Albion's Historic District and was a residence and medical offices for Drs. Frank and Elizabeth Palmer. After the turn of the century, the practice was sold to Dr. Grant. During the early 1900s, the home served as Albion's first hospital. After Dr. Grant's death, the building was a private home into the 1960s. Restored in the 1990s, the building is now a B&B.

AUGUSTA

Fort Custer Museum

Location: 2601 26th Street, Augusta, MI 49012 **Contact Info:** (517) 282-4533 • spackmanj@yahoo.com • www.fortcustermuseum.org **Hours:** By appointment only. **Accessibility:** The museum is nestled among training facilities and offices on the Fort Custer Training Center property. This is a limited-access active-duty military facility.

Site Info: The museum currently fills the lower floor of a renovated World War II barracks that once housed more than 100 soldiers. Much of the construction is intact, including a large open bay for sleeping cots and a row of shared showers, sinks, and toilets. The museum highlights the units that have been part of the Fort Custer history since the post was established in 1917 as Camp Custer.

BARRYTON

Barryton Area Historical Museum

Location: 19730 30th Avenue, Barryton, MI 49305 **Contact Info:** (989) 382-7831 • ikgibbons@hughes.net **Hours:** Memorial Day-Labor Day: Sat-Sun 1-4 p.m. **Admission:** Free.
Site Info: The Barryton Area Historical Commission opened its museum in 1987. It features cameras, pictures, histories, farming equipment, a sleigh, and artifacts from local residents.

BATTLE CREEK

Historic Adventist Village

Location: 480 W. Van Buren St., Battle Creek, MI 49037 **Contact Info:** (269) 965-3000 • adventistvillage@tds.net • www.adventistheritage.org **Hours:** Sun-Fri 10 a.m.-4 p.m., Sat 2-5 p.m. **Admission:** Donations accepted. **Accessibility:** Free on-site parking. Partially wheelchair accessible. Free tour guide available; call ahead.

Site Info: The village comprises an 1870s one-room schoolhouse; an 1850s log cabin; a church built in Parkville, Michigan, in 1860; the home of Harriet Henderson Tucker, a former slave who fled north on the Underground Railroad; and the home of James and Ellen White, two of the early members of the Seventh-Day Adventist Church. Another attraction is the Dr. John Kellogg Discovery Center.

BAY CITY

Antique Toy & Firetruck Museum

Location: 3456 Patterson Rd., Bay City, MI 48706 **Contact Info:** (888) 888-1270 • info@toyandfiretruckmuseum.org • www.toyandfiretruckmuseum.org **Hours:** May-Sep: Tue-Sun 12-4 p.m. **Admission:** $10/adult, $9/senior, $7/child (5-17), children 4 and under free.

Site Info: The museum is home to more than 60 motorized fire trucks—the largest collection of fire trucks in the world. The museum also contains more than 12,000 antique and collectible toys—many of them fire, police, and rescue vehicles. Also included in the toy collection are toys and models from Tonka, Buddy L, Nylent, and Hess to name a few. For the NASCAR fans, one room is dedicated to all things NASCAR.

Historical Museum of Bay County

Location: 321 Washington Ave., Bay City, MI 48708 **Contact Info:** (989) 893-5733 • info@bchsmuseum.org • www.bchsmuseum.org **Hours:** Mon-Fri 10 a.m.-5 p.m.; Sat 12-4 p.m. **Admission:** Donations accepted. **Accessibility:** Free parking. Wheelchair accessible. Tour guide available by appointment. Museum store.

Site Info: Active since 1919, this museum is located in a former armory. It features exhibit galleries that detail the distinctive heritage of Bay County, including major sections on Native Americans and the fur trade, lumbering, military history, and local businesses and industries.

Trombley-Centre House

Location: 901 John F. Kennedy Drive, Bay City, MI 48706 **Contact Info:** (989) 893-5733 • info@bchsmuseum.org • www.bchsmuseum.org **Hours:** By appointment. **Admission:** Donations accepted. **Accessibility:** Free parking. Tour guide available by appointment.

Site Info: Trombley-Centre House is the oldest frame house still standing in Bay County, built circa 1840, and operated by the Bay County Historical Society as an off-site location for some programs. The historic herb garden is managed by Olde Thyme Herb Society, a BCHS affiliate, and the house is open for first-floor viewing during special events, including River of Time and holiday open houses. Interpretive signs and virtual tour coming soon.

USS Edson DD-946

Location: 1680 Martin St., Bay City, MI 48706 **Contact Info:** (989) 684-3946 • vipuss946@sbcglobal.net • www.ussedson.org **Hours:** Mar-Dec: Daily 9 a.m.-5 p.m. **Admission:** $10/adult, $8/children (6-16), children 5 and under free. **Accessibility:** Free on-site parking. Not wheelchair accessible. Tour guide available. Museum store.

Site Info: Visitors to the USS Edson can explore the command and control centers, berthing areas, weapons systems, and hurricane bow of the ship. On-board exhibits show how the men of the Navy lived during the Vietnam War Era. The museum also houses a flag that flew on the USS Selfridge on the seventh of December 1941, when Japan attacked Pearl Harbor.

CENTRAL

BELDING

Belding Museum at the Historic Belrockton

Location: 108 Hanover St., Belding, MI 48809 **Contact Info:** (616) 794-1900 x425 • beldingmuseum@gmail.com • www.ci.belding.mi.us/museum_history.php **Hours:** 1st Sun monthly 1-4 p.m. Labor Day Weekend: Sat-Mon 1-4 p.m. **Admission:** Free.

Accessibility: Free on-site and street parking. Wheelchair accessible. Self-guided.

Site Info: The Belding Museum occupies three floors of the historic Belrockton Dormitory. The Belrockton Dormitory was built in 1906 to house single women employed at the silk mills. The museum focuses on the silk mill industry period, which was from 1880 to 1935, and the history of Belding and the surrounding area.

BELLEVUE

Bellevue Area Historical Museum

Location: 212 N. Main St., Bellevue, MI 49021 **Contact Info:** (269) 763-9136 • bellevue_mi@cox.net • www.rootsweb.com/~mibhs **Hours:** By appointment. **Admission:** Donations accepted. **Accessibility:** Free street parking. Wheelchair accessible. Self-guided.

Site Info: The Bellevue Area Historical Museum houses local artifacts focusing on military, agricultural, domestic, and industrial history. Collections of the museum include genealogy and school records, period clothing, uniforms, scrapbooks, and microfilm newspaper clippings of the Bellevue Gazette.

BIG RAPIDS

Bergelin House Museum

Location: 218 Winter, Big Rapids, MI 49307 **Contact Info:** (231) 796-9507 **Hours:** May-Sep: Sat 2-4 p.m. Also by appointment. **Admission:** Free. Donations accepted.

Site Info: The 1873 Italianate home of the Robert Bergelin family is being restored to display furniture manufactured in Big Rapids. Tours focus on furniture manufacturing at the end of the 19th century. Other collections include memorabilia of Big Rapids and Ferris State University.

Mecosta County Historical Society & Museum

Location: 129 S. Stewart Ave., Big Rapids, MI 49307 **Contact Info:** (231) 592-5091 • verona705@chartermi.net **Hours:** May-Sep: Sat 2-4 p.m. Also by appointment. **Admission:** Free. **Accessibility:** Street parking. Not wheelchair accessible. Tour guide available.

Site Info: The Mecosta County Historical Society operates a museum in the former home of lumberman Fitch Phelps. First opened in 1966, the museum features exhibits that highlight Mecosta County and lumber industry history. The museum also holds local history research collections.

Mecosta County Old Jail

Location: 220 South Stewart, Big Rapids, MI 49307 **Contact Info:** (231) 796-9507 **Hours:** May-Sep: Mon-Sat 9 a.m.-5 p.m. Also by appointment. **Admission:** Free. Donations accepted. **Accessibility:** Free parking in adjacent lot. Partially wheelchair accessible. Self-guided.

Site Info: The Big Rapids Historic Preservation Commission maintains the 1873 Queen Anne Old Jail. Tours focus on the penal system at the end of the 19th century. The site also holds some jail inmate records.

BRECKENRIDGE

Plank Road Museum

Location: 404 E. Saginaw St., Breckenridge, MI 48615 **Contact Info:** (989) 842-1241 • breckenridgewheeler@frontier.com • www.bwahs.org **Hours:** May-Sep: Mon 9 a.m.-12 p.m. Also by appointment. **Admission:** Donations accepted. **Accessibility:** Free on-site parking. Partially wheelchair accessible. Tour guide available.

Site Info: The Plank Road Museum is located in an 1890 Baptist Church and its exhibits change on an annual basis. The Drake Memorial House is set in the 1920s era, with a doctor's office featuring physicians' instruments that were used from 1920 to 1950. There is also a carriage house on-site.

BRIDGEPORT

Bridgeport Historic Village & Museum

Location: 6190 Dixie Hwy., Bridgeport, MI 48722 **Contact Info:** (989) 777-5230 • damccartney2@yahoo.com • www.bridgeporthistorical.blogspot.com **Hours:** Tue-Sat 1-5 p.m. **Admission:** Donations accepted.

Accessibility: Free on-site parking. Wheelchair accessible. Tour guide available. Museum store.

Site Info: The Bridgeport Historic Museum is one of seven buildings maintained by the Historical Society of Bridgeport. Other buildings in the village include an 1896 brick town hall, an 1862 one-room schoolhouse, an 1855 Greek Revival house, a replica 1941 fire hall and truck, an 1888 black barn for storage, and a replica little white church from the late 1860s. All buildings contain historical artifacts of the Bridgeport area, from 1835 to the present.

CHARLOTTE

1845 Eaton County Courthouse

Location: 1305 S. Cochran Ave., Charlotte, MI 48813
Contact Info: (517) 543-6999 • csamuseum@yahoo.com • www.csamuseum.net **Hours:** By appointment. **Admission:** Varies. **Accessibility:** Free on-site parking. Wheelchair accessible. Self-guided.

Site Info: The building served as Eaton County's courthouse from 1846 to 1872. The Greek Revival structure cost $1,000 to build in 1845. The Episcopal Church bought the courthouse in 1872. The building has served many purposes but has been renovated to resemble its original form.

Eaton County's Museum at Courthouse Square

Location: 100 W. Lawrence Ave., Charlotte, MI 48813 **Contact Info:** (517) 543-6999 • csamuseum@yahoo. com • www.csamuseum.net **Hours:** Mon-Thu 9 a.m.-4 p.m. Also by appointment. **Admission:** $1/ individual. **Accessibility:** Free on-site parking. Partially wheelchair accessible; second and third floors require assistance. Tour guide available; for large groups, please call ahead. School tours from within Eaton County are free.

Site Info: The restored 1885 courthouse features 10 exhibit rooms ranging from the restored courtroom to military exhibits. Along with the courthouse, the site includes the 1873 Sheriff's residence that is currently home to the Charlotte Chamber of Commerce, which has the hours of Mon-Thu 8:30am-3:30pm.

CHESANING

Chesaning Historical Museum

Location: 602 W. Broad St., Chesaning, MI 48047 **Contact Info:** (989) 845-3155 • cahs@centurytel.net • www.cahs.chesaning. com **Hours:** Apr-Dec: Mon, Wed 10 a.m.-12 p.m., 1st Sat monthly 1-4 p.m. Also by appointment. **Admission:** Free. **Accessibility:** Street parking. Wheelchair accessible. Tour guide available.

Site Info: The displays and permanent exhibits at the Chesaning Historical Museum focus on the area's history from Native-American habitation to present-day local businesses, industries, schools, and artifacts of local significance.

CLARE

Clare County Museum Complex

Location: 7050 S. Eberhart Ave., Clare, MI 48617 **Contact Info:** (734) 755-2638 • museum@clarecountyhistory.org • www.clarecountyhistory.org **Hours:** May-Sep: Sat 1-4 p.m. **Admission:** Free. Donations accepted. **Accessibility:** Free on-site parking. Wheelchair accessible. Tour guide available. Call for groups.

Site Info: Tour the Clare County Museum Complex, including a one-room schoolhouse and restored log cabin, and even watch a blacksmith in action. Plus, learn about such Clare County characters as Spikehorn Meyers and his bears. There is even a pavilion with tables perfect for a picnic.

COLDWATER

Little Red School House

Location: Branch County Fairgrounds, South Spregue St., Coldwater, MI 49036 **Contact Info:** (517) 278-2870 • bchistorybook@aol.com • www.branchcountyhistoricalsociety.org **Hours:** During Branch County Fair Week. Also by appointment.

Admission: $3/person. **Accessibility:** Free on-site parking. Not wheelchair accessible. Tour guide available.

Site Info: Step back in time as presenters pose as school teachers and demonstrate the creature comforts of a mid-1800s one-room schoolhouse and the learning tools used by educators.

Wing House Museum

Location: 27 S. Jefferson St., Coldwater, MI 49036 **Contact Info:** (517) 278-2870 • bchistorybook@aol.com • www.branchcountyhistoricalsociety.org **Hours:** May-Nov: 3rd Sat monthly. Also by appointment. **Admission:** $3/person. **Accessibility:** Free street parking. Not wheelchair accessible. Tour guide available.

Site Info: Constructed in 1875, the Wing House Museum is an example of Second Empire architecture with a convex mansard roof. It was sold to the Wing family in 1882 and has been restored to reflect the presence of both the

Chandler and Wing families through their periods of ownership up to 1974. Most of the furnishings on display in the museum belonged to the two families and include items dating back to the mid-1800s.

CONCORD

Mann House

Location: 205 Hanover St., Concord, MI 49237 **Contact Info:** (517) 373-3559 • museuminfo@michigan.gov • www.michigan.gov/michiganhistory **Hours:** Memorial Day-Labor Day: Thu-Sun 10 a.m.-4p.m. **Admission:** Free. Donations accepted.
Accessibility: Free street parking. Partially wheelchair accessible. Tour guide available.

Site Info: In 1883, Daniel and Ellen Mann built a two-story house in the small, picturesque farming community of Concord. They taught their daughters, Mary Ida and Jessie, to value education and life-long learning, which ultimately led them to preserve their family's nearly unaltered home and its furnishings. Visitors today can experience the family life and Victorian culture that shaped this pair of independent women.

CRYSTAL

Crystal Township Historical Society Building

Location: 415 S. Main St., Crystal, MI 48818 **Contact Info:** CTHS@CrystalHistory.com • www.rootsweb.ancestry.com/~micryshs/CrystalTownshipHistoricalSociety.html **Hours:** Sat 10 a.m.-3 p.m.
Admission: Donations accepted.

Site Info: The Crystal Township Historical Society's building houses genealogical research information for the area. There are also displays that share the history of Crystal Township and the surrounding area. Visitors have access to computers for research.

DURAND

Michigan Railroad History Museum

Location: 200 Railroad St., Durand, MI 48429 **Contact Info:** (989) 288-3561 • dusi@durandstation.org • www.durandstation.org **Hours:** Tue-Fri, Sun 1-5 p.m., Sat 10 a.m.-5 p.m.
Admission: Free. **Accessibility:** On-site parking. Wheelchair accessible. Tour guide available. Call for groups.

Site Info: The museum collects, preserves, and interprets artifacts, records, and documents related to history of railroads and railroading in Michigan. It engages in activities that encourage interest in railroad industry and is a source of information on railroad groups and structures throughout Michigan. The collection includes a wide variety of print, graphic, and railroading resources.

EAST LANSING

Michigan State University Archives & Historical Collection

Location: 888 Wilson Road, Rm. 101, East Lansing, MI 48824-1327 **Contact Info:** (517) 355-2330 • archives@msu.edu • www.archives.msu.edu **Hours:** Mon-Tue, Thu-Fri 9 a.m.-5 p.m., Wed 10 a.m.-5 p.m. Closed university holidays. **Admission:** Free. **Accessibility:** On-site parking for a fee. Wheelchair accessible. Self-guided. Call for groups.

 Site Info: The Michigan State University Archives & Historical Collection preserves and provides access to the university's historical records. The archives also has an active interest in records pertaining to the state of Michigan and the Great Lakes region, with emphasis on materials that complement existing collections or have a relation of some kind to the university. Changing exhibits are available to the public. See website for current exhibits and archive collections.

Michigan State University Museum

Location: 409 W. Circle Dr., East Lansing, MI 48824 **Contact Info:** (517) 884-6894 • pr@museum.msu.edu • www.museum.msu.edu **Hours:** Mon-Fri 9 a.m.-5 p.m.; Sat 10 a.m.-5 p.m.; Sun 1-5 p.m. Closed university holidays. **Admission:** $5/individual suggested donation. **Accessibility:** Street parking for a fee. Wheelchair accessible. Museum store.

 Site Info: The museum features country store and print shop exhibits and a Michigan fur trade display. Other exhibits include Michigan folk life, historical collections that emphasize rural history, Great Lakes archeology and ethnography collections, and ethnographic material from around the world. The Michigan Traditional Art Program Research Collection is a repository of objects and materials documenting the traditional culture of Michigan, including 3000 audio-taped interviews and 100,000 photographic images of folk life subjects in Michigan.

EATON RAPIDS

GAR Memorial Hall and Museum

Location: 224 S. Main St., Eaton Rapids, MI 48827 **Contact Info:** (517) 694-9394 • garmichigan@gmail.com • www.garmuseum.com **Hours:** 1st and 2nd Wed monthly. Holidays. Also by appointment. **Admission:** Free. Donations accepted. **Accessibility:** Free on-site and street parking. Not wheelchair accessible. Tour guide available upon request, call a day in advance.

Site Info: The location for Michigan's GAR Memorial Hall and Museum is the former James B. Brainerd Post #111 Grand Army of the Republic Hall located in Eaton Rapids, Michigan. The building is listed in the National Register of Historic Places and houses more than 2,900 historical artifacts and records relating primarily to the Grand Army of the Republic. Artifacts include uniforms, ribbons, flags, banners, photos, and printed documents.

EDMORE

Old Fence Rider Historical Center

Location: 222 S Sheldon, Edmore, MI 48829 **Contact Info:** (989) 506-9562 • cjlon49@yahoo.com • www.montcalm.org/culture0015.asp **Hours:** By appointment. **Admission:** $3/individual donation requested. **Accessibility:** Free on-site parking. Wheelchair accessible. Tour guide available; call for appointment.

Site Info: The Old Fence Rider Historical Center contains displays on early America, pioneers, the logging industry, the Civil War, and the major wars of the 20th century. Also included are life-size displays and recreations of old-fashioned drugstores, a 1950s diner, and a gas station. Local history is also displayed.

Pine Forest Historical Museum

Location: 402 E. Home St, Edmore, MI 48829 **Contact Info:** (989) 427-3843 • wshirley2@frontier.com • www.facebook.com/PineForest HistoricalMuseum/ **Hours:** May-Sep: Thu 2-4 p.m., and by appointment. **Admission:** Free. **Accessibility:** Free on-site and street parking. Not wheelchair accessible.

Site Info: Opened in 1983, the museum is located in the former Our Savior's Lutheran Church. Some unique exhibits include Victorian jewelry made from hair and a glass bookcase owned by a former state treasurer of Illinois, a close personal friend of Abraham Lincoln.

ESSEXVILLE

Heritage House Farm Museum

Location: 305 Pine St., Essexville, MI 48732 **Contact Info:** (989) 686-7025 • lenglehardt7025@charter.net **Hours:** Summer: Sun 2-4 p.m.. Also by appointment. **Admission:** Donations accepted. **Accessibility:** Not wheelchair accessible. Nearby parking available. Tours by appointment only.

Site Info: The Heritage House Farm Museum is a fully furnished nine-room home from the early 1890s. The home was built by John Garber, whose family members were the building's only residents. Today, the home features furniture that belonged to both the Garber family and the community. Also on-site are a German-style shed, corn crib, and herb garden.

EVART

Evart Public Library Museum

Location: 105 N. Main St., Evart, MI 49631 **Contact Info:** (231) 734-5542 • evartlibrary@yahoo.com **Hours:** Mon 9 a.m.-6 p.m., Tue-Fri 9 a.m.-4 p.m. **Admission:** Free. **Accessibility:** Street and lot parking. Wheelchair accessible. Tour guide available part-time.

Site Info: The museum has rotating exhibits and freestanding items that relate to the history of the Evart area and the interests of its citizens. Collections include artifacts, records, and archival materials.

FARWELL

Farwell Area Historical Museum

Location: 221 W. Main St., Farwell, MI 48622 **Contact Info:** (989) 588-0580 • trishtom68@yahoo.com • www.farwellmuseum. com **Hours:** Year-round: Mon, Wed, Fri 1:30-5:30 p.m.; May-Sep: Sat 12-4 p.m. **Admission:** Free. **Accessibility:** Free on-site and street parking. Wheelchair accessible. Free tour guide available.

Site Info: The Farwell Area Historical Society maintains a museum in the 1882 Ladies Library Association building. Exhibits highlight local history and include school, mill, post office, and local figures.

FOWLERVILLE

Livingston Centre Historical Village

Location: 8800 W. Grand River Ave., Fowlerville, MI 48836 **Contact Info:** (517) 223-8186 • jrhodes@fowlervillefamilyfair. com • www.fowlervillefamilyfair.com **Hours:** By appointment or during fairground events. **Admission:** Donations accepted. **Accessibility:** Free on-site parking. Partially wheelchair accessible. Call for groups and tours.

Site Info: The Livingston Centre Historical Village includes eight buildings: 1869 home of early settlers, 1872 Pere Marquette Depot, 1906 Methodist Church, 1880s barn and silo, 1910 barber shop, 1870 cobbler shop, and 1882 schoolhouse, and blacksmith shop. Many of the buildings house displays with period artifacts and original collections. There are several model train displays inside the Pere Marquette Depot.

FRANKENMUTH

Frankenmuth Historical Museum

Location: 613 S. Main St., Frankenmuth, MI 48734
Contact Info: (989) 652-9701 • fhaoffice@airadv.net • www.frankenmuthmuseum.org **Hours:** Mon-Thu 10 a.m.-5 p.m., Fri-Sat 10 a.m.-8 p.m., and Sun 12-6 p.m. **Admission:** $2/adult, $1/student, $5/family. Paid admission gives visitor free admission to Lager Mill Museum. **Accessibility:** Free public parking. Wheelchair accessible. Self-guided.

Site Info: The exhibits in the museum focus on the history of Frankenmuth and change quarterly. The Frankenmuth Historical Association also maintains the log cabin in Cross Park as well as Fischer Hall. Built in 1894 as a local gathering place, Fischer Hall is still used for the same purpose today.

Lager Mill Brewing Museum

Location: 701 Mill St., Frankenmuth, MI 48734 **Contact Info:** (989) 652-3377 • fhaoffice@gmail.com • www.frankenmuthmuseum.org **Hours:** Mon-Thu 11 a.m.-7 p.m., Fri-Sat 10 a.m.-9 p.m., Sun 12-6 p.m. **Admission:** $2/adult, $1/student, $5/family. Paid admission gives visitor free admission to Frankenmuth Historical Museum. **Accessibility:** Free public parking. Wheelchair accessible. Self-guided.

Site Info: The Lager Mill Brewing Museum shares Frankenmuth's brewing heritage and explores the brewing process. The two-story brewing museum is housed in the historic Nickless-Hubinger flour mill along the Cass River. Displays include antique signs, glasses, and bottles.

Michigan's Military & Space Heroes Museum

Location: 1250 Weiss St., Frankenmuth, MI 48734 **Contact Info:** (989) 652-8005 • info@michigansmilitarymuseum.com • www.michigansmilitarymuseum.com **Hours:** Daily 10 a.m.-5 p.m. **Admission:** $7/general, $6/senior, $5/college student, $4/active military, $3 age 6-17, children 5 and under free. **Accessibility:** On-site parking. Wheelchair accessible. Tour guides available.

Site Info: Michigan's Military & Space Heroes Museum is home to more than 140 displays and a collection of nearly 700 exhibits. Highlights of the collections include the uniforms of 5 Michigan governors and 13 Michigan astronauts. The museum also features the stories of 30 individual Medal of Honor recipients, making it the nation's largest Medal of Honor collection on display.

GLADWIN

Gladwin County Historical Museum

Location: 221 W. Cedar Ave., Gladwin, MI 48624 **Contact Info:** (989) 426-9277 • historicalsociety@ejourney.com • www.gladwinhistory.org **Hours:** Thu-Sat 10 a.m-4 p.m. Closed major holidays. **Admission:** Free. Donations accepted. **Accessibility:** Free on-site and street parking. Wheelchair accessible; use rear entrance. Self-guided. Museum store.

Site Info: Attractions at the Gladwin County Historical Museum include antiques belonging to the first settlers, World War I memorabilia, an 1850s square grand piano, an antique barbershop, portable embalming table and tools, and antique hand tools. Visitors can view photos and genealogies of four family estates in the county, horse-drawn carriages and farm implements on display, and military uniforms going back to the Black Hawk War of 1832.

Gladwin County Historical Village

Location: 515 E. Cedar, Gladwin, MI 48624 **Contact Info:** (989) 426-9277 • historicalsociety@ejourney.com • www.gladwinhistory.org **Hours:** Memorial Day-Labor Day: Sat 9 a.m.-1 p m. **Admission:** Free. Donations accepted. **Accessibility:** Free on-site parking. Partially wheelchair accessible.

Site Info: The Gladwin County Historical Village is a complex featuring a restored Michigan Central Railroad depot and seven other buildings. Other buildings in the collection include a carriage house built circa 1890, log cabins, and a one-room school.

GRAND LEDGE

Grand Ledge Area Historical Society Museum

Location: 118 W. Lincoln St., Grand Ledge, MI 48837 **Contact Info:** (517) 627-5170 • marnor1@comcast.net • www.gdledgehistsoc.org **Hours:** Sun 2-4 p.m., Festival Days 12-4 p.m. **Admission:** Donations accepted. **Accessibility:** Free street parking.

Wheelchair accessible. Tour guide available. Museum store.

Site Info: The Grand Ledge Area Historical Society Museum is housed in an 1880 Gothic Revival house that was built by local minister Byron S. Pratt. The museum explores a new theme each year. Archives and photographs are housed at the Grand Ledge District Library. The collection includes local photographs and slides, archival materials on businesses, cultural activities, families, schools, churches, and genealogical research materials.

GRASS LAKE

Coe House Museum

Location: 371 W. Michigan Ave., Grass Lake, MI 49240 **Contact Info:** (517) 522-8324 • mkoleary@reagan.com • www.facebook.com/Grass-Lake-Area-Historical-Society-1404304593177794 **Hours:** Mar-Oct: 1st and 3rd Sat. **Admission:** Donations accepted. **Accessibility:** On-site parking. Partially wheelchair accessible. Tour guide available.

Site Info: The museum houses a collection of material from Grass Lake, Waterloo, Sylvan, Norvell, and surrounding areas. The main exhibits include an ever-expanding collection of Michigan-related military items including a 1917 Model T ambulance and a British cannon that was recovered from the Detroit River after nearly 200 years underwater. A 1913 interurban rail car, one of only two known to exist, is also available for tours.

Dewey School Museum

Location: 11501 Territorial Road, Grass Lake, MI 48340 **Contact Info:** (517) 596-2254 • info@waterloofarmmuseum.org • www.waterloofarmmuseum.org **Hours:** By appointment. **Admission:** Donations accepted. **Accessibility:** Free on site parking. Not wheelchair accessible. Tour guide available by appointment.

Site Info: The Dewey School Museum conducts school tours in an effort to help students experience and appreciate 19th-century rural schooling. The Waterloo Area Historical Society also hopes to foster an appreciation of the pioneer farmers of Michigan, their family life, and their children's schooling.

Waterloo Farm Museum

Location: 13493 Waterloo Munith Road, Grass Lake, MI 49240 **Contact Info:** (517) 596-2254 • info@waterloofarmmuseum.org • www.waterloofarmmuseum.org **Hours:** Jun-Aug: Fri, Sat, Sun 1-5 p.m. **Admission:** $5/adult. Memberships available. **Accessibility:** Free on-site parking. Partially wheelchair accessible. Tour guide available.

Site Info: The Waterloo Farm Museum includes several buildings, such as a farmhouse, the Really Barn, a milk house, a log cabin, a workshop and forge, an ice house, and more. Visitors will also get the chance to explore historical artifacts from Michigan farming and country living, including farm equipment, clothing, household items, and quilts, along with 1880s clothing and furnishings and blacksmithing tools.

GREENVILLE

Fighting Falcon Military Museum

Location: 516 W. Cass St., Greenville, MI 48838 **Contact Info:** (616) 225-1940 • bachristensen@charter.net • www.thefightingfalcon.com **Hours:** May-Oct: Sun 2-4:30 p.m. Also by appointment. **Admission:** Donations accepted. **Accessibility:** Free on-site parking. Wheelchair accessible. Tour guide available. Museum store.

Site Info: The main exhibit is the restoration of an Army Air Corps CG4A, known worldwide as the "Fighting Falcon," which was purchased originally by the students of Greenville Public Schools and made locally by the Gibson Refrigerator Company. The primary focus of the exhibits center on WWII, but artifacts from the Civil War, WWI, Korean War, Vietnam, and modern conflicts are also displayed.

Flat River Historical Museum

Location: 213 N. Franklin St., Greenville, MI 48838 **Contact Info:** (616) 754-9950 • kjhudson@chartermi.net • www.flatriverhistoricalsociety.org **Hours:** Apr-Nov: Sat-Sun 2-4:30 p.m. **Admission:** Free. **Accessibility:** Free on-site parking. Wheelchair accessible. Tour guide available by appointment.

Site Info: The museum is located on the banks of the Flat River, where John Green settled and built his sawmill in 1844. The area has a rich history of mastodons and other prehistoric mammals, Native-American settlements, fur trading, and lumbering. In the 1890s, Greenville was known as the Refrigerator Capitol and Potato Capitol of the World. The Greenville area was the destination for many Danish immigrants. Michigan retailer Meijer was started in Greenville in 1934.

HANOVER

Conklin Reed Organ and History Museum

Location: 105 Fairview St., Hanover, MI 49241 **Contact Info:** (517) 563-8927 • hhahs@frontier.com • www.conklinreedorganmuseum.org **Hours:** May-Oct: Sun 1-5 p.m.

Admission: Donations accepted. **Accessibility:** On-site parking. Partially wheelchair accessible. Self-guided. Call for groups. Museum store.

Site Info: Housed in a 1911 Quincy Box-style schoolhouse, the Conklin Reed Organ and History Museum displays a collection of more than 100 playable reed (pump) organs, melodeons, and harmoniums. Other attractions include a restored antique fire apparatus, a 1950s water pump truck, a restored classroom, a printing press, and a Model-T popcorn truck. The building is listed on the National Register of Historic Sites.

Hanover-Horton Heritage Park

Location: 121 Tefft St., Hanover, MI 49241 **Contact Info:** (517) 563-8927 • hhahs@frontier.com • www.conklinreedorganmuseum.org **Hours:** Check website for schedule of events. **Admission:** Donations accepted. **Accessibility:** On-site parking. Self-guided. Call for groups.

Site Info: The Hanover-Horton Area Historical Society farms much of the land's 82-plus acres using antique equipment and holds two annual tractor pulls on a specially built track. Other structures include a vintage working sawmill and planer, lumber drying shed, operation "sugar shack" for refining raw maple sap into maple syrup, and an event center. Nature trails are open year-round.

HILLSDALE

Will Carleton Poorhouse

Location: 180 N. Wolcott Drive, Hillsdale, MI 49242 **Contact Info:** (517) 439-9547 • hillsdalehistoricalsociety@gmail.com • www.hillsdalehistoricalsociety.org **Hours:** Call or see website. **Admission:** Donations accepted. **Accessibility:** Free on-site parking. Wheelchair accessible. Tour guide available upon request.

Site Info: Experience yesteryear at the Will Carleton Poorhouse, which is open for special events and for arranged tours. The museum features many restored artifacts and plays host to several changing exhibits.

HOMER

Blair Historical Farm

Location: 26445 M-60 East, Homer, MI 49245 **Contact Info:** (517) 524-7348 • drcampers94@gmail.com • www.homerhistoricalsociety.org **Hours:** By appointment. **Admission:** Donations accepted. **Accessibility:** Free on-site parking. Partially wheelchair accessible. Tour guide available.

 Site Info: The Blair Historical Farm has an 1870s home on its grounds that had an addition built onto it in the 1880s. A 1920s barn, a more modern barn that houses a Birdsell Clover Huller, the 1889 Albion Township Town Hall, a DT&M way station, a chicken house, and a carriage house are also on the grounds. In addition, a nature trail is available for visitors.

HOWELL

Depot Museum

Location: 128 Wetmore Street, Howell, MI 48844 **Contact Info:** (517) 548-6876 • howellareahistoricalsociety@gmail.com • www.howellareahistoricalsociety.org **Hours:** Memorial Day-Labor Day: Sun 10 a.m.-2 p.m. Also by appointment. **Admission:** Donations accepted. **Accessibility:** Free on-site parking. Wheelchair accessible. Tour guide available by appointment.

 Site Info: Located in the 1886 Historic Ann Arbor Depot, the Howell Area Historical Society's museum houses a replica of an 1890s general store, displays, and artifacts from WWI and WWII. Railroad buffs will be particularly interested in the station master's old telegraph key, hand-operated signal levers, and collection of lanterns. The site also features an 1888 Grand Trunk wooden caboose.

HUBBARDSTON

Hubbardston Area Historical Society Museum

Location: 305 Russell St., Hubbardston, MI 48845 **Contact Info:** (989) 584-3803 • hubb.northplains@gmail.com • www.hubbardston.org **Hours:** Tue-Wed 2-4 pm. Also by appointment. **Admission:** Donations accepted. **Accessibility:** Free on-site parking. Wheelchair accessible. Tour guide available.

 Site Info: The Hubbardston Area Historical Society Museum features local author collections, first-family genealogy completions, files and folders of family histories, plat maps, Irish history collections, antique clothing display, fancy work, albums of pictures, and school class photos.

St. John the Baptist Catholic Church Complex

Location: 324 S. Washington St., Hubbardston, MI 48845 **Contact Info:** (989) 584-3803 • hubb.northplains@gmail.com • www.hubbardston.org **Hours:** Tue-Wed 2-4 p.m. Also by appointment. **Admission:** Donations accepted. **Accessibility:** Free on-site parking. Wheelchair accessible. Tour guide available by appointment.

Site Info: Built in 1868, St. John the Baptist Catholic Church was the largest building—seating 400—in Ionia County at the time of its establishment. It features 17 stained-glass windows, which were installed in 1905 and registered with the Michigan Stained Glass Census Bureau in the late 1990s. Other buildings on-site include the rectory, circa 1907; a former school, circa 1919; and a cemetery that was dedicated in 1884 and is still in use today.

IONIA

John C. Blanchard House

Location: 251 East Main Street, Ionia, MI 48846 **Contact Info:** (616) 527-6281 • kknoop@charter.net • www.ioniahistory.org **Hours:** Jun-Aug and Dec: Sun 1-4 p.m. Also by appointment. **Admission:** $3/individual suggested donation. **Accessibility:** Free on-site and street parking. Not wheelchair accessible. Tour guide available. Museum store.

Site Info: The John C. Blanchard House, which is on the National Register of Historic Places and the Michigan State Register of Historic Places, has been carefully preserved. Elements such as its walnut louvered shutters are still as striking today as they were in the past. The basement of the Blanchard House also serves as the local museum.

ITHACA

Gratiot County Historical Museum

Location: 129 W Center St, Ithaca, MI 48847 **Contact Info:** (989) 875-6232 • carol@gchgs.org • www.gchgs.org **Hours:** Historical Museum: Wed 1-4 p.m. **Admission:** Donations accepted. **Accessibility:** Free street parking. Wheelchair accessible. Tour guide available.

Site Info: The Gratiot County Historical Society Museum is housed in a Victorian house built in 1881, which is on the State Register of Historic Places. Collections include furniture, ceramics, glass, china, kitchenware, clothing, needlework, photographs, and postcards from the 1850s to the 1950s. A barn with small farm implements and tools is also featured.

JACKSON

Cell Block 7

Location: 3455 Cooper St., Jackson, MI 49201 **Contact Info:** (517) 780-5512 • info@ellasharp.org • www.cellblock7.org **Hours:** Mon-Tue Large groups by appointment, Wed-Sun 10 a.m.-5 p.m. **Admission:** $15/adult, $10/senior and military, $8/children (13-17), children 12 and under free. **Accessibility:** Free on-site parking. Not wheelchair accessible. Self-guided. Museum store.

Site Info: The museum is dedicated to the history of the State Prison of Southern Michigan and is located within an active working prison. Exhibits display how Jackson was chosen for the site of Michigan's State Prison and how punishment and overcrowding have changed since the prison first opened in 1839. Learn about the riots, escapes, and establishment of the Michigan Department of Corrections.

Ella Sharp Museum of Art & History

Location: 3225 Fourth St., Jackson, MI 49203 **Contact Info:** (517) 787-2320 • info@ellasharp.org • www.ellasharp.org **Hours:** Tue, Wed, Fri, Sat: 10 a.m.-5 p.m., Thu 10 a.m.-7 p.m. **Admission:** Combined galleries and house: $7/adult, $5/children (5-12), $4/AAA members. Free for museum members. Prices vary for visitation to farmhouse and galley only. See website for current price listings. **Accessibility:** Free on-site parking. Wheelchair accessible. Self-guided.

Site Info: The Ella Sharp Museum includes Ella Sharp's 19th-century Hillside Farmhouse, the Dibble One-Room Schoolhouse, Eli Stilson's Log House, the Merriman-Sharp Tower Barn, and six modern galleries that feature a private Audubon sculpture and art collection, Jackson history, and a private clock collection.

LAKEVIEW

Lakeview Area Museum

Location: 719 South Lincoln Avenue, Lakeview, MI 48850 **Contact Info:** (989) 352-7304 • jimandsharonyoungman@yahoo.com • www.lviewmuseum.com **Hours:** Jun-Sep: Fri-Sat 10 a.m.-1 p.m. **Admission:** Donations accepted. **Accessibility:** Free on-site parking. Wheelchair accessible. Self-guided.

Site Info: Located on the north end of town, the museum will give you a look into the past of the Lakeview area. Exhibits share information about the first settlers to the area and the industries, organizations, and schools of the town throughout the years. Visitors will find many articles, photographs, and artifacts to explore. A self-guided walking tour of the history of the downtown business buildings is available.

LANSING

Library of Michigan

Location: 702 W. Kalamazoo St., Lansing, MI 48909 **Contact Info:** (517) 373-1300 • librarian@michigan.gov • www.michigan.gov/libraryofmichigan **Hours:** Mon-Fri 10 a.m.-5 p.m., Sat 10 a.m.-4 p.m. **Admission:** Free. **Accessibility:** On-site parking for a fee. Free street parking. Wheelchair accessible. Self-guided. Museum store.

Site Info: The library has a Michigan collection, government documents, legal material, and rare book room. Exhibits change throughout the year. Call for current exhibit information.

Michigan Historical Center

Location: 702 W. Kalamazoo St., Lansing, MI 48909 **Contact Info:** (517) 373-1359 • museuminfo@ michigan.gov • www.michigan.gov/ michiganhistory **Hours:** Mon-Fri 9 a.m.-4:30 p.m., Sat 10 a.m.-4 p.m., Sun 1-5 p.m. **Admission:** $6/adult, $4/ senior (65 and older), $2/child (6-17), children under 5 free. **Accessibility:** On-site and street parking for a fee. Wheelchair accessible. Self-guided. Museum store.

Site Info: Experience all of Michigan's history through the center's exhibits, research collections, programs, and online resources. Museum exhibits and archival collections offer a unique statewide perspective. The Archives of Michigan holds government documents, manuscripts, maps, photographs, and major genealogical collections and makes them available to researchers. Educational programs are available for all ages.

Michigan State Capitol

Location: 100 North Captiol Avenue, Lansing, MI 48909 **Contact Info:** (517) 373-0184 • www.capitol. michigan.gov **Hours:** Mon-Fri 8 a.m.-5 p.m., Sat: 10 a.m.-4 p.m. **Admission:** Free. **Accessibility:** Street parking for a fee. Wheelchair accessible. Tour guide available, see website for details.

Site Info: Visit the capitol to watch the legislature meet for session, view hand-painted decorative art, and learn stories from Michigan's past. Two of the most distinctive characteristics of the capitol are its dome—inside and out—and the statue of Civil War Governor Austin Blair that greets visitors at the front of the building. The building has four stories with two grand staircases in the north and south corridors that provide access to all floors.

Michigan Women's Historical Center & Hall of Fame

Location: 213 W. Malcolm X St., Lansing, MI 48933 **Contact Info:** (517) 484-1880 • info@ michiganwomen.org • www. michiganwomenshalloffame.org **Hours:** Wed-Sat 12-4 p.m. 1st Sun monthly 2-4 p.m. Closed holidays. **Admission:** $3/adult, $2/student (6-18), children 5 and under free.

Accessibility: On-site parking. Wheelchair accessible. Tour guide available. Museum store.

Site Info: Opened in 1987 by the Michigan Women's Studies Association, the Michigan Women's Historical Center & Hall of Fame was the nation's first state-level facility to focus on women's history. The Michigan Women's Hall of Fame promotes equality of women by honoring the history and celebrating the accomplishments of Michigan women.

R.E. Olds Transportation Museum

Location: 240 Museum Dr., Lansing, MI 48933 **Contact Info:** (517) 372-0529 • director@reoldsmuseum.org • www.reoldsmuseum.org **Hours:** Tue-Sat 10 a.m.-5 p.m., Sun 12-5 p.m.; Nov-Mar: closed Sun. **Admission:** $7/ adult, $5/senior, $5/student, $5/ military, $15/family, $4/groups of 10 or more (per person).
Accessibility: Limited free on-site parking. Street parking available for a fee. Wheelchair accessible. Tour guide available. Call for groups. Museum store.

Site Info: The museum places emphasis on the automobile and its effect on Lansing and its people. On display are 50-plus cars and trucks, a Curved Dash Olds assembly line, the first automobile built by R.E. Olds, and an EV1.

Turner-Dodge House

Location: 100 E. North St., Lansing, MI 48906 **Contact Info:** (517) 483-4220 • DodgeTurner@gmail.com • www.lansingmi. gov/tdodge **Hours:** Tue-Fri 10 a.m.-5 p.m. Closed for holidays and special events. **Admission:** $5.00 **Accessibility:** Free on-site parking. Partially wheelchair accessible. Tour guide available.

Site Info: This historic house was built in 1858 by Marion and James Turner and enlarged in 1903 by daughter Abby and her husband, Frank Dodge. Guided tours of the house are available.

MARSHALL

Capitol Hill School

Location: 602 E. Washington St., Marshall, MI 49068
Contact Info: (269) 781-8544 • rhodes@msu.edu • www. marshallhistoricalsociety.org **Hours:** By appointment.
Admission: $3.00 **Accessibility:** Free on-site parking. Partially wheelchair accessible. Tour guide available.

Site Info: Built in 1860 and adjacent to the intended Michigan State Capitol, Capitol Hill School is the only survivor of three identical Gothic Revival schools. It was removed from public service in 1961 but now continues to provide a turn-of-the-century classroom experience. The Capitol Hill

School is listed on the National Register of Historic Places and the Historical American Building Survey.

Marshall Historical Museum at the G.A.R. Hall

Location: 402 E. Michigan Ave., Marshall, MI 49068
Contact Info: (269) 781-8544 • rhodes@msu.edu • www.marshallhistoricalsociety.org **Hours:** May 1-Oct 31: Sat, Sun 11 a.m.-4:30 p.m. **Admission:** Free, donations accepted.
Accessibility: Free on-site parking. Partially wheelchair accessible. Tour guide available.

 Site Info: The Marshall Historical Museum at the G.A.R. Hall focuses on telling Marshall's stories and highlighting items made in Marshall. Some items of interest are a Marshall folding bathtub, a buggy made by Page Brothers Buggy Works, and items from the Brewer Dry Goods Store. The museum also has exhibits on Marshall in the Civil War and community life. The building housing the museum's collections was built in 1902 as a meeting place for Civil War veterans.

Honolulu House Museum

Location: 107 N. Kalamazoo Ave., Marshall, MI 49068
Contact Info: (269) 781-8544 • rhodes@msu.edu • www.marshallhistoricalsociety.org **Hours:** Apr, Nov, Dec: Sat-Sun 11 a.m.-4:30 p.m.; May 1-Oct 31: Wed-Mon 11 a.m.-4:30 p.m.
Admission: $5/individual. **Accessibility:** Free on-site parking. Partially wheelchair accessible. Tour guide available.

Site Info: The Honolulu House was built in 1860 by Abner Pratt, then-consul to the Sandwich Islands. The exterior architecture is a blend of Italianate, Gothic, and Polynesian. The interior features paint-on-plaster wall and ceiling paintings restored to the splendor of the 1880s, including period furnishings and authentic replicas of the carpets. The Honolulu House Museum is listed on the National Register of Historic Places and the Historical American Building Survey.

Walters Gasoline and Interurban Railroad Museum

Location: 220 West Michigan Ave., Marshall, MI 49068
Contact Info: (269) 789-2562 **Hours:** May-Oct: Sat 12-5 p.m.; Sun 1-4 p.m. Also by appointment. **Admission:** Free.
Accessibility: Free on-site and street parking. Not wheelchair accessible. Tour guide available.
Site Info: The museum features photos and maps of the Marshall Interurban Railroad that ran through downtown Marshall. Collections include Shell Oil and gasoline artifacts; Marshall and Calhoun Counties historical artifacts; and historic Marshall Interurban Railway maps, coins, books, and many other items.

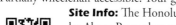

LODGING IN MARSHALL

National House Inn

Location: 102 S Parkview, Marshall, MI 49068 **Contact Info:** (269) 781-7374 • frontdesk@nationalhouseinn.com • www. nationalhouseinn.com **Property Info:** Inn. Seasonal: Feb-Dec. Privately owned; no public tours; pre-booking required. Free on-site and street parking. Not wheelchair accessible. Gift shop. **Price:** $120-$170.

Site Info: The National House Inn is one of the oldest operating hotels in Michigan. The inn was built in 1835 by Colonel Andrew Mann, who used lumber from the Ketchum sawmill and bricks that were molded and fired on the site to construct what has endured as the oldest brick building in Calhoun County. The inn was a stop on the Underground Railroad. Listed on the State and National Register of Historic Places.

MASON

Mason Historical Museum

Location: 200 East Oak Street, Mason, MI 48854 **Contact Info:** (517) 697-9837 • info@masonmuseum.org • www. masonmuseum.com **Hours:** Tue, Thu, Sat 1-3 p.m. **Admission:** Free. **Accessibility:** Free street parking. Wheelchair accessible. Tour guide available. Museum store.

Site Info: Exhibits in the Mason Historical Museum include artifacts related to the history of the Mason area. Also available is a library with information pertaining to the Mason area, photos, books, files, and DVDs of past programs.

The Pink School

Location: 707 W. Ash St., Mason, MI 48854 **Contact Info:** (517) 697-9837 • info@masonmuseum.org • www.masonmuseum. com **Hours:** By appointment. **Admission:** Free. **Accessibility:** Free street parking. Wheelchair accessible. Tour guide available.

Site Info: The Pink School is a one-room school that originally opened in 1854. It displays old school memorabilia, including the original slate blackboard and rope to pull the bell. The school was open for 111 years, and there is a photo for each of the 105 teachers who worked at the school. The school was moved to its current location in 1976.

LODGING IN MASON

Barnes Street Bed & Breakfast

Location: 604 S. Barnes St., Mason, MI 48854 **Contact Info:** (517) 676-9600 • info@barnesbnb.com • www.barnesbnb.com **Property Info:** Bed & Breakfast. Open year-round. Free on-site and street parking. Not

CENTRAL

wheelchair accessible. Food available on-site. **Price:** $95-$125.

Site Info: The Barnes Street Bed & Breakfast is in a preserved Victorian home, circa 1887, including original wallpaper, fixtures, and woodwork.

MIDLAND

Alden B. Dow Home & Studio

Location: 315 Post St., Midland, MI 48640 **Contact Info:** (866) 315-7678 • info@abdow.org • www.abdow.org **Hours:** Tours are held Feb-Dec: Mon-Sat 2 p.m., Fri-Sat 10 a.m. Reservations required. **Admission:** $15/adult, $12/senior, $7/student.

Accessibility: Free on-site parking. Not wheelchair accessible. Guided tours only.

Site Info: The Alden B. Dow Home & Studio was the home of Alden B. Dow, an organic architect. Today, his home, along with his studio, is a National Historic Landmark that is open for tours and educational programming. The home and studio houses original furnishings, a ceramic and glass collection from the 1930s to the 1960s, personal and professional libraries, historic model-scale trains, and mechanical toys.

Chippewa Nature Center

Location: 400 S. Badour Rd., Midland, MI 48640 **Contact Info:** (989) 631-0830 • kbagnall@ chippewanaturecenter.org • www. chippewanaturecenter.org **Hours:** Mon-Sat 8 a.m.-5 p.m., Sun and Holidays 12-5 p.m. **Admission:** Free.

Accessibility: Free on-site parking. Wheelchair accessible. Self-guided. Museum store.

Site Info: Within the Chippewa Nature Center, the ecosystem gallery provides hands-on exhibits. The 1870s homestead farm and log schoolhouse are open Sunday afternoons. Visitors can tour the log cabin, barn, and outbuildings; visit farm animals and an heirloom garden; and participate in historical activities.

Doan Midland County History Center

Location: 3417 West Main St., Midland, MI 48640 **Contact Info:** (989) 631-5930 • skory@mcfta.org • www.mcfta.org **Hours:** Weekdays 8:30 a.m.-5 p.m. **Admission:** Free.
Accessibility: Free on-site parking. Wheelchair accessible. Self-guided.

Site Info: The Herbert D. Doan Midland County History Center is the gateway to Heritage Park. It houses a permanent hands-on gallery of interactive exhibits of Midland County history, from the beginning to today. Among the many features of the center are a gallery of featured exhibitions, a research library for local and general history, and an archival collection of Midland County artifacts.

Heritage Park

 **Location:** 3200 Cook Road, Midland, MI 48640 **Contact Info:** (989) 631-5930 • skory@mcfta.org • www.mcfta.org **Hours:** 3rd Fri 11 a.m.-2 p.m. monthly. Also by appointment. **Admission:** Free. **Accessibility:** Free on-site parking. Partially wheelchair accessible. Self-guided.

 Site Info: Heritage Park is home to multiple historical sites. The 1874 Bradley Home is a beautifully restored, hands-on historic house museum, where visitors enjoy a glimpse of the everyday life of an early Midland family. The adjacent carriage house features a collection of horse-drawn carriages and sleighs and is home to mid-Michigan's largest functioning blacksmith shop. View the multimedia exhibits in the Herbert H. Dow Historical Museum to learn about Midland's largest business.

MOUNT PLEASANT

Bohannon Schoolhouse

Location: Central Michigan University, West Campus Dr. and Preston St., Mount Pleasant, MI 48859 **Contact Info:** (989) 774-3829 • cmuseum@cmich.edu • www.museum.cmich.edu **Hours:** Call for current hours. **Admission:** Free. **Accessibility:** Wheelchair accessible.

 Site Info: With its inkwells, McGuffey readers, and wood-burning stove resting in the corner, the school is reminiscent of a long-ago era. Originally located in Jasper Township near Midland, the school was brought to the Central Michigan University campus in 1970. The Museum of Cultural and Natural History staff and many dedicated friends worked to restore the building to its original state. Donated artifacts helped to make it complete.

Clarke Historical Library

Location: First Floor, Charles V. Park Library, Central Michigan University, Mount Pleasant, MI 48043 **Contact Info:** (989) 774-3352 • clarke@cmich.edu • www.clarke.cmich.edu **Hours:** Mon-Fri 8 a.m.-5 p.m. **Admission:** Free. **Accessibility:** On-site parking for a fee. Wheelchair accessible.

Site Info: The Clarke Historical Library has a comprehensive printed collection regarding the state of Michigan and Michigan history. The archives focus primarily on the geographic region north of Lansing, south of Mackinaw. The library also serves as the archives for the Central Michigan University. The 1,200-square-foot exhibit gallery features two exhibits each year that highlight some aspect of the library's collection.

Museum of Cultural and Natural History

Location: Central Michigan University, 103 Rowe Hall, Mount Pleasant, MI 48859 **Contact Info:** (989) 774-3829 • cmuseum@cmich.edu • www.museum.cmich.edu **Hours:** Mon-Fri 8 a.m.-5 p.m., Sat-Sun 1-5 p.m. **Admission:** $1/adult suggested donation, $0.50/child suggested donation. **Accessibility:** Street parking for a fee. Wheelchair accessible. Tour guide available; call ahead to schedule.

Site Info: A unit of Central Michigan University, the museum features exhibits relating to prehistoric glaciers and mastodons; Native Americans and fur traders; Civil War soldiers and lumbermen; and wildlife, including bats and walleye. It has 13,000 artifacts focused on regional history from the middle of the 1800s on; information about Michigan's lumbering and pioneering eras; and a full range of articles used in everyday life, including bottles, phonograph records, clothing, and woodworking tools.

Ziibiwing Center of Anishinabe Culture & Lifeways

Location: Saginaw Chippewa Indian Tribe of Michigan, 6650 E. Broadway, Mount Pleasant, MI 48858 **Contact Info:** (989) 775-4750 • ggenereaux@sagchip.org • www.sagchip.org/ziibiwing **Hours:** Mon-Sat 10 a.m.-6 p.m. **Admission:** $6.50/adult, $3.75/senior, $4.50/student, $3.75/children (5-17), children 4 and under free. **Accessibility:** On-site parking. Wheelchair accessible. Tour guide available with minimum of 10 people. Museum store.

Site Info: The Ziibiwing Center of Anishinabe Culture & Lifeways is an American-Indian museum that includes the permanent exhibit "Diba Jimooyung," which mean "Telling Our Story"; changing exhibit areas; collections storage area; and research center. Its collection of artifacts includes more than 2,000 pieces of artwork, primarily from Great Lakes Anishinabek, treaty documents, Saginaw Chippewa historical material, and photographs.

OKEMOS

Meridian Historical Village

Location: 5113 Marsh Road, Okemos, MI 48805 **Contact Info:** (517) 347-7300 • meridianhistoricalvillage@gmail.com • www.meridianhistoricalvillage.org **Hours:** May-Oct: Sat 10 a.m.-2 p.m. **Admission:** Free. **Accessibility:** Free on-site parking. Not wheelchair accessible. Tour guide available; check in at general store.

Site Info: This village is a 19th-century living history museum with nine historic structures. It features a small archival collection of local materials. Reference copies of the archival guide are available at the Okemos, Haslett, and East Lansing Public Libraries.

OVID

Mary Myers Museum

Location: 131 East Williams, Ovid, MI 48866 **Contact Info:** (989) 834-5421 • ovidhs67@yahoo.com • www. ovidhistoricalsociety.weebly.com **Hours:** 2nd and 4th Sun monthly 2-4 p.m. Also by appointment. **Admission:** Donations accepted. **Accessibility:** Free street parking.

Site Info: Return to yesteryear in the Mary Myers Museum, which is housed in an 1869 Italianate-style structure that is furnished for the period and operated by the Ovid Historical Society.

OWOSSO

Shiawassee County Historical Society Archives and Museum

Location: 1997 N. M-52 Owosso, MI 48867 **Contact Info:** (989) 723-2371 • archer@charter.net • www. shiawasseecountyhistsoc.org **Hours:** Year-round: Thu 10 a.m.-3 p.m.; Apr-Sep: Sun 1-4 p.m. **Admission:** Donations accepted. **Accessibility:** Free on-site and street parking. Wheelchair accessible. Tour guide available. Museum store.

Site Info: The Shiawassee County Historical Society collects and displays items pertaining to Shiawassee County, especially family histories and the beginning of Shiawassee County. The Shiawassee County Historical Society Archives and Museum contains three rooms plus a long hall full of artifacts pertaining to the county.

REMUS

Remus Area Historical Museum

Location: 324 S. Sheridan Ave., Remus, MI 49340 **Contact Info:** (989) 967-8153 • museum@winntel.net • www.remus.org/historical-society **Hours:** May-Oct: Wed 11 a.m.-3 p.m. **Admission:** Free. **Accessibility:** Free on-site parking. Wheelchair accessible. Self-guided. Museum store.

Site Info: The museum holds local artifacts and pictures of local families, businesses, churches, schools, the Remus Creamery, and items used by persons in bygone periods in the area.

SAGINAW

Castle Museum of Saginaw County History

Location: 500 Federal Ave., Saginaw, MI 48607 **Contact Info:** (989) 752-2861 • ksanta@castlemuseum.org • www.castlemuseum.org **Hours:** Tue-Sat 10 a.m.-4:30 p.m., Sun 1-4:30 p.m. **Admission:** $1/adult, $0.50/child. **Accessibility:** Free on-site and street parking. Wheelchair accessible. Tour guide available by appointment. Museum store.

Site Info: Built in 1898 as a U.S. post office, the museum offers three floors of exhibits. The Historical Society of Saginaw County maintains and preserves a collection of more than 100,000 artifacts used for exhibits and research. The Castle Museum hosts about 40 exhibits—temporary and permanent. One of the largest, working model trains in the region can also be seen here.

Catholic Heritage Museum

Location: 5800 Weiss St., Saginaw, MI 48603 **Contact Info:** (989) 799-7910 • www.saginaw.org/links/catholic-heritage-museum.html **Hours:** By appointment. **Admission:** Free. Donations accepted. **Accessibility:** Free on-site parking. Wheelchair accessible. Tour guide available.

Site Info: Visitors will enjoy Catholic Church artifacts and special exhibitions at the Catholic Heritage Museum. The museum is located in the building that houses the offices of the Catholic Diocese of Saginaw.

Saginaw Railway Museum

Location: 900 Maple St., Saginaw, MI 48602 **Contact Info:** (989) 790-7994 • info@saginawrailwaymuseum.org • www.facebook.com/saginawrailwaymuseum **Hours:** May-Nov: 1st and 3rd Sat 1-4 p.m. **Admission:** Donations accepted. A $20 donation receives a one-year individual membership. **Accessibility:** Free on-site parking. Partially wheelchair accessible. Self-guided. Museum store.

Site Info: Located in a restored 1907 depot, the Saginaw Railway Museum offers photos and artifacts related to railroading, with emphasis on Michigan and the Great Lakes Bay area. A large HO-scale model railroad is displayed in the basement and is loosely based on the region in the 1950s.

SANFORD

Sanford Centennial Museum

Location: 2222 Smith St., Sanford, MI 48657 **Contact Info:** (989) 687-9048 • logmarks@tds.net • www.sanfordhist.org **Hours:** Memorial Day-Labor Day: Sat 10 a.m.-5 p.m., Sun 1-5 p.m. Also by appointment. **Admission:** Free. **Accessibility:** Free on-site parking. Wheelchair accessible. Self-guided.

Site Info: The museum includes eight restored and furnished historic buildings: two schools, a general store, a log cabin, a township hall, a church, an implement barn, and a train depot. Inside are vintage tools, implements from the logging days, political memorabilia, a dentist's office, a barbershop, a doctor's office, a saloon, toys, and household goods. Highlights include a train engine, a boxcar, two cabooses, Michigan logging wheels, a covered bridge, and a windmill.

SARANAC

Saranac Depot

Location: 138 N. Bridge St., Saranac, MI 48881 **Contact Info:** (616) 693-2730 • marilar@att.net **Hours:** May-Sep: 2nd and 4th Sun 1-4 p.m. Also by appointment. **Admission:** Donations accepted. **Accessibility:** Free on-site parking. Wheelchair accessible. Tour guide available. Museum store.

Site Info: The Saranac Depot, located on the banks of the Grand River, is a museum operated by the Boston-Saranac Historical Society. The depot's collections consist of historical artifacts donated from area families. The depot's exhibits highlight artifacts from area doctors, early local businesses, military organizations, rural school pictures, hand tools, and more. A picnic shelter is also located on the grounds.

SHEPHERD

Shepherd Powerhouse Museum

Location: 314 W. Maple St., Shepherd, MI 48883 **Contact Info:** (989) 828-5588 • neema_63@hotmail.com • www.facebook.com/shepherdareahistoricalsociety **Hours:** Last Sat in Apr. Also by appointment. **Admission:** Donations accepted.

Accessibility: Free street parking. Partially wheelchair accessible. Tour guide available.

Site Info: This museum houses artifacts relevant to the Shepherd area community, death notices for Shepherd residents, and multiple scrapbooks and published books for genealogical research on the main floor. The upper floor is composed of mini-scenes from early Shepherd houses, including a kitchen, seamstress shop, dining/living room, and bedroom.

SIDNEY

Montcalm Heritage Village

Location: 2800 College Drive, Sidney, MI 48885 **Contact Info:** (989) 328-2111 • karen.maxfield@montcalm.edu • www.montcalm.edu/heritagevillage **Hours:** May-Oct: 10 a.m.-4 p.m. **Admission:** Free.

Accessibility: Free on-site and street parking. Partially wheelchair accessible. Self-guided. Tour guide available; call ahead to schedule a group or private tour.

Site Info: The village is a collection of 21 buildings, including a schoolhouse, log cabin, hat shop, doctor's house, blacksmith shed, country store, jailhouse, and church. Visitors can tour independently or arrange for a guided tour to view the interiors of the buildings. Docents will explain the historical significance of the buildings and occupants, as well as other relevant information about the village.

ST. CHARLES

St. Charles Area Museum

Location: 603 Chesaning St., St. Charles, MI 48655 **Contact Info:** (989) 865-9115 • stcharlesareamuseum@gmail.com **Hours:** Tue 12-2 p.m., Thu 6-8 p.m., Sat 10 a.m.-12 p.m. Also by appointment. **Admission:** Free. **Accessibility:** Free on-site parking. Wheelchair accessible. Self-guided.

Site Info: The museum is located near the Saginaw Valley Rail Trail and provides a restful stop for those utilizing this beautiful linear county park. Visitors can also see a restored 1941 Chessie Caboose, one of three remaining of its type.

ST. JOHNS

Paine-Gillam-Scott Museum

Location: 106 Maple St., St. Johns, MI 48879 **Contact Info:** (989) 224-2894 • pgsmuseum@hotmail.com • www.pgsmuseum.com **Hours:** May-Dec: Sun 1-4 p.m., Wed 2-6:30 p.m. **Admission:** $2/adult. Members free. **Accessibility:** Free on-site and street parking. Not wheelchair accessible. Tour guide available, call for other tours.

Site Info: Paine-Gillam-Scott campus has three buildings, including the oldest brick house in St. Johns, plus a general store with an old-fashioned dentist's office, a carriage house with many agricultural artifacts, and industrial items manufactured in St. Johns. The house is named after three physicians who had offices there at different times. The campus also has a doctor's office exhibit, military room, Native-American exhibit, and a research room.

ST. LOUIS

St. Louis Historic Park

Location: 110 E. Crawford St., St. Louis, MI 48880 **Contact Info:** (989) 681-3017 • stlouisdda@stlouismi.com • www.stlouismi.com/1/stlouis/Historical_Society.asp **Hours:** Thu 1-4 p.m. **Admission:** Free. **Accessibility:** Free on-site parking. Wheelchair accessible. Tour guide available by appointment.

Site Info: The park includes the St. Louis Area Historical Society's museum, which is located in the restored Pere Marquette Train Depot. It is filled with historic items and displays, including the transportation pavilion that contains a 1917 Republic Truck, a Native-American dugout canoe, and other transportation items. Also available is a restored historic wooden tollbooth from the M-46 Plank Road.

SUNFIELD

Welch Museum

Location: 161 Main St., Sunfield, MI 48890 **Contact Info:** (517) 331-4682 • sunfieldhistoricalsociety@gmail.com • www. sunfieldhistoricalsociety.com **Hours:** Apr-Dec: Mon 10 a.m.-2 p.m., Wed 2-5 p.m., Sat 10 a.m.-2 p.m.; Jan-Mar: Open Sat. **Admission:** Free. **Accessibility:** Free street parking. Wheelchair accessible. Free tour guides available.

 Site Info: A fully furnished 1860 log cabin is built within the museum. The Welch Museum also features a barn replica, a 1927 fire truck, a turn-of-the-century classroom, hands-on displays, and photos of students who graduated from Sunfield High School from 1914 to 1963. A genealogy room is available for research of the local area.

TEKONSHA

Tekonsha Historical Museum

Location: 109 East Canal St., Tekonsha, MI 49092
Contact Info: (517) 765-2588 • bc.arnold765@gmail.com
Hours: By appointment. **Admission:** Free. **Accessibility:** Wheelchair accessible.
Site Info: The museum has many replica hand-built homes from the town, a reference library, photos, and memorabilia. The museum is readily available to anyone wishing to trace his or her family ancestry or to learn more about the history of Tekonsha.

UNION CITY

Hammond House Museum

 **Location:** 210 Charlotte St., Union City, MI 49094 **Contact Info:** (517) 741-7733 • uchistoricalsociety@ yahoo.com **Hours:** Open for special events and by appointment.
Admission: $2/adult.
Site Info: The 150-year-old Hammond House is a Greek Revival-style structure and was one of the first fine homes in Union City. The former Union City School bell, which was used in the late 19th century, is also housed on the premises.

WILLIAMSTON

Williamston Depot Museum

Location: 369 W. Grand River Ave., Williamston, MI 48895
Contact Info: (517) 655-1030 • williamstondepot2013@gmail.com • www.williamstonmuseum.org **Hours:** Mon-Fri 9 a.m.-1 p.m., 2nd Sun monthly 2-4 p.m. **Admission:** Free. **Accessibility:** Free on-site parking. Wheelchair accessible. Self-guided.

Site Info: The museum has a nine-case exhibit that tells the story of Williamston, beginning with the Native Americans up to the present. There is an American Legion exhibit and several displays that change throughout the year. Many volumes of the "Williamston Enterprise" are housed at the museum and are available for reference purposes. In addition, photographs of historic Williamston are on display and in the collection.

ADRIAN

Lenawee County Historical Museum

Location: 110 E. Church St., Adrian, MI 49221 **Contact Info:** (517) 265-6071 • lenaweemuseum@yahoo.com • www.lenaweemuseum.org **Hours:** Tue-Fri 10 a.m.-2 p.m., Sat 10 a.m.-4 p.m. **Admission:** Free. **Accessibility:** Free on-site parking. Wheelchair accessible. Tour guide available; group tours available by appointment.

Site Info: Exhibits in the museum feature the history of Lenawee County; its pioneers, railroads, industries; and other items linked to the county's history. The 100-year-old museum building is listed on the National Register of Historical Places and also includes an auditorium and a large archive of genealogical information.

Madden Hall Historical Area

Location: 1257 E. Siena Heights Dr., Adrian, MI 49221 **Contact Info:** (517) 266-3580 • nfoley@adriandominicans.org • www.adriandominicans.org **Hours:** Mon-Fri 9 a.m.-5 p.m. Also by appointment. **Admission:** Free. **Accessibility:** Parking across the street. Wheelchair accessible. Tour guide available upon request.

Site Info: The historical display in Madden Hall is organized into three time periods: 1879 to 1933, 1933 to 1962, and 1963 to the present. Each contains narrative panels, photos, documents, and artifacts of its respective period. Also located within Madden Hall is the historic Holy Rosary Chapel, which was built 1905 to 1907.

ALGONAC

Algonac-Clay Historical Society Museum

Location: 1240 St. Clair River Dr., Algonac, MI 48001 **Contact Info:** (810) 794-9015 • achs@algonac-clay-history.com • www.achistory.com **Hours:** May-Dec: Sat-Sun 1-4 p.m., Summer: Wed 6-8 p.m. Also by appointment. **Admission:** Donations accepted. **Accessibility:** Free on-site parking. Wheelchair accessible. Free tour guides available.

Site Info: The Algonac-Clay Historical Society Museum features an exhibit of the area's Native-American tribes, a military display, a freighter exhibit, Tall Ship memorabilia display, and an exhibit that changes yearly.

Maritime Museum

Location: 1117 St Clair River Dr., Algonac, MI 48001 **Contact Info:** (810) 794-9015 • achs@algonac-clay-history.com • www.achistory.com **Hours:** May-Dec: Sat-Sun 1-4 p.m.; Summer: Wed 6-8 p.m. Also by appointment. **Admission:** Donations accepted. **Accessibility:** Free on-site parking. Wheelchair accessible. Tour guides available.

Site Info: Exhibits include an ice boat built by Chris Smith and donated by son Alan, a 1949 Chris-Craft runabout, many motors and models, and a kit boat made by the Algonac High School shop class. There is also a race boat patterned after the boats raced in the area in the 1940s and 1950s. The information provided with each display helps highlight the rich maritime history of the area.

ANN ARBOR

Bentley Historical Library

Location: University of Michigan, 1150 Beal Ave., Ann Arbor, MI 48109 **Contact Info:** (734) 764-3482 • kljania@umich.edu • www.bentley.umich.edu **Hours:** Mon-Fri 9 a.m.-5 p.m., Sat 9 a.m.-1 p.m. Closed major holidays. **Admission:** Free. **Accessibility:** Free on-site parking. Wheelchair accessible.

Site Info: Attractions at the Bentley Historical Library include an exhibit in the reading room and "Tappan's Vision" in the Whiting Room. The library includes more than 50,000 linear feet of archives and manuscripts; 90,000 printed volumes; 1.5 million photographs and other visual materials; more than 10,000 maps; and nearly 60 terabytes of digital content.

Detroit Observatory

Location: Detroit Observatory, University of Michigan, 1398 East Ann St., Ann Arbor, MI 48109 **Contact Info:** (734) 764-3482 • kljania@umich.edu • www.bentley.umich.edu/about/detroit-observatory **Hours:** Contact for current hours. **Admission:** By donation. **Accessibility:** Street parking is available for a fee. Not wheelchair accessible. Tour guide available.

Site Info: The Detroit Observatory was the first observatory built in the state of Michigan and is the second-oldest building on the University of Michigan's campus. In 2005, the Detroit Observatory became a division of the Bentley Historical Library. Having undergone a full restoration in 1998, the building stands essentially as it was in 1854.

Gerald R. Ford Presidential Library

Location: 1000 Beal Ave., Ann Arbor, MI 48109 **Contact Info:** (734) 205-0555 • ford.library@nara.gov • www.fordlibrarymuseum.gov **Hours:** Mon-Fri 8:45 a.m.-4:45 p.m. Closed federal holidays. **Admission:**

Free. **Accessibility:** Free on-site parking. Wheelchair accessible. Self-guided.

Site Info: Step inside Michigan's only presidential library, home to Gerald R. Ford's Presidential, Vice Presidential, and Congressional papers, including his Warren Commission files. Visitors can view a video on President Ford's life and career; browse lobby exhibits detailing Gerald Ford's early life, his years at the University of Michigan and Yale, and his years as a congressman, vice president, and president; learn about the role and impact of First Lady Betty Ford; and see President Ford's office.

Kempf House Museum

Location: 312 S. Division St., Ann Arbor, MI 48104 **Contact Info:** (734) 994-4898 • kempfhousemuseum@ gmail.com • www.kempfhousemuseum. org **Hours:** Spring and Fall: Sun 1-4 p.m. Also by appointment.
Admission: Donations accepted.

Accessibility: Parking is available in the structures on S. Fifth or E. Washington. Wheelchair accessible. Tour guide available.

Site Info: The 1853 Greek Revival Kempf House interprets Ann Arbor history and Victorian lifestyles from 1850 to 1910. Trained guides will lead you through restored rooms, including the music studio, where the 1877 Steinway Concert Grand Piano remains as it has for more than 100 years.

Historic Michigan Theater

Location: 603 E. Liberty St., Ann Arbor, MI 48104 **Contact Info:** (734) 668-8397 • info@michtheater.org • www.michtheater.org **Hours:** Mon-Sat 3-10 p.m.; Sun 3-9 p.m. **Admission:** $7-$10/individual for films.
Accessibility: Street parking for a fee; multiple parking structures in area (Maynard and Liberty Square structures are closest). Wheelchair accessible. Tour guide available; by appointment.

Site Info: The Historic Michigan Theater hosts live events and performing art programs, in addition to exhibiting fine films 365 days a year. The Ford Gallery exhibits and highlights the founding of Ann Arbor, the building of the Michigan Theater, and the restoration of the theater.

Museum on Main Street

Location: 500 N. Main St., Ann Arbor, MI 48106 **Contact Info:** (734) 662-9092 • wchs-500@ameritech.net • www.washtenawhistory.org **Hours:** Sat-Sun 2-4 p.m. Weekdays by appointment. **Admission:** Donations accepted. **Accessibility:** Free on-site and street parking. Wheelchair accessible. Tour guide available. Museum store.

 Site Info: The Museum on Main Street features changing exhibits that tell the various stories of Washtenaw County. Using an extensive collection, each exhibit focuses on a particular theme, story, or event. Exhibits have included the county's role in farming, photography, and the Civil War and how Washtenaw County's heritage is interpreted through local museums, historic homes and sites, and the programs and attractions they offer to the public. The archives are open for research by appointment.

Sindecuse Museum of Dentistry

 **Location:** Ground floor of Kellogg Foundation Inst., Corner of N. University & Fletcher, Ann Arbor, MI 48109 **Contact Info:** (734) 763-0767 • dentalmuseum@umich.edu • www. dent.umich.edu/sindecuse **Hours:** Mon-Fri 8 a.m.-6 p.m. Closed university holidays. **Admission:** Free. **Accessibility:** On-site and street parking for a fee. Wheelchair accessible. Self-guided.

 Site Info: The Sindecuse Museum of Dentistry has collected and cataloged more than 18,000 objects with approximately 15 percent on display in permanent and temporary exhibitions. There are 13 museum exhibit cases that feature the history of dentistry, with an emphasis on the United States and Michigan. In addition, displays of dental instruments and equipment, photos of dentistry alumni and faculty, dental trade catalogs, and consumer oral hygiene products can be viewed.

Sutherland-Wilson Farm Museum

 **Location:** 797 Textile Rd., Ann Arbor, MI 48108 **Contact Info:** (734) 668-2607 • pittsfieldhistory@yahoo. com • www.pittsfieldhistory.org **Hours:** By appointment. **Admission:** Free. **Accessibility:** Free on-site parking. Wheelchair accessible. Tour guide available by appointment. Museum store.

 Site Info: The Sutherland-Wilson Farm Museum is located in an 1830s Greek Revival home and features furniture from the 1830s to 1900s. Also available are plat maps, newspaper clippings, and historical information about the township. Outbuildings consist of a barn, a carriage house, an ice house, a wood shed, and a pump house.

The Argus Museum

Location: 525 West William St., Ann Arbor, MI 48103 **Contact Info:** (734) 769-0770 • cchidester@ onealconstruction.com • www. washtenawhistory.org **Hours:** Mon-Fri 9 a.m-5 p.m. Closed holidays.
Admission: Free. Donations accepted.
Accessibility: Free on-site parking. Self-guided.

Site Info: Founded in Ann Arbor during the Depression Era as a radio manufacturer, Argus Inc. grew to become an international organization that held numerous patents and created iconic products, including the Argus C3 camera, "the brick."

Promoting the art and medium of photography, the museum is housed in one of the company's former factory buildings and exhibits photography equipment, including still and movie cameras, projectors, accessories, and darkroom equipment.

William L. Clements Library

Location: University of Michigan, 909 S. University Ave., Ann Arbor, MI 48109 **Contact Info:** (734) 764-2347 • www. clements.umich.edu **Hours:** Mon–Wed: 9 a.m. – 4:45 p.m.; Thu: 9 a.m. – 7:45 p.m. **Admission:** Free. **Accessibility:** Free street parking. Wheelchair accessible. Self-guided.

Site Info: The front hall's changing exhibits focus on different aspects of collections that would interest both an expert bibliophile and the casual reader.

LODGING IN ANN ARBOR

Stone Chalet Bed & Breakfast Inn and Event Center

Location: 1917 Washtenaw Ave., Ann Arbor, MI 48104 **Contact Info:** (734) 417-7223 • lana@stonechalet.com • www.stonechalet.com **Property Info:** Bed & Breakfast. Open year-round. Privately owned; no public tours; pre-booking required. Free street parking. Not wheelchair accessible. **Price:** $159-$300.

Site Info: The Stone Chalet has 10 guest rooms and an event center for 100 people. The three-story Swiss Chalet with one-foot-thick fieldstone walls and leaded glass windows was built in 1917 as the family home of Dr. Dean Myers. The Unitarian Church purchased the property in 1946 and built a parsonage in 1948. A mid-century modern sanctuary was designed in 1956 by Dr. George Brigham. The grounds include a garden with a gazebo and water lily pond.

BAD AXE

Pioneer Log Cabin Village

Location: 205 S. Hanselman St., Bad Axe, MI 48413 **Contact Info:** (989) 550-2733 • badaxehistorical@yahoo.com • www.thehchs.org **Hours:** Memorial Day-Labor Day: Sun 2-4 p.m. **Admission:** Donations accepted. **Accessibility:** Free street parking. Partially wheelchair accessible; grounds only. Tour guide available.

Site Info: The Pioneer Log Cabin Village is the largest collection of authentically restored pioneer log buildings in Michigan. The six individual museums include a pioneer home, general store, one-room school, chapel, barn, and blacksmith shop. They were originally built between 1875 and 1900 and moved to this site from elsewhere around Huron County in the 1980s.

The Allen House Museum

Location: 303 N. Port Crescent, Bad Axe, MI 48413 **Contact Info:** (989) 550-2733 • badaxehistorical@yahoo.com • www.thehchs.org **Hours:** Memorial Day-Labor Day: Sun 2-4 p.m. **Admission:** Donations accepted. **Accessibility:** Free street parking. Not wheelchair accessible. Tour guide available.

Site Info: The museum is located within a 1902 Dutch colonial home that was built by Wallace E. Allen, the town's longest-serving mayor. Owned by only one family, the home is virtually the same structure it was originally. As a result, many of the original features are still as they were in 1902. The museum depicts life as it would be at the turn of the century and is furnished with period antiques.

BELLEVILLE

Belleville Area Museum

Location: 405 Main St., Belleville, MI 48111 **Contact Info:** (734) 697-1944 • kdallos@provide.net • www.facebook.com/BellevilleAreaMuseum **Hours:** Jan-Mar: Tue 3-7 p.m., Wed-Sat 12-4 p.m.; Apr-Aug: Tue 3-7 p.m. Mon, Wed, Fri 12-4 p.m.; Sep-mid-Nov: Tue-Wed 3-7 p.m., Thu-Sat 12-4 p.m.; Late Nov-Dec: Tue, Wed, Fri 3-7 p.m., Thu, Sat 12-4 p.m. **Admission:** $2/adult, $1/student (7-12). **Accessibility:** Free street parking. Wheelchair accessible. Self-guided. Museum store.

Site Info: See life as it was long ago at the Belleville Area Museum, which is housed in the 1875 Van Buren Township Hall. Exhibits highlight local history of Belleville as well as Van Buren and Sumpter Townships.

Yankee Air Museum

Location: 47884 D St., Belleville, MI 48111 **Contact Info:** (734) 483-4030 • supportyankee@yankeeairmuseum.org • www.yankeeairmuseum.org **Hours:** Tue-Sat 10 a.m.-4 p.m. **Admission:** $8/adult, $5/students, seniors, and military. Free for members and children under 2. **Accessibility:** Free on-site parking. Wheelchair accessible. Tour guide available. Museum store.

Site Info: The museum challenges, educates, and inspires visitors to embrace aviation's past as a vehicle to the future. Exhibits center on the Willow Run Bomber Plants, along with more recent conflicts, such as the Vietnam War. Come take a ride in one of the historic WWII-Era bombers—the B-17 "Yankee Lady" or the B-25 "Yankee Warrior!"

BERKLEY

Berkley Historical Museum

Location: 3338 Coolidge Hwy., Berkley, MI 48072 **Contact Info:** (248) 658-3335 • museum@berkleymich.net • www.berkleymich.org/community_museum.shtm **Hours:** Sun 2-4 p.m., Wed 10 a.m-1 p.m. **Admission:** Free. **Accessibility:** Free on-site parking. Wheelchair accessible. Tour guide available. Call for groups. Museum store.

Site Info: The Berkley Historical Museum has a fascinating collection of items and historical information from the town's rich and colorful past. The museum is located in a historic 1928 fire hall and has a large collection of treasures from both the police and fire departments' past, including hats, boots, and clothing.

BIRMINGHAM

Birmingham Museum

Location: 556 W. Maple, Birmingham, MI 48009 **Contact Info:** (248) 530-1928 • museum@bhamgov.org • www.bhamgov.org/museum **Hours:** Wed-Sat 1-4 p.m. 2nd Thu of the month 1-8 p.m. Also by appointment. **Admission:** $7/adults, $5/seniors, $5/students, children under 5 free. Admission fees may be higher during special exhibitions. **Accessibility:** Free street parking. Partially wheelchair accessible. Tour guide available. Museum store.

Site Info: The museum shares personal stories about the history and heritage of the Birmingham area, from pre-settlement Native-American presence to contemporary culture. The museum is located in a beautiful park setting near downtown Birmingham and has something for all ages.

BLOOMFIELD HILLS

Cranbrook Archives

Location: 380 Lone Pine Rd., Bloomfield Hills, MI 48304
Contact Info: (248) 645-3583 • www.cranbrook.edu/ archives **Hours:** Tue-Fri 10 a.m.-5 p.m. and by appointment.
Admission: Free. **Accessibility:** Free on-site parking. Wheelchair accessible.

 Site Info: The archive manages the care and conservation of Cranbrook's cultural properties. It also fosters greater public awareness of Cranbrook's history and cultural heritage through temporary exhibits. Check the website to see current and future exhibits. The archive also maintains an extensive collection of architectural records and audio-visual materials pertaining to Cranbrook. The archives are located in the Cranbrook Art Museum.

BRIGHTON

1885 Lyon One-Room Schoolhouse

 **Location:** 14455 Buno Rd., Brighton, MI 48114 **Contact Info:** (810) 250-7276 • info@brightonareahistorical. com • www.brightonareahistorical.com **Hours:** Thu 9 a.m.-12 p.m. Also by appointment. **Admission:** Free. **Accessibility:** Free on-site parking. Wheelchair accessible. Tour guide available. Museum store.

 Site Info: The Lyon One-Room Schoolhouse is a completely restored one-room school. Originally, a log school occupied the site from 1842 until the existing frame school was built in 1885. The small museum highlights local memorabilia, including early veterinarian tools and early photos of Brighton.

City of Brighton Arts, Culture, and History (CoBACH) Center

 **Location:** 202 W. Main St., Brighton, MI 48116 **Contact Info:** (810) 250-7276 • info@brightonareahistorical. com • www.brightonareahistorical.com **Hours:** Sun-Fri 5-8 p.m., Sat 11 a.m.-5 p.m. **Admission:** Free. **Accessibility:** Free street parking. Partially wheelchair accessible. Tour guide available. Museum store.

 Site Info: With educational exhibits changing every two months, the CoBACH provides a wonderful opportunity for both children and adults to experience the past and to discuss how life, work, and home have changed.

The 1838 Old Village Cemetery

Location: 200 W. St. Paul Street, Brighton, MI 48116 **Contact Info:** (810) 250-7276 • info@ brightonareahistorical.com • www. brightonareahistorical.com **Hours:** Dawn to dusk. **Admission:** Free. **Accessibility:** Free on-site parking. Wheelchair accessible. Self-guided. Call for other tours.

Site Info: This beautiful burial ground located above the tranquil waters of Brighton's millpond and under a canopy of mature trees offers a unique view looking down on the town. Enter this city cemetery through the double-arched entrance gates located adjacent to St. Paul Episcopal Church. This outdoor museum of history is a walk into Brighton's past. Many names that appear on the gravestones are also found on street signs throughout the city and neighboring townships.

BROOKLYN

Walker Tavern Historic Complex

Location: 13220 M-50, Brooklyn, MI 49230 **Contact Info:** (517) 241-0731 • museuminfo@michigan.gov • www. michigan.gov/walkertavern **Hours:** See website. **Admission:** Free. Michigan State Parks Recreation Passport required for park entry. **Accessibility:** Free on-site parking. Partially wheelchair accessible. Tour guide available.

Site Info: From 1843 to 1855, Lucy and Sylvester Walker's farmhouse tavern welcomed travelers who stopped at Cambridge Junction. When the Detroit-Chicago Road, today's US-12, began seeing auto traffic, another entrepreneur, Frederick Hewitt, spotted an opportunity and created a tourist attraction. The 1830s tavern, a reconstructed barn, and the 1929 Hewitt residence offer period settings and interpretive exhibits.

CANTON

Canton Historical Museum

Location: 1022 S Canton Center Rd., Canton, MI 48187 **Contact Info:** (734) 397-0088 • cantonhist@comcast. net • www.cantonhistoricalsociety.org **Hours:** Mid-Apr-Dec: Sun 9 a.m.-1 p.m. Also by appointment. **Admission:** Donations accepted. **Accessibility:** Free on-site parking. Wheelchair accessible. Tour guide available. Museum store.

Site Info: The Canton Historical Society's main museum is a one-room schoolhouse. There is also the Bartlett-Travis House, a Victorian-style home, and a pole barn with old farm equipment all at Preservation Park.

CAPAC

Capac Community Historical Museum

Location: 401 E. Kempf Ct., Capac, MI 48014 **Contact Info:** (810) 395-2859 • capacmuseum@hotmail.com • www. capachistoricalsocietymuseum.wordpress.com **Hours:** Mon-Fri 12-3 p.m., Sun 1-4 p.m. Also by appointment. **Admission:** Donations accepted. **Accessibility:** Free on-site parking. Wheelchair accessible. Tour guide available.

Site Info: The Capac Community Historical Society maintains a museum in the restored Grand Trunk Western Depot, which features exhibits relating to Capac and the Thumb. On display is the Kempf Model City, a mechanical city that is 40 feet long and four feet wide. A Grand Truck Western caboose is also on-site, which includes several railroad artifacts.

CASEVILLE

Maccabees Hall Museum

Location: 6733 Prospect St., Caseville, MI 48725 **Contact Info:** (989) 856-9090 • chscm@comcast.net • www.thehchs. org/caseville **Hours:** Wed-Sat 12-4:30 p.m. **Admission:** Free. **Accessibility:** Free on-site parking. Wheelchair accessible. Tour guide available.

Site Info: The Historical Society of Caseville maintains a museum in the 1890s Maccabees Hall. Displays include fishing, farming, lumbering, school, and household exhibits. The society also has a collection of newspapers and yearbooks. Come to see the items and materials that illustrate the life, conditions, events, and activities of the past.

CASS CITY

Sanilac Petroglyphs Historic Site

Location: 2501 Germania Rd., Cass City, MI 48909 **Contact Info:** (989) 856-4411 • museuminfo@michigan.gov • www.michigan.gov/sanilacpetroglyphs **Hours:** End of May-early Sep: Wed-Sun 10 a.m.-4 p.m. **Admission:** Free. **Accessibility:** Free on-site parking. Partially wheelchair accessible. Tour guide available.

Site Info: The focal point of the site is a sandstone outcrop with more than 100 petroglyphs carved into its surface. The park also includes other early Native-American archaeological sites as well as later historic period sites and a portion of the Cass River floodplain forest landscape. There is a mile-long, self-guided walking trail with two river crossings. This is the most extensive grouping of petroglyphs known in the state.

CHELSEA

Chelsea Area Historical Museum

Location: 128 Jackson St., Chelsea, MI 48118 **Contact Info:** (734) 476-2010 • info@chelseahistory.org • www.chelseahistory. org **Hours:** Winter: Sat-Sun 12-3 p.m.; Summer: Sat 11 a.m.-3 p.m., Sun 12-3 p.m. **Admission:** Donations accepted. **Accessibility:** Call for groups.

 Site Info: This museum collects, manages, displays, and maintains area artifacts, archival information, photographs, genealogy records, and oral histories of local citizens.

CHESTERFIELD

Chesterfield Historical Village

 **Location:** 47275 Sugarbush Road, Chesterfield, MI 48047 **Contact Info:** (586) 747-1970 • chesterfieldhistory@yahoo.com • www. chesterfieldhistoricalsociety.org **Hours:** 2nd Sun monthly 10 a.m.-4 p.m. **Admission:** Donations accepted. $1/ adult and $2/family suggested donation. **Accessibility:** Free on-site parking. Wheelchair accessible. Self guided. Museum store.

 **Site Info:** The historical village has a one-room school, working blacksmith shop, museum store, and log cabin. It is operated by the Chesterfield Township Historical Society, which maintains and stores the Trinity Collection, dedicated to the history of Chesterfield Township. The village is located next to a one-mile paved walking trail.

Stahls Automotive Museum

 Location: 56516 N. Bay Dr., Chesterfield, MI 48051 **Contact Info:** (586) 749-1078 • info@stahlsauto.com • www.stahlsauto.com **Hours:** Tue 1-4 p.m., 1st Sat of the month 11 a.m-4 p.m. **Admission:** Donations accepted. **Accessibility:** Free on-site and street parking. Self-guided.

Site Info: Stahls Automotive Museum helps visitors gain a better understanding of how the automobile developed from a novelty to a main form of transportation. In addition to the beautiful cars, enjoy the collection of gas pumps, road signs, oil cans, and other car-related accessories from the Depression Era.

CLARKSTON

Clarkston Heritage Museum

Location: 6495 Clarkston Rd., Clarkston, MI 48346 **Contact Info:** (248) 922-0270 • info@clarkstonhistorical.org • www.clarkstonhistorical.org **Hours:** Mon-Thu 10 a.m.-9 p.m., Fri-Sat 10 a.m.-6 p.m., Sun 1-6 p.m. **Admission:** Free. **Accessibility:** Free on-site parking. Wheelchair accessible. Self-guided.

Site Info: Located in the library, the museum offers displays that focus on Clarkston history. The museum has featured exhibits detailing every aspect of early life in Clarkston. Exhibits change approximately twice a year and have covered everything from village businesses and local farms to summer tourists and the area's long-standing tradition of 4th of July parades.

CLAWSON

Clawson Historical Museum

Location: 41 Fisher Ct., Clawson, MI 48017 **Contact Info:** (248) 588-9169 • historicalmuseum@cityofclawson.com • www.clawsonhistoricalsociety.org **Hours:** Sun, Wed 1-4 p.m. **Admission:** Free. **Accessibility:** Free parking. Not wheelchair accessible. Call for groups.

Site Info: The museum building is a three-story house built by Oswald and Deborah Fischer in the 1920s. It features 11 rooms furnished to reflect that era. The collection includes furniture, decorative arts, textiles, clothing, tools, and ephemera from the 1920s. The museum also includes high school and city yearbooks, genealogical materials, newspaper clippings, and more than 3,000 photographs.

CLAY TOWNSHIP

Log Cabin and Detroit Urban Railway Wait Station and Annex

Location: 4710 Point Tremble Road, Clay Township, MI 48001 **Contact Info:** (810) 794-9015 • achs@algonac-clay-history.com • www.achistory.com **Hours:** Open Log Cabin Day (last Sun in Jun). Also by appointment. **Admission:** Donations accepted. **Accessibility:** Free on-site parking. Wheelchair accessible. Tour guides available.

Site Info: The log cabin shows life as it was in 1850. On display are many artifacts donated by community members. The log cabin was moved to its current location in 1984. The DUR Wait Station and section of tracks show where people waited for the train from Detroit to Port Huron. The annex has boats and farming implements.

CLINTON

Southern Michigan Railroad Museum

Location: 320 S. Division St., Clinton, MI 49236 **Contact Info:** (517) 456-7677 • www.southernmichiganrailroad.com **Hours:** Museum open during scheduled train excursions or by appointment. **Admission:** Train fares vary; museum admission is free. **Accessibility:** Free on-site and street parking. Not wheelchair accessible. Self-guided.

Site Info: The Southern Michigan Railroad Society (SMRS) is dedicated to building an operating museum railroad using one of the first railroad branch lines in Michigan—a rail corridor that connected the Michigan Southern line with the Michigan Central line in Jackson—and preserving its historical railroad era, which was 1838 to 1982. The society also maintains the SMRS Tecumseh South and North Rail Yards.

CLINTON TOWNSHIP

Albert L. Lorenzo Cultural Center

Location: 44575 Garfield Rd., Clinton Township, MI 48038 **Contact Info:** (586) 445-7348 • culturalcenter@macomb.edu • www. lorenzoculturalcenter.com **Hours:** Wed-Sat 10 a.m.-4 p.m., Thu 10 a.m.-8 p.m. **Admission:** Free. **Accessibility:** Free on-site parking. Wheelchair accessible. Tour guides available. Call for groups.

Site Info: Located on the center campus of Macomb Community College, the center provides multidimensional cultural experiences in the areas of history, science, literature, current events, visual and performing arts, and popular culture. Each year, the center presents a themed anchor program and numerous presentations that explore the influences and experiences that shape the community's heritage; examine topics from a variety of perspectives; and create interactive opportunities for learning, celebration, and entertainment.

COLUMBIAVILLE

Columbiaville Historical Society Museum

Location: 4718 First St., Columbiaville, MI 48619 **Contact Info:** (810) 793-2932 • cville.historical.society.2@gmail.com • www.columbiavillehistoricalsociety.blogspot.com **Hours:** May-Oct: 1st and 3rd Fri monthly 1-4 p.m. Also by appointment. **Admission:** Donations accepted. **Accessibility:** Free on-site parking. Wheelchair accessible. Tour guide available.

Site Info: Attractions at the Columbiaville Historical Society Museum include Native-American arrowheads, mounted birds, quilts, furniture, books, photographs, and antique household and farm implements.

DAVISON
Davison Area Historical Museum

Location: 263 E. Fourth St., Davison, MI 48423 **Contact Info:** (810) 658-2286 • info@davisonmuseum.org • www.davisonmuseum.org **Hours:** Thu 10 a.m.-2 p.m. **Admission:** Donations accepted. **Accessibility:** Free on-site parking. Partially wheelchair accessible. Tour guides available.

Site Info: Exhibits include a display of a kitchen, circa 1900; toys; a dry goods store; a millinery shop; Davison's first "post office"; military uniforms; artifacts from area veterans; a scale of Davison Village as it was about 1903; and school artifacts. The Woolley Veterinarian Building is next to the museum. This local veterinary building has all its original medicines, equipment, and other artifacts. The building was built in 1893 and had several uses before becoming a vet's office in 1905.

Kitchen School

Location: 4010 S. State Rd, Davison, MI 48423 **Contact Info:** (810) 658-2286 • info@davisonmuseum.org • www.davisonmuseum.org **Hours:** By appointment. **Admission:** Donations accepted. **Accessibility:** Free on-site parking. Partially wheelchair accessible. Tour guides available.

Site Info: This 150-year-old building is a one-room school as it would have appeared in 1940. It includes an outhouse, a wood stove, and playground equipment. Lumber dimensions and nail type were used to determine the age of the building. The school was named for Silas Kitchen, one of Davis Township's homesteaders.

DEARBORN
Arab American National Museum

Location: 13624 Michigan Ave., Dearborn, MI 48126 **Contact Info:** (313) 582-2266 • ksilarski@accesscommunity.org • www.arabamericanmuseum.org **Hours:** Wed-Sat 10 a.m.-6 p.m., Sun 12-5 p.m. **Admission:** $8/adult, $4/senior (59 and older), $4/student and educator, children 6 and under free. **Accessibility:** Free on-site and street parking. Wheelchair accessible. Self-guided. Museum store.

Site Info: The Arab American National Museum (AANM) is devoted to Arab-American history and culture. Arab Americans have enriched the economic, political, and cultural landscape of American life. By bringing the voices and faces of Arab Americans to mainstream audiences, the museum continues the commitment to dispel misconceptions about Arab Americans and other minorities. The museum presents exhibitions and public programs in Michigan and the nation. AANM is Southeast Michigan's only affiliate of the Smithsonian Institution.

Commandant's Quarters

Location: 21950 Michigan Ave, Dearborn, MI 48124 **Contact Info:** (313) 565-3000 • jtate@ci.dearborn.mi.us • www.thedhm.com **Hours:** Tue-Thu 10 a.m.-3 p.m. **Admission:** Free. **Accessibility:** Free on-site and street parking. Not wheelchair accessible. Tour guide available.

Site Info: Built in 1833, the Commandant's Quarters was one of eleven buildings that were part of the Detroit Arsenal at Dearborn. The period rooms in the building reflect how the commandants and their families would have lived during the Civil War. In addition, a selection of Civil War memorabilia and material is on display at the house.

Ford Rouge Factory Tour

Location: 20900 Oakwood Blvd., Dearborn, MI 48124 **Contact Info:** (800) 835-5237 • research.center@thehenryford.org • www.thehenryford.org **Hours:** Mon-Sat 9:30 a.m.-5 p.m. **Admission:** $17/adult, $15.25/senior (62+), $12.75/children (3-12), children 2 and under free. Combo ticket prices with the Henry Ford Museum are available. **Accessibility:** On-site parking; $6/vehicle except for members. No public parking on factory grounds, shuttle bus service from the Henry Ford Museum is provided. Wheelchair accessible. Self-guided. Museum store.

Site Info: The Ford Rouge Factory Tour allows visitors to walk through a working truck plant and view a gallery of Ford vehicles produced at the factory. There are two theater experiences available to visitors. Observation decks above the factory floor allow visitors to watch production of Ford trucks. Check the website for non-production dates.

Greenfield Village

Location: 20900 Oakwood Blvd., Dearborn, MI 48124 **Contact Info:** (800) 835-5237 • research.center@thehenryford.org • www.thehenryford.org **Hours:** Mid-Apr-Oct: Daily 9:30 a.m.-5 p.m.; Nov: Fri-Sun 9:30 a.m.-5 p.m.; Dec: Select nights. **Admission:** $26/adult, $23.50/senior (62+), $19.50/children (5-12), children 4 and under free. Members free. **Accessibility:** On-site parking; $6/vehicle except for members. Wheelchair accessible. Self-guided.

Site Info: Greenfield Village is an outdoor experience that includes 83 authentic historic structures spread across more than 80 acres. Visitors can walk through Noah Webster's home, Thomas Edison's Menlo Park laboratory, and the courthouse where Abraham Lincoln practiced law. Jump aboard a Model T, take a leisurely ride on a steam-powered locomotive, or watch an 1867 baseball game. Greenfield Village brings history to life and has something for everyone.

Henry Ford Museum

Location: 20900 Oakwood Blvd., Dearborn, MI 48124 **Contact Info:** (800) 835-5237 • research.center@ thehenryford.org • www.thehenryford. org **Hours:** Daily 9:30 a.m.-5 p.m. **Admission:** $21/adult, $19/senior (62+), $15.75/children (5-12), children 4 and under free. Members free. **Accessibility:** On-site parking; $6/vehicle except for members. Wheelchair accessible. Self-guided. Museum store.

Site Info: The Henry Ford Museum showcases exhibits in the areas of transportation, technology, agriculture, industry, domestic life, public life, design, and decorative arts. Items big and small that have changed the world are the focus of the museum. For an additional fee, visitors can experience Greenfield Village, the Ford Rouge Factory Tour, and an IMAX Theatre.

McFadden-Ross House & Gardner House

Location: 915 S. Brady, Dearborn, MI 48124 **Contact Info:** (313) 565-3000 • jtate@ci.dearborn.mi.us • www.thedhm. com **Hours:** Tue-Thu 10 a.m.-4 p.m. **Admission:** Free. **Accessibility:** Free on-site parking. Not wheelchair accessible. Self-guided. Museum store.

Site Info: The Gardner House, which once belonged to a childhood friend of Henry Ford, has three rooms and is Dearborn's oldest building located outside of Greenfield Village at The Henry Ford. The McFadden-Ross House has a variety of photos, papers, and books. In addition, visitors can explore exhibits and an archive with genealogical resources.

DETROIT

Charles H. Wright Museum of African American History

Location: 315 E. Warren Ave., Detroit, MI 48201 **Contact Info:** (313) 494-5800 • ted@chwmuseum.org • www.thewright. org **Hours:** Tue-Sat 9 a.m.-5 p.m.; Sun 1-5 p.m. **Admission:**

$8/adult (13-61), $5/senior (62+), $5/youth (3-12), members and children 3 and under free. **Accessibility:** On-site and street parking. Wheelchair accessible. Guided tours available.

Site Info: Founded in 1965, the Charles H. Wright Museum of African American History is the world's-largest institution dedicated to the African-American experience. The permanent exhibit at the museum focuses on African-American history and culture. Visitors can explore displays on early civilizations in Africa, the tragedy of the middle passage and horrors of slavery, stories of courage along the Underground Railroad, and more. Check the website to view current and upcoming temporary exhibits.

Detroit Historical Museum

Location: 5401 Woodward Ave., Detroit, MI 48202 **Contact Info:** (313) 833-1805 • www.detroithistorical.org **Hours:** Tue-Fri 9:30 a.m.-4 p.m., Sat-Sun 10 a.m.-5 p.m. **Admission:** Free. **Accessibility:** Lot parking available for a fee. Partially wheelchair accessible. Self-guided.

Site Info: The Detroit Historical Museum has 11 signature exhibits, plus changing exhibits, that allow visitors to explore more than 300 years of the city's history. Visitors can see how automobiles helped shape the city by exploring the "America's Motor City" exhibition, and music lovers can check out the interactive Kid Rock Music Lab. Other exhibits, such as the streets of old Detroit, allow guests to "walk" through history and learn about industrial, sports, and domestic life.

Dossin Great Lakes Museum

Location: 100 Strand Dr., Belle Isle, Detroit, MI 48207 **Contact Info:** (313) 833-5538 • www.detroithistorical.org **Hours:** Sat-Sun 11 a.m.-4 p.m. **Admission:** Free. Michigan State Parks Recreation Passport is required for entry. **Accessibility:** Free on-site and street parking. Wheelchair accessible. Self-guided.

Site Info: Permanent exhibits include "built by the river," the Miss Pepsi vintage 1950s championship hydroplane, the Gothic room from the City of Detroit III, a bow anchor from the S.S. Edmund Fitzgerald, the pilothouse from the Great Lakes freighter S.S. William Clay Ford, and one of the largest known collections of scale model ships in the world.

Ford Piquette Avenue Plant

Location: 461 Piquette Ave., Detroit, MI 48202 **Contact Info:** (313) 872-8759 • nancy.darga@tplex.org • www.fordpiquetteavenueplant.org **Hours:** Wed-Sun 10 a.m.-4 p.m. **Admission:** $12/adult, $10/senior, $5/student (w/ID), children 12 and under free. **Accessibility:** Free parking. Wheelchair accessible. Tour guide available. Call for groups.

Site Info: The 67,000-square-foot, three-story plant is located in the Milwaukee Junction Industrial District, the birthplace of Detroit's auto industry. Changing exhibits and vintage vehicles tell the story of Ford Motor Company during the Piquette Era. This National Historic Landmark is listed on the U.S. Department of Interior Registered Historic Places and State Register of Historic Sites.

Historic Fort Wayne

Location: 6325 Jefferson, Detroit, MI 48209 **Contact Info:** (810) 793-6739 • info@historicfortwaynecoalition.com • www.historicfortwaynecoalition.com **Hours:** May-Oct: Sat-Sun 10 a.m.-4 p.m. **Admission:** Free. **Accessibility:** On-site parking for a fee.

Site Info: The site has multiple structures including barracks, a post hospital, parade grounds, warehouses, stables, the commanding officer's house, officer's row, and post headquarters. Visitors can see the preservation and restoration work being done on the fort's structures and facilities. The site also includes the National Museum of the Tuskegee Airmen, which is open only by appointment. Call (313) 833-8849.

Motown Museum

Location: 2648 W. Grand Blvd., Detroit, MI 48208 **Contact Info:** (313) 875-2264 • arawls@motownmuseum.org • www.motownmuseum.org **Hours:** Sep-May: Tue-Sat 10 a.m.-6 p.m.; Jun-Aug: Mon-Fri 10 a.m.-6 p.m., Sat 10 a.m.-8 p.m., Sun 10 a.m.-6 p.m. **Admission:** Call for current prices. **Accessibility:** Free street parking. Wheelchair accessible. Tours included in price of admission. Museum store.

Site Info: The Motown Museum, which was founded by Esther Gordy Edwards in 1985, is one of Southeast Michigan's most popular tourist destinations. Visitors come from across America and throughout the world to stand in Studio A, where their favorite artists and groups recorded much-loved music and to view the restored upper flat where Berry Gordy lived with his young family during the company's earliest days.

DEXTER

Dexter Area Historical Museum

Location: 3443 Inverness St., Dexter, MI 48130 **Contact Info:** (734) 426-2519 • dexmuseum@aol.com • www.dexterhistory.org **Hours:** May-early Dec: Fri-Sat 1-3 p.m. **Admission:** Free. **Accessibility:** Free on-site parking. Not wheelchair accessible. Self-guided. Museum store.

Site Info: The museum is located in the old St. Andrews Church, circa 1883, which was moved to its current location in 1971. Displays include furniture; clothing; toys; medical equipment; a dentist office; military artifacts from the Civil War to World War II; a carriage; farm implements; school materials; a model railroad layout replicating the village of Dexter; and artifacts of Dexter's founder, Judge Samuel W. Dexter.

Gordon Hall

Location: 8341 Island Lake Rd., Dexter, MI 48130 **Contact Info:** (734) 426-2519 • dexmuseum@aol.com • www.dexterhistory.org **Hours:** By appointment. **Admission:** $5/ individual. **Accessibility:** Free on-site parking. Partially wheelchair accessible. Tour guide available. Call for groups.

Site Info: Built in 1843 for Judge Samuel Dexter, Gordon Hall was once known as one of the most beautiful Greek Revival buildings in Michigan. It was donated to the University of Michigan in 1950 to be used as an apartment building. In 2005, the Dexter Area Historical Society acquired the building and now provides tours discussing its history.

Webster Corners

Location: Corner of Webster Church Rd. and Farrell Rd., Dexter, MI 48130 **Contact Info:** (734) 426-4892 • jkgmbrig@yahoo.com • www.twp.webster.mi.us/history_of_webster_township.aspx **Hours:** Tours of village buildings can be arranged by contacting through e-mail. **Admission:** Donations accepted. **Accessibility:** Free on-site parking. Not wheelchair accessible.

Site Info: The Webster Township Historical Society maintains a collection of historical buildings located at an area known locally as "Webster Corners." Buildings include the Kleinschmidt General Store, Wheeler Wheelwright & Blacksmith Shop, old township hall, Podunk School, May's Old North Barn, and Crossroads Community Center. Some of the buildings are restored and others are recreations.

DRYDEN

Dryden Historical Depot

Location: 5488 Main St., Dryden, MI 48428 **Contact Info:** (810) 796-3611 • drydenhistoricalsociety@gmail.com • www.drydenhistoricalsociety.webs.com **Hours:** Mon 5:30-7 p.m. Also by appointment. Closed Jan-Apr. **Admission:** Donations accepted.

Site Info: Built in 1883, the Dryden Historical Depot moved to its current location in 1970 and is now used as a museum by the Dryden Historical Society. The museum has a large collection of historical photos, graduation information from Dryden High School from 1881 to 2013, and a General Squier's personal effects display.

DUNDEE

Old Mill Museum

Location: 242 Toledo St., Dundee, MI 48131 **Contact Info:** (734) 529-8596 • museum@dundeeoldmill.com • www.dundeeoldmill.com **Hours:** Fri-Mon 12-4 p.m. **Admission:** Donations accepted. **Accessibility:** Free on-site and street parking. Wheelchair accessible. Tour guide available; call ahead to schedule a group or private tour. Museum store.

Site Info: The Old Mill Museum features three floors of exhibits chronicling local history. Learn about the Ford Village Industries, farm and small town life in the 19th century, and Native-American life on the Macon Reserve. Adjacent to Wolverine Park, you'll find a scenic view of the River Raisin and its dam and a lovely spot to picnic or just relax. The museum's archive room is open to the public for research.

EASTPOINTE

Halfway Schoolhouse

Location: 15500 Nine Mile Rd., Eastpointe, MI 48021 **Contact Info:** (586) 775-1414 • www.edhs1929.blogspot.com **Hours:** Open for special events and by request. **Admission:** Free. **Accessibility:** On-site parking. Wheelchair accessible.

Site Info: The East Detroit Historical Society maintains a museum in the 1872 Halfway Schoolhouse. Some of the items in the school are a teacher's desk from 1844, reflector kerosene lamps, and globe lights. Collections include pictures and biographies related to early Halfway, later East Detroit, now Eastpointe.

Michigan Military Technical & Historical Society Museum

Location: 16600 Stephens Rd., Eastpointe, MI 48021 **Contact Info:** (586) 872-2581 • chris.causley@mimths.org • www.mimths.org **Hours:** Sat 10 a.m.-5 p.m., Sun 12-5 p.m. **Admission:** $5/individual, $7/family, $3 senior/military/student, children 15 and under free. **Accessibility:** Free on-site parking. Wheelchair accessible. Tour guide available. Call for groups.

Site Info: The Michigan Military Technical & Historical Society is dedicated to portraying and preserving the stories of Michigan's civilian and military personnel in 20th-century conflicts and showcasing the products of Michigan's "Arsenal of Democracy." The society's museum features exhibits of Michigan-related military production, units, and veterans dating back to the 1900s.

FARMINGTON

Governor Warner Mansion

Location: 33805 Grand River Ave., Farmington, MI 48335 **Contact Info:** (248) 474-5500 • kshay@farmgov.com • www.facebook.com/FarmingtonHistoricalCommission **Hours:** Apr-Dec: Wed 1-5 p.m.; 1st Sun monthly 1-5 p.m. **Admission:** $3/adult, $1/child (7-12), children 6 and under free. **Accessibility:** Free on-site parking. Not wheelchair accessible. Tour guide available. Museum store.

Site Info: This historic house collects and preserves the artifacts of Farmington and the Warner family from 1867 to 1911. The Governor Warner Mansion is a Victorian home, where visitors learn about Governor Warner and his family. The carriage house houses a classroom, 19th-century tools, and an early 20th-century printing press and loom.

FARMINGTON HILLS

Holocaust Memorial Center

Location: 28123 Orchard Lake Rd., Farmington Hills, MI 48334 **Contact Info:** (248) 553-2400 • info@holocaustcenter.org • www.holocaustcenter.org **Hours:** Sun-Thu 9:30 a.m.-5 p.m. (last admission 3:30 p.m.), Fri 9:30 a.m.-3 p.m. (last admission 1:30 p.m.). Closed Jewish holidays. **Admission:** $8/

adult, $6/student, $6/senior, $5/children. **Accessibility:** Free on-site parking. Wheelchair accessible. Tour guide available Sun-Thu at 1 p.m., reservations for groups of six or more.

Site Info: Highlights at the museum include the interactive "portraits of honor," where visitors can read and hear the stories of many of Michigan's survivors, and the "institute of the righteous," which provides an exploration of those who took responsibility and risked their lives for Holocaust resistance. The museum and archives house videotapes, memorial books, photographs, maps, artifacts, an art collection, newspapers, periodicals, and the John J. Mames Oral History Collection.

The Heritage & History Center of Farmington Hills

Location: 24725 Farmington Rd., Farmington Hills, MI 48335
Contact Info: (248) 701-8112 • bgolden@pastways.info • www.pastways.info/home.html **Hours:** Tue-Thu Sat 10 a.m.-2 p.m.
Admission: Donations accepted.
Accessibility: Free on-site parking. Not wheelchair accessible. Tour guide available. Museum store.

Site Info: The Heritage & History Center offers visitors the opportunity to experience and learn about Farmington Township, the city of Farmington, and the city of Farmington Hills. The Farmington area is the oldest settlement in western Oakland County. A resource library and a museum annex with a collection of agricultural equipment are available to visitors.

FERNDALE

Ferndale Historical Museum

Location: 1651 Livernois, Ferndale, MI 48220 **Contact Info:** (248) 545-7606 • garryandrewsmich@comcast.net • www.ferndalehistoricalsociety.org **Hours:** Mon-Wed 10 a.m.-1 p.m., Sat 1-4 p.m. Appointments available. **Admission:** Donations accepted. **Accessibility:** On-site parking. Partially wheelchair accessible. Tour guides available; 24 hours notice needed for special tours.

Site Info: The Ferndale Historical Museum is housed in a building given to the city by Canadian Legion Post No. 71. Collections date from the 1800s to the present and include a large military installation covering all of America's greatest wars, histories of all 8,000 structures in Ferndale, and local historical and genealogical information.

FLAT ROCK

Memory Lane Village

Location: 25200 Gibraltar Road, Flat Rock, MI 48134 **Contact Info:** (734) 782-5220 • lesley@flatrockhistory.org • www.flatrockhistory.org **Hours:** Wed 1-3 p.m., 2nd Sun monthly 1-4 p.m., 3rd Fri monthly 7-9 p.m. **Admission:** Free. **Accessibility:** Free on-site parking. Wheelchair accessible. Tour guide available. Museum store.

Site Info: The museum offers a large collection of old newspapers, yearbooks, and pictures from the area. Also included is an exhibit featuring a buffalo hide from the 1800s, which was killed locally.

FLINT

Alfred P. Sloan Museum

Location: 1221 E. Kearsley St., Flint, MI 48503 **Contact Info:** (810) 237-3450 • sloan@sloanlongway.org • www.sloanlongway.org **Hours:** Mon-Fri 10 a.m.-5 p.m., Sat-Sun 12-5 p.m. **Admission:** $9/adult, $8/senior, $6/youth (2-11), children 1 and under free. **Accessibility:** Free on-site parking. Wheelchair accessible. Museum store.

Site Info: The museum features exhibits relating to regional history, historic automobiles, and hands-on science. In the "Flint and the American dream" exhibit, dramatic settings, video programs, and hundreds of artifacts and photographs portray the area's tumultuous 20th-century history. The museum's collection includes 100,000 artifacts ranging from prehistoric stone implements to antique textiles and prototype automobiles. Visitors will also find photographs and papers of Flint and Genesee County history and Buick engineering papers, service manuals, and sales literature.

Applewood Estate

Location: 1400 E. Kearsley St., Flint, MI 48503 **Contact Info:** (810) 233-3835 • delliott@ruthmott.org • www.applewood.org **Hours:** Early May-late Oct: Thu-Sun 10 a.m.-6 p.m. **Admission:** Free. Please consider bringing food or personal care items to be donated to local shelters. **Accessibility:** On-site parking. Free guided tours are available for groups of 10 or more; call ahead.

Site Info: Applewood is the estate of the Charles Stewart Mott family, built by Mr. Mott in 1916. The estate is listed on the National Register of Historic Places. Ruth Mott gave Applewood to the Ruth Mott Foundation upon her passing in 1999. It features the original home and barn, 34 acres of stately trees, and the heritage apple orchard for which it was named. Buildings include the Jacobean-Revival residence, gatehouse, barn, and chicken coop.

Buick Automotive Gallery and Research Center

Location: 303 Walnut St., Flint, MI 48503 **Contact Info:** (810) 237-3450 • BuickGallery@SloanLongway.org • www. sloanlongway.org **Hours:** Mon-Fri 10 a.m.-5 p.m., Sat-Sun 12-5 p.m. **Admission:** $9/adult, $8/senior, $6/youth (2-11), children 1 and under free. **Accessibility:** Free on-site parking. Wheelchair accessible. Self-guided.

Site Info: The Buick Automotive Gallery and Research Center features more than 25 classic and concept Buicks, Chevrolets, and other locally built automobiles. Automobiles exhibited include five concept cars designed by Buick: 1951 XP-300, 1954 Wildcat II, 1956 Centurion, 1963 Silver Arrow I, and 1977 Phantom. A Hellcat Tank Destroyer built by Buick during World War II is also on display.

Durant-Dort Carriage Company Headquarters

Location: 316 Water St., Flint, MI 48503 **Contact Info:** (810) 410-4605 • gchs1@comcast.net • www.geneseehistory.org **Hours:** Memorial Day-Labor Day by appointment. **Admission:** Free. **Accessibility:** Free parking behind building. Wheelchair accessible. Tour guide available by appointment.

Site Info: The Genesee County Historical Society's museum is located in the restored Durant-Dort Carriage Company Headquarters, the birthplace of the General Motors Corporation. Today, the building is a National Historic Landmark that features photo exhibits, carriages, and furniture.

Longway Planetarium

Location: 1310 E. Kearsley St., Flint, MI 48503 **Contact Info:** (810) 237-3450 • sloan@sloanlongway.org • www. sloanlongway.org **Hours:** Check website for planetarium showtimes. **Admission:** $6/adult, $4/senior, $4/youth (2-11), children 1 and under free. **Accessibility:** Free on-site parking. Wheelchair accessible.

Site Info: The planetarium is used for school field trips but also provides public shows, family science workshops, and community events. The site has been recently renovated and gives visitors the opportunity to explore the universe. The museum provides live discussions and immersive virtual journeys to help visitors study history and science.

Stockton Center at Spring Grove

Location: 720 Ann Arbor St., Flint, MI 48503 **Contact Info:** (810) 238-9140 • freemantgreer@gmail.com • www.stocktoncenter.weebly.com **Hours:** 3rd Sun of every month: 1-4 p.m. Also by appointment.
Admission: $5/adult, $3/children (6-18). **Accessibility:** Free on-site parking. Wheelchair accessible. Tour guide available. Museum store.

Site Info: The museum is housed in the 1872 Italianate Victorian home built by Colonel Stockton and his wife, Maria Smith Stockton. It has been restored in cooperation with the National Parks Guidelines for Historical Restoration. In-depth research was conducted to ensure the home was restored appropriately. Guests will find period furniture inside and stunning gardens surrounding the site with a natural spring park area.

Whaley Historic House Museum

Location: 624 E. Kearsley St., Flint, MI 48503 **Contact Info:** (810) 471-4714 • 1885@whaleyhouse.com • www.whaleyhouse.com **Hours:** 1st and 3rd Sat of month 10 a.m.-1 p.m. Mon-Fri by appointment. **Admission:** $5/adult, $3/student, $3/children.
Accessibility: Free on-site parking. Partially wheelchair accessible; first floor only. Tour guide available.

Site Info: The Whaley Historic House Museum was once the home of the prominent Whaley family of Flint. The home, which is listed on the National Register of Historic Places, contains many items once owned by the Whaley family, as well as by other prominent Flint families. All items are, however, true to the Gilded Age. At the time of printing, this museum was closed due to a fire. Please call ahead before visiting.

FLUSHING

Flushing Area Museum and Cultural Center

Location: 431 W. Main St., Flushing, MI 48433 **Contact Info:** (810) 487-0814 • fahs@att.net • www.flushinghistorical.org **Hours:** Tue 10 a.m.-1 p.m.; May-Dec: Sun 1-4 p.m. Closed all holiday weekends.
Admission: Free. **Accessibility:** Free on-site and street parking. Wheelchair accessible. Tour guide available. Museum store.

Site Info: The Flushing Area Historical Society maintains the Flushing Depot and operates it as a museum and cultural center. The restored 1888 Grand Trunk depot museum features railroading and local history, veterinary medical equipment, drugstore items, 1930s kitchen appliances, and a shaving mug display.

GAGETOWN

Thumb Agricultural Museum

Location: 6948 Richie Rd., Gagetown, MI 48735 **Contact Info:** (989) 665-0081 • www.thumboctagonbarn.org **Hours:** May-Sep: Wed-Sat 11 a.m.-5 p.m. **Admission:** $5/guided tour, children 6 and under free. **Accessibility:** Free on-site parking. Wheelchair accessible. Tour guide available. Museum store.

Site Info: The 70-foot-high, 8,000-square-foot Octagon Barn was part of "Mud Lake Estate" built by banker James Purdy in the 1920s. The site includes the Craftsman-style Purdy home, a one-room school, a grain elevator, and a blacksmith shop. Visitors will see a milk parlor, a milk wagon, a fire truck, antique hand tools, hay equipment, sugar beet equipment, buggies, hand plows, bean sorters and separators, working legs in the grain elevator, and the Thumb-Two Cylinder display.

GARDEN CITY

The Straight Farmhouse

Location: 6221 Merriman Rd., Garden City, MI 48135 **Contact Info:** (734) 838-0650 • straight.farmhouse@yahoo.com • www.sfhonline.org **Hours:** Wed, Sat 12-3 p.m. **Admission:** Donations accepted. **Accessibility:** Free on-site parking. Wheelchair accessible. Tour guide available. Museum store.

Site Info: The Garden City Historical Museum is located inside the 1866 Straight Farmhouse. It includes the Lathers General Store and the Grande Parlour Banquet Room. There are currently three floors of archives and exhibits available to the general public.

GOODELLS

Historic Village at Goodells County Park

Location: 8345 County Park Dr., Goodells, MI 48207 **Contact Info:** (810) 325-1146 • hermweng@gmail.com • www.waleshistoricalsociety.org **Hours:** Open by appointment. **Admission:** Donations accepted. **Accessibility:** Free on-site parking. Wheelchair accessible. Tour guide available.

Site Info: The Wales Historical Society collaborates with St. Clair County at the Historic Village in Goodells County Park. Attractions include C.C. Peck Bank, circa 1900; Lynn School, circa 1882; Mudge Log Cabin, circa 1860; and

Murphy-Ryan Farm, circa 1871. Local family archives are on display in the C.C. Peck Bank. There is also an extensive library of local history books located in the Lynn School. The park was once the location of the county's poor farm.

St. Clair County Farm Museum

Location: 8310 County Park Dr., Goodells, MI 48027 **Contact Info:** (810) 325-1737 • info.farmmuseum@gmail.com • www.stclaircountyfarmmuseum.org **Hours:** Call for current hours. **Admission:** Free. **Accessibility:** Free on-site parking. Not wheelchair accessible. Tour guide available by appointment. Museum store.

 Site Info: The St. Clair County Farm Museum, located in a restored farmhouse, has a large collection of antique and vintage farming equipment. Collections also include domestic items ranging from handmade and muscle-powered through factory-made and electrified, focusing on the period between 1880 and 1965.

GRAND BLANC

Grand Blanc Heritage Museum

 **Location:** 203 E. Grand Blanc Rd., Grand Blanc, MI 48439 **Contact Info:** (810) 694-7274 • dharrett@tir.com • www.cityofgrandblanc.com/Departments/HeritageMuseum.aspx **Hours:** Wed 10 a.m.-2 p.m. **Admission:** Donations accepted.

Accessibility: Free on-site and street parking. Partially wheelchair accessible. Tour guide available; call ahead to schedule a group tour. Museum store.

 Site Info: Located in a historic 1885 church building attached to the Grand Blanc City Hall complex, the Grand Blanc Heritage Museum has two floors of exhibits, photographs, and documents that serve to illustrate the community's nearly 175-year history. A series of public programs invite the general public to learn more about the growth of the community.

GROSSE ILE

Gross Ile North Channel Light

Location: Lighthouse Point Rd., Grosse Ile, MI 48138 **Contact Info:** (734) 675-1250 • info@gihistory.org • www.gihistory.org **Hours:** 2nd Sun in Sep. Also by appointment. **Admission:** Varies. **Accessibility:** Not wheelchair accessible. Tour guide available; call (734) 675-1250 for more information.

 Site Info: Built in 1894, the North Channel Light is the only remaining light on Grosse Ile. The light is under the protection of the Grosse Ile Historical Society. Tours share the history of the light and its importance to the area.

Michigan Central Railroad Depot Museum & Customs House

Location: 25020 E. River Rd., Grosse Ile, MI 48138 **Contact Info:** (734) 675-1250 • info@gihistory.org • www.gihistory.org **Hours:** Sun 1-4 p.m., Thu 10 a.m.-12 p.m. **Admission:** Free. **Accessibility:** Free on-site parking. Not wheelchair accessible. Self-guided.

 Site Info: The Michigan Central Depot Museum & Customs House features displays on railroad, community life, and significant Grosse Ile artifacts. The 1870s Customs House was moved to a spot just behind the depot in 1979, greatly expanding the Grosse Ile Historical Society's meeting and museum facilities.

Naval Air Station GI Museum

Location: 9601 Groh Rd., Grosse Ile, MI 48138 **Contact Info:** (734) 675-1250 • info@gihistory.org • www.gihistory.org **Hours:** Mon-Fri 8 a.m.-5 p.m. **Admission:** Free. **Accessibility:** Free on-site parking. Wheelchair accessible. Self-guided.

 Site Info: Located in the lobby of the Grosse Ile Township Hall, the Naval Air Station GI Museum has exhibits that focus on naval history and Grosse Ile's legacy as a Naval Air Station through artifacts and photographs. Also on-site is a memorial garden.

GROSSE POINTE FARMS

Provencal-Weir House

 **Location:** 376 Kercheval Ave., Grosse Pointe Farms, MI 48236 **Contact Info:** (313) 884-7010 • info@gphistorical.org • www.gphistorical.org **Hours:** 2nd Sat monthly 1-4 p.m. Group tours by appointment. **Admission:** Free. **Accessibility:** Not wheelchair accessible. Free street parking.

 Site Info: The Provencal-Weir House, built circa 1823, is believed to be the oldest-surviving residence in the community. Since its construction, it has served as a home, summer cottage, rental unit, grocery store, and real estate office. Restoration of the home was completed in 1996. Visitors will also find an 1840s log cabin on the property.

GROSSE POINTE SHORES

Edsel & Eleanor Ford House

 **Location:** 1100 Lake Shore Rd., Grosse Pointe Shores, MI 48236 **Contact Info:** (313) 884-4222 • info@fordhouse.org • www.fordhouse.org **Hours:** Tue-Sat 10 a.m.-4 p.m., Sun 12-4 p.m. Business office: Mon-Fri 8:30

a.m.-4:30 p.m. **Admission:** $12/adult, $11/senior, $8/child (6-12), children 5 and under free. **Accessibility:** Parking adjacent to Activities Center (free, except during large grounds events). Partially wheelchair accessible. Tour guide available. Museum store.

Site Info: Visitors can tour the historic home of automotive pioneer Edsel Ford and his family. Collections include paintings, graphic arts, French and English period furniture, glass, ceramics, and historic textiles. Permanent exhibits include the historic garage with Ford family vehicles. Changing exhibits occur throughout the year. Visitors can also enjoy the gardens and grounds of the house.

HADLEY

Hadley Hill Museum

Location: 3633 Hadley Rd., Hadley, MI 48440 **Contact Info:** (810) 797-4026 • krc@centurytel.net • www.hadleytownship.org/HISTORICALSOCIETY.html **Hours:** Jun-July: 2nd and 4th Sat 1-3 p.m.; 4th of Jul 1-3 p.m. **Admission:** Free.

Accessibility: Free on-site parking. Partially wheelchair accessible. Tour guide available.

Site Info: The Hadley Hill Museum is in the grist mill as part of the Hartwig Community Park. It features the mill's turbine, chutes, grain elevators, a line shaft, and a large engine.

HAMBURG

Hamburg Township Historical Museum

Location: 7225 Stone St., Hamburg, MI 48139 **Contact Info:** (810) 986-0190 • hamburgmuseumtearoom@outlook.com • www.hamburg.mi.us/hamburg_historical_museum/index.html **Hours:** Mon 1-4 p.m., Wed 4-7 p.m., Sat 11 a.m.-3 p.m.

Admission: Free. **Accessibility:** Free on-site parking. Wheelchair accessible. Tour guides available; call ahead to schedule a group tour. Museum store.

Site Info: The museum is located in the original site of Hamburg village, settled in 1835. In addition to the history displays, several other rooms are available, including a tea room, which is available by reservation; a gift shop; and the "basement treasures," a by-donation resale shop. The Wayne Burkhardt Train Gallery houses a layout depicting Hamburg in 1910—the village with two railroads.

HAMTRAMCK

Hamtramck Historical Museum

Location: 9525 Jos. Campau, Hamtramck, MI 48212 **Contact Info:** (313) 893-5027 • hamtramckhistory@gmail.com • www.hamtramckhistory.org **Hours:** Sat-Sun 11 a.m.-4 p.m. and by appointment. **Admission:** Free. Donations accepted. **Accessibility:** Street parking available for a fee. Wheelchair accessible. Tour guide available. Museum store.

Site Info: Hamtramck has an amazing history that had a national and even international impact in many ways. The museum also reaches out to the many diverse nationalities represented in the city. The Friends of Historic Hamtramck conducts walking and bus tours of the city on request and is available for off-site slide presentations and lectures on the rich history of Hamtramck.

HARBOR BEACH

Grice House Museum

Location: 865 N. Huron Ave., Harbor Beach, MI 48441 **Contact Info:** (9890 479-3363 • tntoneil@speednetllc.com • www.harborbeachmi.org/ParksRecreation/Museums.aspx **Hours:** Memorial Day-Labor Day: Wed-Fri 1-5 p.m., Sat 10 a.m.-4 p.m., Sun 1-5 p.m. **Admission:** $5/individual, children 12 and under free. **Accessibility:** Free on-site parking. Partially wheelchair accessible. Tour guide available. Museum store.

Site Info: On the beautiful shore of Lake Huron at the north city limit, the Grice Museum complex has something for everyone. The museum has exhibits on family life in the late 1800s, plus military, industrial development, education, and maritime. Also on-site is the 1920s Adams School with furnishings typical of one-room schoolhouses. The building is adjacent to the USCG station and the Harbor Beach Marina. Take a stroll on the breakwater, part of the world's-largest man-made harbor.

HARSENS ISLAND

Harsens Island St. Clair Flats Historical Society Museum

Location: 3058 South Channel Drive, Harsens Island, MI 48028 **Contact Info:** (586) 530-7100 • chairman@hiscfhs.org • www.stewartfarm.org/hiscfhs **Hours:** May: Sat 10 a.m.-3 p.m., Sun 12-4 p.m.; Jun-Sep: 2nd Fri

6-8 p.m., Sat 10 a.m.-3 p.m., Sun 12-4 p.m.; Nov-Apr: Appointment only. **Admission:** Free. **Accessibility:** Free on-site parking. Wheelchair accessible. Self-guided. Museum store.

 Site Info: The museum houses history and artifacts from the Tashmoo Steamer and Park, plus information on ferry service, hotels, personal and commercial traffic along the St. Clair River's South Channel, and more. The museum also holds the personal histories of Jacob Harsen and his descendants. Visitors can view the anchor and propeller of the steamer John N. Glidden, as well as explore the history of the ship and its sinking in 1903.

HOLLY

Hadley House Museum

 **Location:** 306 S. Saginaw St., Holly, MI 48442 **Contact Info:** (248) 634-9233 • hollyhistoricalsoc@comcast.net • www.hsmichigan.org/holly **Hours:** Sat 1-4 p.m. Call for exact dates. **Admission:** $2/adult. **Accessibility:** Limited parking. Not wheelchair accessible. Self-guided.

 Site Info: The Holly Historical Society organized in 1965 and acquired the 1873 Italianate Hadley House in 1986. The house has its original interior with period furniture. Many rooms have historical displays.

HUDSON

Thompson House Museum

 **Location:** 101 Summit St., Hudson, MI 49247 **Contact Info:** (517) 448-8125 • rlennard@thompsonmuseum.org • www.thompsonmuseum.org **Hours:** Mon, Wed, Fri 12-4 p.m. Also by appointment. **Admission:** $7.50/adult, $5/senior and student. **Accessibility:** Free on-site and street parking. Partially wheelchair accessible. Tour guide available. Museum store.

 Site Info: The interior of the Thompson House Museum is filled to the brim with the collections of three generations of Thompsons, including oriental art, antiques, and paintings. Visitors have the unique opportunity to see the changes that have occurred in the home as personal styles of individuals have changed over the years.

IMLAY CITY

Imlay City Historical Museum

Location: 77 Main St., Imlay City, MI 48444 **Contact Info:** (8100 724-1904 • bswihart1904@charter.net **Hours:** Apr-Dec: Sat 1-4 p.m. Also by appointment. **Admission:** Donations accepted. **Accessibility:** Free street parking. Wheelchair accessible. Self-guided.

Site Info: The Imlay City Historical Museum opened in 1978 in the Historic Grand Trunk Depot. Displays include military, farm tools, country doctor's operating room equipment, photos of Imlay City, and race car driver Bob Burman.

LAPEER

Davis Brothers Farm Shop Museum

Location: 3520 Davis Lake Road, Lapeer, MI 48446 **Contact Info:** (810) 245-5808 • LCHS.POBOX72@gmail.com • www.lapeercountyhistoricalsociety.com **Hours:** Call for current hours. **Admission:** Donations accepted. **Accessibility:** Free on-site parking. Wheelchair accessible. Tour guide available.

Site Info: The Farm Shop Museum offers demonstrations of farming practices of the 1930s and 1940s, including the harvesting of grains, a working sawmill, a blacksmith shop and lathe, and other exhibits and demonstrations. An education program for elementary students provides hands-on learning activities to introduce children to farm life in an earlier time. Take a peaceful walk through the Maple Sugar Bush Memorial Grove or belt of native white pines planted by Chatfield students.

Lapeer County Heritage Museum

Location: 518 W. Nepessing St., Lapeer, MI 48446 **Contact Info:** (810) 245-5808 • LCHS.POBOX72@gmail.com • www.lapeercountyhistoricalsociety.com **Hours:** Wed, Sat 10 a.m.-3 p.m. **Admission:** Donations accepted. **Accessibility:** Free on-site and street parking. Not wheelchair accessible. Self-guided. Museum store.

Site Info: Exhibits are rotated and are designed to introduce visitors to the people, events, and circumstances that shaped the history of Lapeer County. Also, notable individuals whose influence extended beyond the community are represented. In addition, the museum has displays on logging, farming, state institutions, and wars at home and aboard, and more.

LINCOLN PARK

Lincoln Park Historical Museum

Location: 1335 Southfield Rd., Lincoln Park, MI 48146 **Contact Info:** (313) 386-3137 • lpmuseum@gmail.com • www.lphistorical.org **Hours:** Wed, Sat 1-6 p.m. Also by appointment. **Admission:** Free. **Accessibility:** Free on-site parking. Wheelchair accessible. Self-guided. Museum store.

Site Info: The Lincoln Park Historical Museum is housed in the historic 1938 Depression-Era post office building. Permanent exhibits reflect the community's long heritage, including the influence of the automobile industry and a tribute to 1920s city policeman and automotive pioneer Preston Tucker. Specially featured is a recently installed permanent exhibit on hometown 1960s rock-and-roll band MC5. Visitors may tour the museum and visit the library of local history.

LINDEN

Linden Mills Historical Society & Museum

Location: 201 N. Main, Linden, MI 48451 **Contact Info:** (810) 735-2860 • lindenmills@yahoo.com • www.freewebs.com/lindenmichiganhistoricalsociety **Hours:** Jun-Sep: 2nd and 4th Sun 2-4 p.m. Also by appointment. **Admission:** Donations accepted. **Accessibility:** Free on-site parking. Wheelchair accessible. Call for tours.

Site Info: The museum is located in an 1871 grist mill building. Exhibits include a Beach Buggy carriage made at Linden's Joe Beach Buggy Factory, a vintage clothing section, a military display, and many unique vintage items in the general store exhibit. Children can view antique toys and can experience what school was like in the pioneer days in the old schoolroom.

LIVONIA

Greenmead Historical Park

Location: 20501 Newburgh Road, Livonia, MI 48152 **Contact Info:** (248) 477-7375 • greenmead@ci.livonia.mi.us • www.facebook.com/Greenmead **Hours:** Jun-Oct and Dec: 1-4 p.m. (no holiday tours). Also by appointment. **Admission:** $3/adult, $2/youth. **Accessibility:** Free on-site parking. Partially wheelchair accessible. Tour guide available. Museum store.

Site Info: Greenmead Historical Park was once the homestead of Michigan pioneer Joshua Simmons. The 1841 Greek Revival farmhouse and its outbuildings are listed on the National Register of Historic Places. Nine of the farm's eleven original outbuildings still stand today.

MANCHESTER
John Schneider Blacksmith Shop

Location: 324 E. Main St., Manchester, MI 48158 **Contact Info:** (517) 536-0775 • mahs-info@manchesterareahistoricalsociety.org • www.manchesterareahistoricalsociety.org **Hours:** By appointment. **Admission:** Donations accepted. **Accessibility:** Free street parking. Not wheelchair accessible. Tour guide available with appointment.

Site Info: The John Schneider Blacksmith Shop is a complete shop with a working forge and tools of the trade. It remained after John Schneider died in 1952. He was the last full-time blacksmith in Manchester. The shop is one of the last remaining, intact, "main street" blacksmith shops. The blacksmith shop also houses and displays various artifacts of the Manchester area that have been collected by the Manchester Area Historical Society.

MARINE CITY
Community Pride & Heritage Museum

Location: 405 South Main St., Marine City, MI 48039 **Contact Info:** (810) 765-5446 • marinecitymuseum@hotmail.com • www.marinecitymuseum.org **Hours:** Jun-Oct: Sat-Sun 1-4 p.m. **Admission:** Free. Under 14 must be accompanied by an adult. **Accessibility:** Free street parking. Partially wheelchair accessible. Tour guide available.

Site Info: The Community Pride & Heritage Museum provides information on local history and shipbuilding in the area and helps teachers educate their students about the history of their community. The museum is located in a building constructed in 1847 by Eber Brock Ward to house the Newport Academy, run by his sister Emily Ward. Exhibits touch on shipbuilding, Americana, business, farming, and genealogy research.

MARLETTE
Train Depot Museum

Location: 3225 Main St., Marlette, MI 48453 **Contact Info:** (989) 635-3041 • dianne.ca41@gmail.com • www.facebook.com/MarletteTrainDepot **Hours:** May-Sep: Sun 2-5 p.m. **Admission:** Donation. **Accessibility:** Wheelchair accessible. Museum store.

Site Info: The Marlette Historical Society has restored the Marlette Train Depot, which is on the Michigan Registry of Historic Places. The museum rotates historic items on display according to season. The society runs an operating Lionel train and the ticket office to buy a ticket. View collections devoted to local businesses of the past, farming in the community, and local schools.

MILAN

Friend-Hack House Museum

Location: 775 County St., Milan, MI 48160 **Contact Info:** (734) 439-1297 • farmera44@att.net • www.historicmilan.com **Hours:** May-Oct: Sun 1-4 p.m. **Admission:** Free. **Accessibility:** Free on-site parking. Not wheelchair accessible. Tour guide available. Museum store.

Site Info: The beautiful 127-year-old Victorian farm home was built with funds obtained by fraudulent means. The Friend-Hack house is referred to as "The House that Sugar built" by locals.

The Old Fire Barn

Location: Corner of Court and Main Street, Milan, MI 48160 **Contact Info:** (734) 439-1297 • farmera44@att.net • www.historicmilan.com **Hours:** Call for current hours. **Admission:** Free. **Accessibility:** Free street parking. Wheelchair accessible. Tour guide available.

Site Info: The old Milan Fire Barn was built in 1897 and served as a fire station until 1979. The building housed the fire department and some of the city's fire vehicles, including a 1938 Ford Fire Truck. Over time, it also housed the police department, a jail—which consisted of a single jail cell—and the city library.

MILFORD

Mary Jackson's Childhood Home

Location: 642 Canal St., Milford, MI 48381 **Contact Info:** (248) 685-7308 • milfordhistory@hotmail.com • www.milfordhistory.org **Hours:** By appointment. **Admission:** Donations accepted. **Accessibility:** Free on-site and metered street parking. Wheelchair accessible. Tour guide available.

Site Info: Mary Jackson was best known as a stage, screen, and TV actress, with many movie credits and a role as one of the Baldwin sisters on the TV show "Walton's Mountain." Her home was willed to the Milford Historical Society after her passing in 2005. The home is full of memorabilia of Mary Jackson's life and is preserved to be just as it was when she lived there.

Milford Historical Museum

Location: 124 E. Commerce St., (248) 685-7308 • milfordhistory@hotmail.com • www.milfordhistory.org **Hours:** May-Dec: Wed, Sat 1-4 p.m. **Admission:** Donations accepted. **Accessibility:** Free on-site and metered street parking. Wheelchair accessible. Tour guide available.

Site Info: Located in an 1853 Greek Revival home, the entire second floor of the Milford Historical Museum is a display that is furnished as a home would have been in the late Victorian Era, complete with a living room, dining room, kitchen, and bedroom from that period. Many of the furnishings in the display are items that were manufactured in Milford.

MILLINGTON

Millington-Arbela Historical Society & Museum

Location: 8534 State St. (M-15 Heritage Route), Millington, MI 48746 **Contact Info:** (989) 871-5508 • millingtonarbelahistoricalsociety@hotmail.com • www.millington-arbela-historical-society.webs.com **Hours:** Apr-Nov: Fri 1-4 p.m. Also by appointment. **Admission:** Free. **Accessibility:** Free on-site and street parking. Partially wheelchair accessible. Tour guide available. Call for other tours. Museum store.

Site Info: The Millington-Arbela Historical Museum is home to research collections and historical artifacts from Millington and Arbela Townships. The museum is located in the Millington Bank, a nationally registered, split fieldstone building constructed in 1898.

MONROE

Monroe County Museum

Location: 126 S. Monroe St., Monroe, MI 48161 **Contact Info:** (734) 240-7780 • history@monroemi.org • www.historicmonroecounty.org **Hours:** Sun 12-5 p.m., Mon, Tue, Wed, Fri, Sat 11 a.m.-5 p.m., Thu 11 a.m.-7 p.m. **Admission:** Suggested donation of $5/adult, $2.50/child. Free to Monroe County residents.

Accessibility: Free on-site parking. Street parking available for a fee. Wheelchair accessible. Self-guided. Museum store.

 Site Info: Housed in a stately former post office in downtown Monroe, the Monroe County Museum collects, preserves, and presents the cultural, social, and natural history of Michigan's second-oldest county. Signature exhibits focus on Native culture, French-Canadian settlement, George and Libbie Custer, and life on the region's rivers and Lake Erie. The museum also features a series of temporary and seasonal exhibits throughout the year.

River Raisin National Battlefield Park

 **Location:** 1403 E Elm Ave, Monroe, MI 48162 **Contact Info:** (734) 243-7136 • sheilah_larnhart@nps.gov • www.battlefieldfoundation.com/about **Hours:** 9 a.m.-5 p.m. weekly. **Admission:** Free. **Accessibility:** Free on-site parking. Wheelchair accessible. Tour guide available. Museum store.

 Site Info: The only National Battlefield Park dedicated solely to the War of 1812, the River Raisin National Battlefield Park works to illustrate the viewpoints of all the conflicting interests involved in the War of 1812.

River Raisin Territorial Park

 **Location:** 3815 North Custer Rd., Monroe, MI 48162 **Contact Info:** (734) 240-7780 • history@monroemi.org • www.historicmonroecounty.org **Hours:** Buildings open May-Oct: Fri, Sat 12-5 p.m. Grounds open year round. **Admission:** Suggested donation of $5/adult, $2.50/children. Free to Monroe County residents. **Accessibility:** Free on-site parking. Partially wheelchair accessible. Self-guided.

 Site Info: Located on the north bank of its namesake river, the park explores the region's role during Michigan's settlement and territorial eras. The Navarre-Anderson Trading Post and Navarre-Morris Cabin are accompanied by a replica 1790s barn, bake oven, and orchard to recreate a long lot farm. River Raisin Territorial Park is a popular destination for fishing and birdwatching and a great place to stop with your canoe or kayak.

Vietnam Veterans Memorial and Museum

Location: 1095 N Dixie Hwy., Monroe, MI 48161 **Contact Info:** (734) 240-7780 • history@monroemi.org • www. historicmonroecounty.org **Hours:** Buildings open May-Oct: Fri, Sat 12-5 p.m. Grounds open year round. **Admission:** Donations accepted. **Accessibility:** Free on-site parking. Wheelchair accessible. Self-guided.

Site Info: The Vietnam Veterans Memorial and Museum at Heck Park is dedicated to the memory of the Monroe County veterans who served in the Vietnam War. The museum houses exhibits, models, military gear, and mementos from the conflict and serves as a place of reflection for veterans and education for the general public. The grounds are host to several memorials and static exhibits of Vietnam-Era military equipment.

MONTROSE

Montrose Historical & Telephone Pioneer Museum

Location: 144 East Hickory Street, Montrose, MI 48457 **Contact Info:** (810) 639-6644 • staff@montrosemuseum.com • www.montrosemuseum.com **Hours:** Sun 1-5 p.m., Mon-Tue 9:30 a.m.-3:30 p.m. **Admission:** Free admission. Group tours: $2/adult, children free. **Accessibility:** Free on-site and street parking. Wheelchair accessible. Tour guide available; call ahead to schedule a group or private tour.

Site Info: The Montrose Historical & Telephone Pioneer Museum is home to one of the best collections of telephones and related items in the United States. In addition to an extensive collection of telephones, the museum also houses local history collections as well as a large genealogical database.

MOUNT CLEMENS

Crocker House Museum

Location: 15 Union St., Mount Clemens, MI 48043 **Contact Info:** (586) 465-2488 • crockerhousemuseum@sbcglobal.net • www.crockerhousemuseum.com **Hours:** Mar-Dec: Tue-Thu 10 a.m.-4 p.m., 1st Sun monthly 1-4 p.m. Closed holidays. **Admission:** $4/adult, $2/child suggested donation. **Accessibility:** On-site parking for a fee. Free street parking. Not wheelchair accessible. Tour guide available.

Site Info: Visitors to the Crocker House Museum can explore historical Mount Clemens, which was known worldwide for its mineral water, and experience the city's bath era through exhibits, photos, and artifacts. The museum is located in an 1869 Italianate-style house, which was home to the first two mayors of Mount Clemens. Rooms throughout the house depict life as was during the 1880s, and a large garden outside is reminiscent of a Victorian park.

Michigan Transit Museum

Location: 200 Grand Ave., Mount Clemens, MI 48043 **Contact Info:** (586) 463-1863 • mtm1973@juno.com • www.michigantransitmuseum.org **Hours:** Sat-Sun 1-4 p.m. Train rides also offered Sun (Jun-Oct). **Admission:** Donations accepted. Train rides $7/adult, $4/child. **Accessibility:** Free on-site parking. Wheelchair accessible. Train rides not wheelchair accessible. Tour guide available. Call for other tours. Museum store.

Site Info: One of the original Grand Trunk Railway stations, the Mount Clemens Depot originally opened for business on November 21, 1859. Today, it is home to the Michigan Transit Museum. Visitors can view full-size locomotives, freight cars, electric trolleys, and rapid transit cars. The museum also has a railroad-related archival collection.

NEW BALTIMORE

Grand Pacific House Museum

Location: 51065 Washington St., New Baltimore, MI 48047 **Contact Info:** (586) 725-4755 • www.newbaltimorehistorical. org **Hours:** Wed, Sat 12-2 p.m. **Admission:** Donations accepted. **Accessibility:** Free parking. Tour guide available. Museum store.

Site Info: The Grand Pacific House Museum is operated by the New Baltimore Historical Society, which strives to preserve all historical aspects of the Anchor Bay area. Originally built in 1881 for use as a hotel and later used as a boarding house and a soda fountain and candy store, the museum building now contains exhibits about New Baltimore's history.

NEW BOSTON

Samuel Adams Historical Museum

Location: 37236 Huron River Drive, New Boston, MI 48164 **Contact Info:** (734) 775-4747 • nfaydee@yahoo.com **Hours:** 1st Sun monthly 1-3 p.m. **Admission:** Free. **Accessibility:** Free on-site parking. Wheelchair accessible. Tour guide available. **Site Info:** The Huron Township Historical Society is dedicated to the promotion of history and historical preservation at a local and global level through its Samuel Adams Historical Museum.

NORTHVILLE

Mill Race Historical Village

Location: 215 N. Griswold Street, Northville, MI 48167 **Contact Info:** (248) 348-1845 • office@ millracenorthville.org • www. millracenorthville.org **Hours:** Grounds

open dawn to dusk. Buildings open Jun-Oct: Sun 1-4 p.m.
Admission: Donations accepted. **Accessibility:** Free
on-site parking. Partially wheelchair accessible. Tour guide
available. Museum store.

 Site Info: The Northville Historical Society created
Mill Race Historical Village to preserve examples of
architectural styles common to Northville pre-1900.
The village is home to 10 relocated, reproduced,
and/or reconstructed buildings: a church and school,
a blacksmith shop and general store, a gazebo, an interurban
station, a Georgian home, a Victorian home furnished in the style
of 1880, and a small weaving studio.

OAKLAND

Caretaker House at Cranberry Lake Historic District Park

 **Location:** 384 W. Predmore Rd.,
Oakland, MI 48363 **Contact
Info:** (248) 652-0712 •
othsmember@comcast.net • www.
oaklandtownshiphistoricalsociety.org
Hours: By appointment and during
events. **Admission:** $2/person. Free at
events. **Accessibility:** Free on-site parking. Wheelchair
accessible. Tour guide available. Museum store.

 **Site Info:** The Oakland Township Historical leases
part of the 16-acre Cranberry Lake Farm Historic
District in township-owned Cranberry Lake Park.
The society's museum is located in the tenant house
and the archives are available for research on the
second floor of the main house.

Cranberry Lake Farm Historic District

Location: 388 West Predmore Rd.,
Oakland, MI 48363 **Contact Info:**
(248) 608-6807 • bbarber@
oaklandtownship.org • www.
oaklandtownship.org **Hours:** Call for
current hours. **Admission:** Call for
current admission prices. **Accessibility:**
Free on-site parking. Wheelchair accessible. Self-guided.

 Site Info: Cranberry Lake Farm Historic District
is listed in the National Register of Historic Places.
The farmstead remains substantially intact and
reflects the architectural and social history for the
period of 1840s to 1951. The property is an
example of an older farmstead in a rural setting modified into a
recreational retreat of the 1930s that still exists today. The
Oakland Township Historical Society provides tours and has an
archives room at the site.

ORTONVILLE

The Old Mill Museum

Location: 366 Mill St., Ortonville, MI 48462 **Contact Info:** (248) 627-3893 • jmiracle60@comcast.net • www.ortonvillecommunityhistoricalsoc.weebly.com **Hours:** Apr-Dec: Sat 10 a.m.-2 p.m. **Admission:** Donations accepted. **Accessibility:** Free on-site and street parking. Partially wheelchair accessible. Tour guide available. Museum store.

Site Info: The Old Mill Museum is housed in a repurposed grist mill built in 1856 from hand-hewn timbers taken from the property. The museum now houses an extensive military exhibit, a 1920s fire truck, and many local farming artifacts.

OTISVILLE

Otisville Area Museum

Location: 122 E Main St., Otisville, MI 48463 **Contact Info:** (810) 714-0323 • oaha1982@yahoo.com • www.facebook.com/otisvillemuseum.oaha **Hours:** Apr-Oct: Wed 3-6 p.m., 2nd Sunday 2-6 p.m. Also by appointment. **Admission:** Free.
Accessibility: Free on-site parking. Wheelchair accessible. Self-guided. Museum store.

Site Info: The Otisville Area Museum project began in 2010. Now in full operation, it features a variety of displays, including farming, military, lumbering, Otisville sports, Otisville High School class composite pictures, and so much more.

PIGEON

Pigeon Historical Depot Museum

Location: 59 S. Main St., Pigeon, MI 48755 **Contact Info:** (989) 453-3242 • depotmuseum1903@gmail.com • www.pigeonhistoricalsociety.com **Hours:** Jun-Aug: Thu-Fri 10 a.m.-3 p.m., Sat 10 a.m.-1 p.m. Also by appointment. **Admission:** Donations accepted. **Accessibility:** Free on-site parking. Wheelchair accessible. Self-guided. Museum store.

Site Info: This museum is in a 1903 railroad depot that houses many artifacts from the Pigeon area. The depot is designated as a Michigan Historical Landmark.

PLYMOUTH

Jarvis Stone School Local Historic District

Location: 7991 N. Territorial Rd., Plymouth, MI 48170 **Contact Info:** (248) 486-0669 • salem_area_hs@yahoo.com • www.sahshistory.org **Hours:** 4th Wed of Apr, May, Jun, Sep, Oct 7-10 p.m. **Admission:** Free. **Accessibility:** Free on-site and street parking. Wheelchair accessible. Self-guided.

Site Info: The Jarvis Stone School in Salem Township, a one-room school, was used from 1857 to 1967 and was restored in 1995. It is occasionally still used for teaching. In 1999, the Salem Area Historical Society acquired the Dickerson Barn, the oldest barn in Washtenaw County. From 2006 to 2008, the society raised the barn on its property, which, in 2013, was designated by Washtenaw County as The Jarvis Stone School Local Historic District.

Plymouth Historical Museum

Location: 155 S. Main St., Plymouth, MI 48170 **Contact Info:** (734) 455-8940 • director@plymouthhistory.org • www.plymouthhistory.org **Hours:** Wed, Fri, Sun 1-4 p.m. **Admission:** $5/adult, $2/student (6-17), children under 6 free. **Accessibility:** Free street parking. Wheelchair accessible. Self-guided. Museum store.

Site Info: The Plymouth Historical Museum features a late 19th-century Victorian recreation of Main Street, tracing the growth of the small town from the railroad depot to the general store. The largest Lincoln collection in Michigan is housed in a separate room off Main Street. A permanent exhibit depicting a time line of Plymouth is also included, featuring displays on the Daisy Air Rifle, Ford Village Industries, the Alter Motor Car, World War II, and more.

PONTIAC

Pine Grove Museum/Governor Moses Wisner Home

Location: 405 Cesar E. Chavez Ave., Pontiac, MI 48342 **Contact Info:** (248) 338-6732 • office@ocphs.org • www.ocphs.org **Hours:** Tue-Thu 11 a.m.-4 p.m. Also by appointment. **Admission:** $5/adult, $3/children 12 and under. **Accessibility:** Free on-site parking. Partially wheelchair accessible. Tour guide available by appointment.

Site Info: Pine Grove consists of 4 1/2 acres of land; the Wisner mansion; and several outbuildings, including a summer kitchen, an outhouse, a smokehouse, and a root cellar. In addition to the outbuildings, there are the Drayton Plains One-Room Schoolhouse and the carriage house, which is home to the research library and archives, office, and the Pioneer Museum.

PORT AUSTIN

Port Austin History Center

 **Location:** 1424 Pte. Aux Barques Rd, Port Austin, MI 48467
Contact Info: (989) 550-1586 • portaustinhistorycenter@gmail.com • www.portaustinhistorycenter.com
Hours: Apr-May: Sat-Sun 1-4 p.m.; Jun-Aug: Daily 1-4 p.m.; Sep-Oct: Sat-Sun 1-4 p.m. **Admission:** Free. **Accessibility:** Free on-site parking. Wheelchair accessible. Tour guide available. Museum store.

 Site Info: The Port Austin History Center is located in the renovated civic center. Exhibits include Port Austin merchants and businesses, Port Austin manufacturing, Port Austin school items, Port Austin Air Force Station, Port Austin Reef Lighthouse, local agriculture, local homemaking, Great Lakes Storm of 1913 and Howard M. Hanna Jr., a Union Rug Loom, and an 1890 cutter.

PORT HOPE

Pointe aux Barques Lighthouse Museum
Location: 7320 Lighthouse Road, Port Hope, MI 48468
Contact Info: www.pointeauxbarqueslighthouse.org/index.cfm
Hours: Memorial Day-Oct 15: 10 a.m.-7 p.m. **Admission:** Donations accepted. **Accessibility:** Free on-site parking.

 Site Info: Originally constructed in 1848, the original Pointe aux Barques Lighthouse lasted only nine years due to the ravages of shoreline weather and a fire. The new keeper's house and attached 89-foot tower were built of the finest brick available in 1857. The light is still an active aid to navigation, making Pointe aux Barques one of the oldest continuously operating lighthouses on the Great Lakes.

PORT HURON

Carnegie Center Museum
Location: 1115 Sixth St., Port Huron, MI 48060 **Contact Info:** (810) 982-0891 • info@phmuseum.org • www.phmuseum.org **Hours:** Wed-Sun 10 a.m.-4 p.m. **Admission:** $7/adult, $5/senior, $5/student, children 4 and under are free.
Accessibility: Free on-site and street parking. Wheelchair accessible. Self-guided.

Site Info: The museum features more than 16,000 items focusing on the culture, art, and history of St. Clair County, with a portion of the collection dedicated specifically to Great Lakes maritime history. The Carnegie Center Museum inspires knowledge through exhibitions, education, and public programs.

Fort Gratiot Light Station

Location: 2802 Omar St., Port Huron, MI 48060 **Contact Info:** (810) 982-0891 • info@phmuseum.org • www.phmuseum.org **Hours:** May-Jun, Sep-Oct: Sat, Sun 11 a.m.-5 p.m.; Jun-Sep: 10 a.m-5 p.m. daily. **Admission:** $7/adult, $5/senior, $5/student, children 4 and under free. **Accessibility:** Free street parking. Not wheelchair accessible. Self-guided.

Site Info: The Fort Gratiot Light Station, circa 1829, is the oldest lighthouse in Michigan and was re-opened to the public in 2012. The original structure was 65 feet tall but was extended to its present height of 82 feet in the early 1860s. Visitors need closed-toe shoes to climb to the top of the tower.

Huron Lightship

Location: 800 Prospect Place, Port Huron, MI 48060 **Contact Info:** (810) 982-0891 • info@phmuseum.org • www.phmuseum.org **Hours:** May-Jun, Sep-Oct: Sat, Sun 11 a.m.-5 p.m.; Jun-Sep: 10 a.m-5 p.m. daily. **Admission:** $7/adult, $5/senior, $5/student, children 4 and under free. **Accessibility:** Free street parking. Not wheelchair accessible. Self-guided.

Site Info: The Huron Lightship was a "floating lighthouse" and spent its entire career on the Great Lakes with 36 years in Port Huron. Retired in 1970, the ship has been refinished as a museum and traces the history of its service and those who served. There is a fog horn sounding on Memorial Day, Independence Day, and Labor Day.

Knowlton's Ice Museum of North America

Location: 317 Grand River Ave., Port Huron, MI 48060 **Contact Info:** (810) 987-5441 • knowltonsicemuseum@yahoo.com • www.knowltonsicemuseum.org **Hours:** Jun-Sep: Thu-Sat 11 a.m.-5 p.m.; Oct-May: Sat 11 a.m.-5 p.m. **Admission:** $5/adult, $4/senior, $2/children (6-12), children 6 and under free. **Accessibility:** Free on-site and street parking. Wheelchair accessible. Tour guide available. Call for groups.

Site Info: At 10,000 square feet, the Knowlton's Ice Museum houses more than 5,000 items. The ice museum depicts the natural ice-harvesting industry of long ago. Through video, narrative, ice tools, memorabilia, and hands-on interactive displays, the museum tells the history of one of the largest industries in the United States around 1880 using the water/ice resources of the Great Lakes. All items are displayed out in the open and not behind glass displays.

Port Huron & Detroit Railroad Historical Society Museum
Location: 2100 32nd St., Port Huron, MI 48060 **Contact Info:** info@phdrailroad.com • www.phdrailroad.com **Hours:** Call for current hours. **Admission:** Free.

 Site Info: The Port Huron & Detroit Railroad Historical Society's Museum was founded in April 2007. The museum features historical documents, photographs, drawings, artifacts, and equipment relating to the Port Huron & Detroit Railroad Company and its predecessors.

Thomas Edison Depot Museum
Location: 510 Edison Parkway, Port Huron, MI 48060 **Contact Info:** (810) 982-0891 • info@phmuseum.org • www.phmuseum.org **Hours:** May-Jun, Sep-Oct: Sat, Sun 11 a.m.-5 p.m.; Jun-Sep: 10 a.m-5 p.m. daily. **Admission:** $7/adult, $5/senior, $5/student, children 4 and under free. **Accessibility:** Free on-site parking. Wheelchair accessible. Self-guided.

 Site Info: The Thomas Edison Depot is where a teenaged Thomas Edison worked during his years in Port Huron. A restored baggage car recreates his mobile chemistry lab, where some of his early experiments were conducted. The Black Mariah movie theater shows films about Edison, and there are also interactive displays and experiments. The museum is housed in the Fort Gratiot Station, which was built in 1858 by the Grand Trunk Railroad.

PORT SANILAC

Sanilac County Historic Village and Museum

Location: 228 S. Ridge St. (M25), Port Sanilac, MI 48469 **Contact Info:** (810) 622-9946 • sanilacmuseum@gmail.com • www.sanilaccountymuseum.org **Hours:** Jun-Aug: 11 a.m.-4 p.m. **Admission:** Varies by event. **Accessibility:** Free on-site parking. Wheelchair accessible. Tour guide available.

 Site Info: This extensive village—17 buildings in all—surrounds the 2 1/2-story Victorian Loop-Harrison Mansion, built in 1872. Many of the structures were moved to the village from surrounding communities, giving visitors the chance to discover what life was like in Sanilac County in the 1800s and early 1900s. Along with the mansion, you can experience a carriage barn, a dairy museum, several log cabins, a schoolhouse and church, a train depot, a general store, and more.

RICHMOND

Richmond Historic Village

Location: 36045 Park St., Richmond, MI 48062 **Contact Info:** (586) 727-7773 • richmondareahistoricalsociety@gmail.com • www.richmondhistoricalsociety.org **Hours:** By appointment only; call ahead for special event exceptions.

Admission: Donations accepted. **Accessibility:** Free on-site and street parking. Wheelchair accessible. Tour guide available.

Site Info: The Richmond Historic Village consists of a one-room schoolhouse, circa 1886; train depot, circa 1915; log cabin, circa 1850; and museum with displays that change bi-annually.

RIVES JUNCTION

Sheridan Stewart Museum

Location: 10138 Tompkins Road, Rives Junction, MI 49277 **Contact Info:** (517) 569-3263 • johnandpattuttle@yahoo.com • www.tompkinshistorical.org **Hours:** 2nd Sat monthly 12-3 p.m. **Admission:** $2/individual. **Accessibility:** Free on-site parking. Wheelchair accessible. Tour guide available.

Site Info: The Sheridan Stewart Museum, located in a restored family farmhouse, features collections and exhibits dedicated to preserving and teaching the history of Tompkins Township. The museum features a fully furnished frontier cabin and a replica schoolhouse, in addition to a windmill, a barn, a pavilion, and nature trails.

ROCHESTER HILLS

Rochester Hills Museum at Van Hoosen Farm

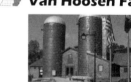

Location: 1005 Van Hoosen Rd., Rochester Hills, MI 48306 **Contact Info:** (248) 656-4663 • rhmuseum@rochesterhills.org • www.rochesterhills.org/museum **Hours:** Fri-Sat 1-4 p.m. and by appointment. **Admission:** $5/adult, $3/senior, $3/student, members free. **Accessibility:** Free on-site parking. Wheelchair accessible. Tour guide available.

Site Info: Located in Stoney Creek Village, this 16-acre museum complex was home to the Taylor and Van Hoosen families dating back to 1823. It features structures original to the property from 1840 to the early 20th century. Presented in a restored 1927 dairy barn are well-designed and informative exhibits highlighting the settlement, agriculture, industry, and cultural evolution of the community. The museum serves as the repository for artifacts and archives related to the greater Rochester area.

ROMEO

Bancroft-Stranahan Museum

Location: 132 Church St., Romeo, MI 48065 **Contact Info:**
(586) 752-4111 • www.romeohistoricalsociety.org **Hours:** Tue 7-9
p.m. Also by appointment. **Admission:** Free. **Accessibility:** On-
site and street parking. Wheelchair accessible. Tour guide available.

Site Info: This 1868 Greek Revival house was used
by the Bancroft and Stranahan families of Romeo.
It has period settings, including furniture, clothing,
kitchenware, and changing displays. It also has a
collection of oil paintings by William Gibbs.

Clyde Craig Blacksmith Shop Museum

Location: 301 N. Bailey St., Romeo, MI 48065 **Contact Info:**
(586) 752-4111 • www.romeohistoricalsociety.org **Hours:** By
appointment only. **Admission:** Free. **Accessibility:** On-site and
street parking. Wheelchair accessible. Tour guide available.

Site Info: The Craig shop was first a carriage barn.
In 1881, it became a tinsmith shop owned by Fritz
Engle. In 1920, Clyde Craig opened a blacksmith,
farrier, fur-trading station and veterinarian and
wheelwright shop. When Craig died in 1970, the
shop was moved and turned into a working blacksmith shop and
museum. Using the 2,800-degree forge, smiths still use the old
tools to shape metal, just as in the past.

Romeo Arts & Archives Center

Location: 290 N. Main St., Romeo, MI 48065 **Contact Info:**
(586) 752-4111 • www.romeohistoricalsociety.org **Hours:** Tue
7-9 p.m. Also by appointment. **Admission:** Free. **Accessibility:**
On-site and street parking. Wheelchair accessible. Tour guide
available.

Site Info: The Romeo Arts & Archives Center
building operated as the Romeo Michigan State
Police Post from 1936 to 2000. The Romeo
Historical Society then purchased it, and it now
houses archives and serves as a small research
library for those interested in Romeo's history. Visitors will also
see a number of oil paintings by William Gibbs on display.

ROSEVILLE

Leon Buyse Memorial Library and Museum

Location: 18740 E. Thirteen Mile Rd., Roseville, MI 48066
Contact Info: (586) 777-2720 • flemishlibrary@gmail.com • www.
flemishlibrary.org **Hours:** Sep-Jun: 2nd and 4th Sat 10:30 a.m.-3
p.m.; Jul-Aug: 4th Sat 10:30 a.m.-3 p.m.; Dec: 2nd Sat 10:30 a.m.-3
p.m. Also by appointment. **Admission:** Free. **Accessibility:** Free
on-site parking. Wheelchair accessible. Self-guided.

Site Info: The Leon Buyse Memorial Library and
Museum specializes in Flemish history. Among the
collections are handmade lace samples; death
memorial cards and obituaries; and the "Gazette

Van Detroit," in paper and microfilm. The Genealogical Society of Flemish Americans also holds the only copy of the "Gazette Van Moline" on microfilm.

ROYAL OAK

Royal Oak Historical Society Museum

Location: 1415 West Webster, Royal Oak, MI 48067 **Contact Info:** (248) 439-1501 • curator@ royaloakhistoricalsociety.org • www. royaloakhistoricalsociety.org **Hours:** Tue, Thu, Sat 1-4 p.m. **Admission:** $2/individual donation. **Accessibility:** Free on-site parking. Wheelchair accessible. Tour guide available; $2 donation/person. Tours are scheduled during hours when the museum is not open to the general public; groups should e-mail or call the society to arrange a tour.

Site Info: Located in the former Northwood Fire Station, the Royal Oak Historical Society Museum displays rotating exhibits covering the history of Royal Oak from its beginnings as a township in the early 1820s to today as a city. The Royal Oak Historical Society Museum maintains a small research library with local history written by residents, a collection of family histories, and a collection of Royal Oak High School yearbooks and newsletters dating back to 1913.

SALINE

Rentschler Farm Museum

Location: 1265 E. Michigan Ave., Saline, MI 48176 **Contact Info:** (734) 944-0442 • salinehistory@frontier.com • www.salinehistory.org **Hours:** May-mid-Dec: Sat 11 a.m.-3 p.m. **Admission:** Free. **Accessibility:** Free on-site parking. Partially wheelchair accessible. Tour guide available. Call for groups.

Site Info: The Rentschler Farm Museum features 12 farm buildings with early 20th-century furnishings. The structure of the farmhouse has never been changed, only paint color and wallpaper. Furnishings show the Great Depression Era of the 1930s.

SEBEWAING

Charles W. Liken Museum

Location: 325 N. Center St., Sebewaing, MI 48759 **Contact Info:** (989) 883-2753 • beegee38@gmail.com • www.thehchs.org **Hours:** May-Sep: 1st Sat-Sun monthly 12-3 p.m. **Admission:** Free. **Accessibility:** Free on-site and street parking. Not wheelchair accessible. Tour guide available.

EASTERN

Site Info: The Charles W. Liken House was built in the early 1880s by the town's founding father. The home has since been renovated and is now a museum that features replicated versions of the original furnishings. Visitors will also find displays about churches, newspapers, sports, outdoor activities, barns, and businesses.

Old Sebewaing Township Hall

Location: 325 N. Center St., Sebewaing, MI 48759 **Contact Info:** (989) 883-2753 • beegee38@gmail.com • www.thehchs.org/sebewaing/index.htm **Hours:** May-Sep: 1st Sat-Sun monthly 12-3 p.m. **Admission:** Free. **Accessibility:** Free on-site and street parking. Partially wheelchair accessible. Tour guide available.

Site Info: The Old Sebewaing Township Hall features exhibits on printing, the fire department water tank, and Sebewaing Beer. The history of daily life in Sebewaing is shared through displays on the post office, township office, jail, and high school.

SHELBY TOWNSHIP

Packard Proving Grounds Historic Site

Location: 49965 Van Dyke Ave., Shelby Township, MI 48317 **Contact Info:** (586) 739-4800 • www.packardmotorfdn.org **Hours:** Call for current hours. **Admission:** Donations accepted. **Accessibility:** Free on-site parking. Wheelchair accessible. Tour group available by appointment; costs vary.

Site Info: The Packard Proving Grounds Historic Site features seven buildings built between 1929 and 1942—six were designed by Albert Kahn. On display are a collection of Packard automobiles and marine engines, Miss America X mahogany racing boat, and more.

SOUTH LYON

Green Oak Township Historical Society Heritage Museum

Location: 10789 Silver Lake Road, South Lyon, MI 48178 **Contact Info:** (248) 446-0789 • stephenharrington@att.net • www.greenoaktownshiphistoricalsociety.org **Hours:** Call for current hours. **Admission:** Donations accepted. **Accessibility:** On-site parking. Wheelchair accessible. Free tour guides available upon request.

Site Info: Organized in 1974, the Green Oak Township Historical Society maintains a heritage museum, featuring artifacts from the 1800s. The museum is located adjacent to the 1856 Green Oak Township Hall, which was restored by the society.

SOUTHFIELD

Mary Thompson Farmhouse

Location: 25630 Evergreen Road, Southfield, MI 48076 **Contact Info:** (248) 796-4624 • historicsouthfield@gmail.com

EASTERN

• www.southfieldhistoricalsociety.wordpress.com **Hours:** By appointment. **Admission:** Donations accepted. **Accessibility:** Free on-site parking. Partially wheelchair accessible. Tour guide available; call ahead to schedule a group or private tour.

Site Info: The farmhouse has furniture and belongings of Southfield teacher and benefactor Mary Thompson and Southfield's first councilwoman, Jean McDonnell. The house features post-and-beam construction, was built in 1840, and was renovated in the 1960s and 1970s.

Town Hall Museum

Location: 26080 Berg Road, Southfield, MI 48033 **Contact Info:** (248) 796-4624 • historicsouthfield@gmail.com • www.southfieldhistoricalsociety.wordpress.com **Hours:** During summer concerts Jul-Aug; check wwww.cityofsouthfield.com for dates. Also by appointment. **Admission:** Donations accepted. **Accessibility:** Free on-site parking. Wheelchair accessible. Tour guide available during summer concerts or by appointment; donations accepted.

Site Info: Town Hall Museum, the original site of the 1872 Southfield Town Hall, features many exhibits including a 1920s kitchen, World War I, the Martin Luther King Task Force, and schools in Southfield. Artifacts reflect early Southfield Township, including its agricultural society and daily life. Archives are housed in the history room at the Southfield Public Library.

ST. CLAIR

St. Clair Historical Museum and Research Center

Location: 308 S. Fourth St., St. Clair, MI 48079 **Contact Info:** (810) 329-6888 • robert.freehan@gmail.com • www.historicstclair.com **Hours:** Open year-round: Tue 9:30 a.m.-12 p.m.; May-Oct: Sat-Sun 1:30-4:30 p.m. **Admission:** Donations accepted. **Accessibility:** Free on-site parking. Partially wheelchair accessible. Tour guide available. Call for other tours. Museum store.

Site Info: The museum features a Fort Sinclair model; specialty rooms highlighting artifacts from the local area, including shipbuilding tools and shoe manufacture; a period kitchen and living room; and a Diamond Crystal Salt Company room. The area's wooden and steel shipbuilding history is highlighted in the museum's maritime room.

ST. CLAIR SHORES

Selinsky-Green Farmhouse Museum

Location: 22500 Eleven Mile Road, St. Clair Shores, MI 48081 **Contact Info:** (586) 771-9020 • stachowm@libcoop.net • www.scslibrary.org/sgfm.html **Hours:** Sep-May: Wed, Sat 1-4 p.m.; Jun-Aug: Wed 1-4 p.m. **Admission:** Donations accepted.

Accessibility: Free on-site parking. Not wheelchair accessible. Tour guide available.

Site Info: The Selinsky-Green Farmhouse Museum represents the history of a typical family of the late 19th century. Prussian immigrants John and Mary Selinsky came to St. Clair Shores, then Erin Township, in 1868 and, by 1874, had built a log, salt-box farmhouse. The home was moved and restored by volunteers and now houses changing exhibits, period-decorated rooms, and special events.

STERLING HEIGHTS

William Upton House

Location: 40433 Dodge Park, Sterling Heights, MI 48313 **Contact Info:** (586) 446-2640 • turgeont@libcoop.net • www.sterling-heights.net/506/Historical-Commission **Hours:** Open during Sterlingfest (Jul) and Sterling Christmas (Dec). Also by appointment.

Admission: Donations accepted. **Accessibility:** Free on site parking. Partially wheelchair accessible.

Site Info: The William Upton House features household accessories, personal artifacts, maps, photographs, and documents relating to personal, business, educational, cultural, and recreational activities. The Sterling Heights Historical Commission solicits and accepts items that depict growth and change within the municipality from inception as a township in 1835 to the present.

TAYLOR

Taylor Historical Museum

Location: 12405 Pardee Rd, Taylor, MI 48180 **Contact Info:** (734) 287-3835 **Hours:** Call for current hours. **Admission:** Free. **Accessibility:** Free on-site parking. Wheelchair accessible. Tour guide available.

Site Info: The Taylor Historical Museum uses exhibits and history artifacts to showcase early Taylor businesses and family life in rural Taylor Township. The museum features farm tools, historical records, published maps, and site information.

TECUMSEH

Tecumseh Historical Museum

Location: 302 E. Chicago Blvd., Tecumseh, MI 49286 **Contact Info:** (517) 423-2374 • historictecumseh@gmail.com • www.historictecumseh.org **Hours:** Apr-Dec: Sat 10:30 a.m.-3:30 p.m. Also by appointment. **Admission:** Free. Donations accepted. **Accessibility:** Free on-site and street parking. Not wheelchair accessible. Self-guided. Museum store.

Site Info: Housed in the town's "old stone church," built circa 1913, the Tecumseh Historical Museum welcomes all to discover the history of the community, from "Dynamic Kernels" with Perry Hayden and Henry Ford to becoming the "refrigeration capital" under the Herrick family's Tecumseh Products. The town's history continues in the many homes and buildings dating from the 1800s, and it's on display in the museum for all to enjoy.

TEMPERANCE

Banner Oak School

Location: Sterns Rd and Crabb Rd, Temperance, MI 48182 **Contact Info:** (734) 847-0922 • lindaski@buckeye-access.com **Hours:** Apr-Oct: By appointment. **Admission:** Free. **Accessibility:** Free on-site parking. Wheelchair accessible. Tour guide available.

Site Info: Established in 1840, Banner Oak School accommodated 35 students between the ages of 5 and 17. The school building is available to teachers and their students to spend a day experiencing what it was like in a one-room school. The school was restored and refurnished in 1871.

TRENTON

Trenton Historical Museum

Location: 306 St. Joseph, Trenton, MI 48183 **Contact Info:** (734) 675-2130 • www.trentonhistoricalcommission.org **Hours:** Mar-Dec: Sat 1-4 p.m. **Admission:** Donations accepted. **Accessibility:** Free street parking. Not wheelchair accessible. Self-guided.

Site Info: The Trenton Historical Museum is a Victorian-style home, built in 1881 by John and Sarah Moore. The museum is decorated in Victorian period and contains information on the history of Trenton and area artifacts.

TROY

Troy Historic Village

Location: 60 W. Wattles Road, Troy, MI 48098 **Contact Info:** (248) 524-3570 • info@thvmail.org • www.troyhistoricvillage.org **Hours:** Mon-Fri 10 a.m.-3 p.m. **Admission:** $5/adult, $3/senior, $3/child, children 6 and under free. **Accessibility:** Free on-site and street parking. Wheelchair accessible. Self-guided. Museum Store.

Site Info: Troy Historic Village showcases 10 historic structures on a five-acre complex. Visitors can explore Michigan history by witnessing and sharing the lifestyles of the pioneers who established homes and farms in rural Troy Township during the 1800s. Offering a wide variety of activities for children and a diverse range of lectures and events for adults, the village aims to enhance appreciation of history while using Troy's rich and evolving story as a backdrop.

UBLY

The Ten Cent Barn

Location: 1 Longuski Drive, Ubly, MI 48475 **Contact Info:** (989) 553-4892 • ublyareahistoricalsociety@gmail.com • www. thehchs.org **Hours:** Memorial Day-Labor Day: Sun 1-4 p.m. **Admission:** Donations accepted. **Accessibility:** Free on-site parking. Partially wheelchair accessible. Tour guide available; call ahead to schedule a group or private tour.

Site Info: The Ten Cent Barn's attractions include a blacksmith shop, farm tools, household items, and historical furniture. The museum is also home to collections relating to Ubly history, including village records, school yearbooks, and cemetery information. During "Homecoming Weekend in July," the museum has a "people mover" pulled by an antique tractor that takes visitors to and from Memorial Park.

VASSAR

Watrousville Museum

Location: 4607 W. Caro Road (M-81), Vassar, MI 48768 **Contact Info:** (989) 823-2360 • dave@watrousville.com • www.watrousville.com **Hours:** Jun-Sep: Thu 1-4 p.m. Also by appointment. **Admission:** Free. **Accessibility:** Free on-site and street parking. Not wheelchair accessible. Self-guided. Museum store.

Site Info: The Watrousville Museum is located in the former Watrousville General Store, which is now a registered Michigan Historic Site. A "Lincoln Flagpole," installed to entice Abraham Lincoln to run for a second term, is located on the museum lawn. This is believed to be the last Lincoln Flagpole still standing.

WALES

Wales Township Hall

Location: 1372 Wales Center Rd., Wales, MI 48027
Contact Info: (810) 325-1146 • hermweng@gmail.com • www.waleshistoricalsociety.org **Hours:** Open by appointment.
Admission: Donations accepted. **Accessibility:** Free on-site parking.

Site Info: The Wales Historical Society stores its archives at the Wales Township Hall, which is listed on the State Register of Historic Sites. The archives include local township history dating from 1848 to the 1900s, available on the society's website. There are also documents from Dr. Horace Modge, a Civil War doctor and director of the county's poor farm.

WARREN

Warren Historical & Genealogical Society Historical Gallery

Location: 5460 Arden, Warren, MI 48092 **Contact Info:** (586) 258-2056 • histcomm@cityofwarren.org • www.cityofwarren.org/index.php/historical-commission **Hours:** Mon-Sat 9 a.m.-9 p.m. Also by appointment.
Admission: Free. **Accessibility:** Free on-site and street parking. Wheelchair accessible. Self-guided.

Site Info: The historical gallery, located within the Warren Community Center, is available for self-guided tours. The gallery shows a visual history of the city of Warren from the swamp to the present. Guided tours are available for scouts, schools, and other groups by appointment.

WASHINGTON

Loren Andrus Octagon House

Location: 57500 Van Dyke Ave., Washington, MI 48094 **Contact Info:** (586) 781-0084 • info@octagonhouse.org • www.octagonhouse.org **Hours:** May-Oct: 3rd Sun 1-4 p.m.
Admission: $5/individual.
Accessibility: Free on-site parking. Partially wheelchair accessible. Self-guided, call ahead to schedule a group or private tour. Museum store.

Site Info: Built in 1860, the Lauren Andrus Octagon House is furnished in a variety of periods beginning with the 1860s. Visitors can self-tour the house, venturing from the basement with its tool display all the way to the cupola for a dramatic vista of the area. Docents are available to answer questions about the house and its many occupants.

Washington Historical Society Museum

Location: 58230 VanDyke, Washington, MI 48094-2765 **Contact Info:** (586) 786-5404 • holcomi@comcast.net • www.washhistsoc.org **Hours:** Jun-Nov: 2nd and 4th Sun 1-4 p.m. **Admission:** Free. Donations accepted. **Accessibility:** Free on-site parking. Not wheelchair accessible. Self-guided.

Site Info: The museum features an extensive display on George Washington, which includes many pictures and commemorative items from the country's bicentennial. The war room has items from the Civil War, World War I, World War II, and Desert Storm. Many models of army vehicles have been placed on display. Within the museum is a Boy Scout Museum, which contains what is believed to be the largest collection of Boy Scout paraphernalia in Michigan.

WATERFORD

Historic Waterford Village

Location: 4490 Hatchery Road, Waterford, MI 48330 **Contact Info:** (248) 683-2697 • sstrait649@comcast.net • www.waterfordhistoricalsociety.org **Hours:** Wed 10:30 a.m.-2 p.m. **Admission:** Free. **Accessibility:** Free on-site parking. Wheelchair accessible. Self-guided; call ahead to schedule a group tour.

Site Info: Gracing the banks of the Clinton River and adjacent to the beautiful Fish Hatchery Park is the Waterford Township Historical Society's Historic Village. Some buildings are original, others are exact replicas, and a few are representations of village buildings from the 1900s. Discover all the village has to offer, such as the Hatchery House, Jacober's general store, Drayton Plains Depot, Grand Trunk caboose, hardware store, Lohff print shop, Gulf filling station, and many more.

WAYNE

Wayne Historical Museum

Location: North East Biddle and Main Street, Wayne, MI 48184 **Contact Info:** (734) 722-0113 • historical-society@ci.wayne.

mi.us • www.ci.wayne.mi.us/index.php/community/historical-museum **Hours:** Wed 12-3 p.m., Thu 4-7 p.m. **Admission:** Free. **Accessibility:** Free on-site and street parking. Wheelchair accessible. Tour guide available.

Site Info: The Wayne Historical Museum, located in the former city offices building, circa 1878, opened in 1964 and features more than 100 exhibits tracing the path from village to city. Artifacts include early Nankin Township history and records; first landowning documents; genealogies; documents; histories; pictures of early businesses, industries, postmasters, and community leaders; and local cemetery records.

WEST BLOOMFIELD

Chaldean Cultural Center
Location: 5600 Walnut Lake Road, West Bloomfield, MI 48323 **Contact Info:** (248) 681-5050 • mromaya@chaldeanculturalcenter.org • www.chaldeanculturalcenter.org **Hours:** Call for current hours. **Admission:** Donations accepted. **Accessibility:** Free on-site parking. Tour guide available; call ahead to schedule a group or private tour.

Site Info: At the heart of the Chaldean Cultural Center is an exhibition that takes visitors from the court of Nebuchadnezzar to an immigrant grocery store in Detroit and beyond. Multimedia presentations, sophisticated hands-on activities, artifacts both ancient and modern, and evocative environments tell a distinctive, engaging, and powerful story.

Orchard Lake Museum
Location: 3951 Orchard Lake Rd., West Bloomfield, MI 48325 **Contact Info:** (248) 757-2451 • contact@gwbhs.org • www.gwbhs.org **Hours:** 2nd Sun monthly 1-4 p.m. Also by appointment. **Admission:** Free. **Accessibility:** Free on-site parking. Wheelchair accessible. Tour guide available. Museum store.

Site Info: The Orchard Lake Museum houses a collection of local artifacts, historical photos, and documents. Regular items on display include a 17th-century dugout canoe and a Keego Cinema sign that was a neon landmark for 60 years.

WIXOM

Wixom-Wire Museum
Location: 687 Wixom Road, Wixom, MI 48393 **Contact Info:** (248) 624-3950 • laure.dorchak@wixomhistoricalsociety.org • www.wixomhistoricalsociety.org **Hours:** By appointment. **Admission:** Free. **Accessibility:** Free on-site parking. Not wheelchair accessible. Guide available by appointment.

Site Info: The Wixom-Wire House was originally built in 1855 as a parsonage. Visitors will observe a simpler lifestyle and meet strong-minded settlers who made a difference.

WYANDOTTE

Ford-MacNichol Home

Location: 2610 Biddle Ave., Wyandotte, MI 48192
Contact Info: (734) 324-7284 • museum@wyan.org • www.
wyandottemuseums.org **Hours:** Apr-Oct, Dec: Thu-Sun 12-4
p.m. **Admission:** $5/adult, $2.50/children (5-12), children 4
and under free. **Accessibility:** Free on-site and street parking.
Not wheelchair accessible.

 Site Info: The 1896 Ford-MacNichol Home
is the main exhibit building of the Wyandotte
Museums' campus and houses the majority of
the artifact collection. In this historic house
setting, a vivid picture of early 20th-century
Wyandotte is recreated with elegantly appointed rooms and
rotating exhibits on local history.

YPSILANTI

Ypsilanti Automotive Heritage Museum

 **Location:** 100 E. Cross St., Ypsilanti,
MI 48198 **Contact Info:** (734)
482-5200 • info@ypsiautoheritage.org •
www.ypsiautoheritage.org **Hours:**
Tue-Sun 1-4 p.m. **Admission:** $5/
adult, children 12 and under free.
Accessibility: Free on-site parking.
Wheelchair accessible. Self-guided.

 Site Info: Located in the world's-last-operating
Hudson auto dealership building, the museum
houses records dating back to 1927 and displays
30 vehicles and 18 cut-a-way automatic
transmissions.

Ypsilanti Historical Society, Museum, & Archives

Location: 220 N. Huron St., Ypsilanti, MI 48197 **Contact
Info:** (734) 217-8236 • yhs.archives@gmail.com • www.
ypsilantihistoricalsociety.org **Hours:** Tue-Sun 2-5 p.m.
Admission: Free. **Accessibility:** Free on-site parking. Wheelchair
accessible. Tour guide available. Tour groups by appointment.

 Site Info: The Ypsilanti Historical Society's
museum is located in the Asa Dow House, an
1860s brick Victorian mansion, with artifacts from
the 19th and 20th centuries in a variety of displays
and exhibits depicting Ypsilanti's heritage.

EASTERN

ALPENA

Besser Museum for Northeast Michigan

Location: 491 Johnson St., Alpena, MI 49707 **Contact Info:** (989) 356-2202 • besser@bessermuseum.org • www.bessermuseum.org **Hours:** Mon-Sat 10 a.m.-5 p.m., Sun 12-4 p.m. **Admission:** $5/adult, $3/senior (60+), $3/children (5-18). **Accessibility:** On-site parking. Wheelchair accessible. Self-guided.

Site Info: Through research, Besser Museum for Northeast Michigan collects, preserves, and interprets artifacts and information concerning 15 counties in Northeast Michigan. Through programs and exhibits, it promotes understanding and appreciation. The museum hosts four permanent and five rotating exhibits. Exhibits include Native-American artifacts, historic Alpena, natural history, and more.

Great Lakes Maritime Heritage Center

Location: 500 West Fletcher St., Alpena, MI 49707 **Contact Info:** (989) 356-8805 • thunderbay@noaa.gov • www.thunderbay.noaa.gov **Hours:** Memorial Day-Jun: Daily 9 a.m.-5 p.m.; Jul-Aug: Daily 9 a.m.-7 p.m.; Sep-May: Mon-Sat 10 a.m.-5 p.m., Sun 12-5 p.m. **Admission:** Free. Donations accepted. **Accessibility:** Free on-site and street parking. Wheelchair accessible. Self-guided. Museum store.

Site Info: The Great Lakes Maritime Heritage Center is a visitor center for the Thunder Bay National Marine Sanctuary, which protects one of America's best-preserved collections of 200-plus shipwrecks. At the heritage center, visitors learn how the sanctuary studies the resources on the lake floor and works to protect the Great Lakes and their rich maritime history, along with why the adjacent stretch of Lake Huron was known as "Shipwreck Alley." Glass-bottom boat tours are also available.

ATLANTA

McKenzie One-Room School

Location: M-33 N (Montmorency County Fair Grounds), Atlanta, MI 49709 **Contact Info:** (989) 742-4218 **Hours:** 3rd week in Aug 10 a.m.-9 p.m. **Admission:** Fair entry fee. **Accessibility:** On-site parking for a fee. Wheelchair accessible. **Site Info:** The McKenzie One-Room School houses local newspapers from 1900 to 1991 on microfilm and also has a large collection of old photographs and family histories. In addition, it has documents pertaining to the one-room schools of Montmorency County and the early timber period.

BEAVER ISLAND

Beaver Island Marine Museum

Location: 38105 Michigan Avenue, Beaver Island, MI 49782
Contact Info: (231) 448-2254 • history@beaverisland.net
• www.beaverislandhistory.org **Hours:** Jun-Aug: Mon-Sat 11
a.m.-5 p.m., Sun 12-3 p.m. **Admission:** Donations accepted.
Accessibility: Free on-site parking. Wheelchair accessible. Tour
guide available. Museum store.

Site Info: Located in an authentic 1906 net
shed overlooking a functioning Lake Michigan
harbor, the Beaver Island Marine Museum
features displays on the island's commercial
fishing, shipbuilding, diving activities, and
shipping history. Additional exhibits share the memories of
the disasters that overtook the men and ships of the island.
Visitors can view information about the other islands in the
Beaver Archipelago as well.

Mormon Print Shop Museum

Location: 26275 Main Street, Beaver Island, MI 49782
Contact Info: (231) 448-2254 • history@beaverisland.net
• www.beaverislandhistory.org **Hours:** Jun-Aug: Mon-Sat 11
a.m.-5 p.m., Sun 12-3 p.m. **Admission:** Donations accepted.
Accessibility: Free on-site parking. Wheelchair accessible. Tour
guides available. Museum store.

Site Info: The Mormon Print Shop Museum
is located in a historic building that housed the
presses for the first newspaper north of Grand
Rapids. Visitors enter through the covered porch
overlooking Paradise Bay in northern Lake
Michigan. Visitors will enjoy exhibits showcasing island life
over the centuries, including Native-American artifacts, the
only "kingdom" in the United States, the Irish and other
immigrant connections, an old classroom, and many artifacts
related to logging.

BRETHREN

Brethren Heritage Museum

Location: 14300 Cart Ave., Brethren, MI 49619 **Contact Info:**
(231) 477-5526 • janetdonstroup@gmail.com **Hours:** Jun-Sep:
Sun 1-4 p.m. Also by appointment. **Admission:** Donations
accepted. **Accessibility:** Free on-site parking. Wheelchair
accessible. Tour guide available by appointment.
Site Info: Four buildings on the site include a reconstructed
authentic cabin from the 1940s, a reconstructed store from
the 1930s, and a tool shed containing many artifacts from the
lumbering era.

CENTRAL LAKE

Knowles Historical Museum

Location: 2238 S. Main, Highway M-88, Central Lake, MI 49032 **Contact Info:** http://eldenq.angelfire.com/#photo2428161 **Hours:** Wed-Fri 1-4 p.m. Also by appointment. **Admission:** Free. **Accessibility:** Free street parking. Not wheelchair accessible.

Site Info: The Central Lake Area Historical Society maintains the Knowles Historical Museum in a restored home that is furnished with local period furniture, including a 1904 pump organ. The museum also offers a 100-year collection of a local newspaper, "The Central Lake Torch," and many tapes, pictures, books by local authors, and genealogy research materials.

CHARLEVOIX

Castle Farms

Location: 5052 M-66, Charlevoix, MI 49720 **Contact Info:** (231) 237-0884 • info@castlefarms.com • www.castlefarms.com **Hours:** May-Oct: Daily 9 a.m.-5 p.m.; Nov-Apr: Mon-Sat 9 a.m.-4 p.m. Early closures on event days. Closed some major holidays.

Admission: Summer: $10/person. Winter: $7/person.
Accessibility: Free on-site parking. Wheelchair accessible. Self-guided. Tour guide available for groups of 10 or more for an additional fee if scheduled in advance.

Site Info: Visit the beautiful castle and gardens, discover the story of this historic property built in 1918, and learn fascinating details about its restoration. Play giant chess, feed the fish, interact with the largest model railroad in Michigan, and enjoy the extensive gardens. Visit the museum that has collections of 1918 memorabilia, antique toys, and royal family memorabilia.

Charlevoix Railroad Depot

Location: 307 Chicago Ave., Charlevoix, MI 49720 **Contact Info:** (231) 547-0373 • info@chxhistory.com • www.chxhistory.com **Hours:** Call for current hours. **Admission:** Donations accepted. **Accessibility:** Free on-site and street parking. Wheelchair accessible. Self-guided.

Site Info: Built by the Chicago & West Michigan Railway in 1892, the depot is used for meetings, events, and occasional exhibits. The depot is listed on the National Historic Register and the interior may be viewed upon request. On the exterior, the Charlevoix Area Garden Club has developed an award-winning heritage garden along the entire west exterior using historic cuttings and design methods. That area is open to the public at all times.

Charlevoix South Pier Lighthouse

Location: Lake Michigan Municipal Beach, Charlevoix, MI 49720 **Contact Info:** (231) 547-0373 • info@chxhistory.com • www.chxhistory.com **Hours:** Interior not open to the public. Exterior may be visited at anytime. **Admission:** Free. **Accessibility:** Free street parking. Partially wheelchair accessible. Self-guided.

Site Info: The Charlevoix Historical Society is responsible for the preservation, restoration, and maintenance of the Charlevoix South Pier Lighthouse. The federal government owns the pier, the city of Charlevoix owns the light, and the Coast Guard maintains the light as an aid to navigation. The lower portion was built in 1948. The black lens housing at the top is from the original Charlevoix light that was built in 1885.

Harsha House Museum

Location: 103 State St., Charlevoix, MI 49720 **Contact Info:** (231) 547-0373 • info@chxhistory.com • www.chxhistory.com **Hours:** Mar-Dec: Tue-Sat 12-4 p.m. **Admission:** $1/individual suggested donation. **Accessibility:** Free on-site and street parking. Wheelchair accessible. Tour guide available. Museum store.

Site Info: The Harsha House Museum includes three restored 1891 Victorian parlors with vintage furnishings and original works of art by Charlevoix artists. It has kitchen and household objects on display. Other attractions include a large one-horse open sleigh, rotating exhibits, a working player piano, a pedal pump reed organ, a working wind-up Victrola, 3 1/2-order Fresnel lens from the Gray's Reef Lighthouse, and a furnished Victorian-style dollhouse.

Norwood Schoolhouse

Location: 742 Fourth St., Charlevoix, MI 49720 **Contact Info:** (231) 547-6220 • secretary@norwoodhistory.org • www.norwoodhistory.org **Admission:** Free.

Site Info: Collections include documents and photos relating to 19th-century settlement and lumbering, local schools, and famous personages. Also includes some oral history transcripts and tapes. During the summer, the Norwood Area Historical Society hosts educational events and social gatherings.

CHEBOYGAN

Cheboygan River Front Range Lighthouse

Location: 606 Water Street, Cheboygan, MI 49721 **Contact Info:** (231) 436-5580 • info@gllka.com • www.gllka.com **Hours:** Memorial Day-Labor Day: Weekends and Holidays 9 a.m.-5 p.m. **Admission:** Donations requested. **Accessibility:** Free on-site parking. Not wheelchair accessible. Tour guide available.

Site Info: The Great Lakes Lighthouse Keepers Association obtained the Cheboygan River Front Range Lighthouse in 2004 under the National Historic Lighthouse Preservation Act. The lighthouse is currently being restored to its circa 1910 appearance, a time when Cheboygan lumber mills were shipping a large amount of products throughout the Great Lakes.

Spies Heritage Hall

 **Location:** 427 Court Street, Cheboygan, MI 49721 **Contact Info:** (231) 627-9597 • museum@ cheboyganhistory.org • www. cheboyganhistorycenter.org **Hours:** Jun-Oct: Tue-Sat 1-4 p.m. **Admission:** $5/adult, children 18 and under free.

Accessibility: Free on-site parking. Partially wheelchair accessible. Tour guide available. Museum store.

 Site Info: The History Center of Cheboygan County seeks to engage, educate, and entertain visitors in the experience of the area's rich cultural commonwealth by collecting, preserving, and presenting the history of Cheboygan County. Exhibits portray the various historic eras of the county through the use of artifacts and period display settings. Visitors will discover Cheboygan County's place in the history of Northern Michigan, the Straits of Mackinac, and the larger Great Lakes region.

COPEMISH

Marilla Museum & Pioneer Place

 **Location:** 9991 Marilla Road, Copemish, MI 49625 **Contact Info:** (231) 362-3430 • boja@kaltelnet. net • www.marillahistory.org **Hours:** May-Oct: Sat 1-5 p.m. **Admission:** $3/adult, $1/children. **Accessibility:** Free on-site parking. Partially wheelchair accessible. Tour guide available.

 Site Info: Marilla Museum & Pioneer Place consists of four unique historic buildings that are all beautifully furnished with artifacts that represent the rich logging and agricultural history of the area. An 1870s two-story log house, the Nels Johnson Logger/Trapper Cabin, the 1900 mortise-and-tenon pioneer barn, and the 1920 Marilla Standard School complete the complex.

EAST JORDAN

East Jordan City Hall

Location: 201 Main St., East Jordan, MI 49727 **Contact Info:** (231) 536-3282 • kprebble@ejps.org • www.portsideartsfair.org

Hours: Mon-Fri 8 a.m.-4 p.m. **Admission:** Free. Donations accepted. **Accessibility:** Free street parking. Not wheelchair accessible. Self-guided.

 Site Info: Collections include ladies furnishings, train memorabilia, woodworking tools, newspaper typeset, and revolving displays. Exhibits include information on local historian George Secord and his contribution to preserving the history of East Jordan, memorabilia from the Hite and Gidley Drug Stores, a game display, and womens fashions and accessories from bygone eras. Exhibits are updated annually, so each visit is a new experience.

East Jordan Portside Art & Historical Society Museum

Location: 1656 S M 66, East Jordan, MI 49727 **Contact Info:** (231) 536-3282 • kprebble@ejps.org • www.portsideartsfair. org **Hours:** Jun-Sep: Sat-Sun 1:30-4:30 p.m. **Admission:** Free. Donations accepted. **Accessibility:** Free on-site parking. Wheelchair accessible. Tour guide available.

 Site Info: The East Jordan Portside Art & Historical Society's museum is located in Elm Pointe Park, a Michigan historic site located on Lake Charlevoix. It is known as the first historical museum in Charlevoix County and was established in 1976 to preserve the history of the local area. Collections include the lumbering era, trains, agriculture, home life, military, and industries.

Raven Hill Discovery Center

Location: 4737 Fuller Rd., East Jordan, MI 49727 **Contact Info:** (231) 536-3369 • info@ravenhilldiscoverycenter.org • www. miravenhill.org **Hours:** Apr-Oct: Mon-Fri 10 a.m.-4 p.m., Sat 12-4 p.m., Sun 2-4 p.m.; Nov-Mar: Sat 12-4 p.m., Sun 2-4 p.m. **Admission:** $10/individual. **Accessibility:** Free on-site parking. Wheelchair accessible. Self-guided. Museum store.

 Site Info: The Raven Hill Discovery Center provides opportunities for all ages to learn, create, grow, and play through classes, exhibits, and facilities. The center creates meaningful learning connections by linking history, science, and the arts. The site serves as a regional science and technology center, as well as a cultural, historical, and art center.

EAST TAWAS

Iosco County Historical Society & Museum

Location: 405 W. Bay St., East Tawas, MI 48730 **Contact Info:** (989) 362-8911 • iosco.history@gmail.com • www.ioscomuseum. org **Hours:** Call for hours. **Admission:** Free. Donations accepted. **Accessibility:** Public parking lot adjacent to museum. Wheelchair accessible. Free tour guide.

Site Info: In 1978, the Iosco County Historical Society opened its museum as a depository of historic artifacts reflecting Iosco County's history and growth. Historical displays and exhibits change regularly and include class pictures; a Victorian parlor; an early kitchen; medical displays; a Western States ship; and the military during World War I, World War II, and the Spanish American and Civil Wars.

Tawas Point Lighthouse

 **Location:** 686 Tawas Beach Rd., East Tawas, MI 48730 **Contact Info:** (989) 362-5658 • museuminfo@michigan.gov • www.michigan.gov/tawaslighthouse **Hours:** See website. **Admission:** $5/ adult, $2/children (6-17), children 5 and under free. Michigan State Parks Recreation Passport is required for entry. **Accessibility:** Free on-site parking. Partially wheelchair accessible. Tour guide available. Call for groups. Museum store.

 Site Info: In service since 1877, the Tawas Point Lighthouse was built to guide vessels safely into Tawas Bay. Tours interpret life at the lighthouse and the area's maritime history. Tawas Point is also a mecca for birders, especially during the spring and fall migration seasons. The point offers spectacular views of Lake Huron sunrises and sunsets over Tawas Bay. Other historic structures on-site include an oil house and a fog signal area.

ELK RAPIDS

Elk Rapids Area Historical Museum

 **Location:** 301 Traverse St., Elk Rapids, MI 48629 **Contact Info:** (231) 264-5692 • president@ elkrapidshistory.org • www. elkrapidshistory.org **Hours:** Jun-Aug: Wed, Sat 1-4 p.m.; May-Sep by appointment. Closed holidays. **Admission:** Donations accepted. **Accessibility:** Free street parking. Partially wheelchair accessible. Tour guide available. Call for groups. After hours call (231) 264-8984.

 Site Info: Exhibits and displays at the Elk Rapids Area Historical Museum focus on the village of Elk Rapids' role in the "Chain of Lakes Region" during the 19th and 20th centuries as an important lumbering, cement, and pig iron smelting center. Collections include artifacts from the pig iron and lumber industries, vintage clothing, antique tools, old office furniture, and machines. There is also a regional photo collection of 3,000 images.

EMPIRE

Empire Area Museum Complex

Location: 11544 S. LaCore St., Empire, MI 49630 **Contact Info:** (231) 326-5568 • empiremuseum@ yahoo.com • www.empiremimuseum. org **Hours:** Memorial Day-Jul 1: Sat-Sun 1-4 p.m. Jul-Aug: Daily 1-4 p.m. Labor Day-mid Oct: Sat-Sun 1-4 p.m. **Admission:** Donations accepted. **Accessibility:** Free on-site parking. Wheelchair accessible. Self-guided. Museum store.

Site Info: The Empire Area Museum Complex includes four buildings featuring a turn-of-the-century saloon, a sail and rail display, a 1924 vintage gas station, several horse-drawn vehicles, and a "hit and miss" engine display. The museum also features a one-room school, a 1911 "hose house" firehouse, a set of original "Big Wheels" for logging, and a barn full of all kinds of farming and lumbering equipment. The store features many publications as well as several locally produced DVDs of the region.

FAIRVIEW

Steiner Logging and Pioneer Museum

Location: 1980 E. Reber Rd., Fairview, MI 48621 **Contact Info:** (989) 889-1742 • nccsurveyor@yahoo.com **Hours:** May-Oct: Sat-Sun 12-4 p.m. Tour groups by appointment. **Admission:** Donations accepted. **Accessibility:** Free on-site parking. Wheelchair accessible. Tour guide available.

Site Info: The museum collects, maintains, renovates, and places on exhibit the "tools of the trade" of Northern Michigan logging operations and the remaining assets by early pioneers who settled in the area. This includes mechanical devices ranging from the "Big Wheels" to early chainsaws, plus farming equipment from the early 1900s.

FIFE LAKE

Fife Lake Historical Museum

Location: 136 E State St., Fife Lake, MI 49633 **Contact Info:** (231) 879-3342 • www.fifelake.com/chamber/historical. htm **Hours:** Summer: Wed, Sat, Sun 1-4 p.m. **Admission:** Free. **Accessibility:** On-site parking. Wheelchair accessible. Guides available.

Site Info: The museum houses collections that include local archaeology, late 19th-century and early 20th-century artifacts, genealogical records, store inventories, and fraternal group records. Nearby are the Fife Lake Historical Fire Barn, which features a 1936 fire truck, uniforms, and large wheeled fire-fighting equipment, and an 1878 one-room school. There is also a Fife Lake Historical Walk that includes 27 display plaques throughout the town. Brochures and maps for the historic walk are available in the museum.

FRANKFORT
Friends of Point Betsie Lighthouse, Inc.

Location: 3701 Point Betsie Road, Frankfort, MI 49635 **Contact Info:** (231) 352-7644 • pointbetsie@gmail.com • www.pointbetsie.org **Hours:** May-Oct: Sat 10 a.m-5 p.m., Sun 12-5 p.m.; Jul-Aug: Wed, Thu 10 a.m.-5 p.m. **Admission:** $5/adult, $2/child, children 6 and under free. **Accessibility:** Free street parking. Wheelchair accessible. Tour guide available. Museum store.

Site Info: All of the historic buildings operated by the Friends of Point Betsie Lighthouse, Inc., have been completely restored, including the inside of the lighthouse and fog signal building. A new building was finished in 2014 that includes the Maritime Museum, gift shop, and public restrooms. The Assistant Keeper's Apartment is available for rent.

LODGING IN FRANKFORT
The Hotel Frankfort

Location: 231 Main St., Frankfort, MI 49635 **Contact Info:** (231) 352-8090 • frontdesk@thehotelfrankfort.com • www.thehotelfrankfort.com **Property Info:** Hotel/Inn. Open year-round. Restaurant open May-Oct. Privately owned; no public tours; pre-booking required. Free on-site and street parking. Partially wheelchair accessible. Food available on-site. **Price:** $80-$280.

Site Info: There has been a hotel on this site since 1865. The current building was built in 1932 after a fire leveled the original building in 1929. The Hotel Frankfort is a boutique hotel with 17 rooms, a full-service restaurant, a bar, a wine cellar, and two banquet rooms.

GRAYLING
Crawford County Historical Society & Museum Complex

Location: 97 E. Michigan Ave., Grayling, MI 49738 **Contact Info:** (989) 348-4461 • www.grayling-area.com/museum **Hours:** 12-4 p.m. **Admission:** Donations accepted. **Accessibility:** Free street parking. Partially wheelchair accessible; the second story of the railroad depot is not accessible. Tour guides available upon request.

Site Info: The Crawford County Historical Society maintains a museum complex that includes an 1882 historic train depot, a 1900 schoolhouse that is used to exhibit the military history of Crawford County, a log trapper's cabin, a firehouse with two restored fire engines, a farm building with a restored tractor, an early 1900 cutter sleigh, and a retired 1920s caboose. Rooms in the depot represent a general store, schoolroom, ladies sewing room, saloon, one-room cabin, and R.R. Crew quarters.

Hartwick Pines Logging Museum

Location: 2833 Monarch Dr., Grayling, MI 49738 **Contact Info:** (989) 348-2537 • burger@michigan.gov • www.michigan.gov/loggingmuseum **Hours:** Apr 27-May 27: Daily 9 a.m.-4 p.m.; May 28-Sep 5: Daily 9 a.m.-5 p.m.; Sep 6-Oct 23: Daily 9 a.m.-4 p.m. **Admission:** Free. Michigan State Parks Recreation Passport is required for entry. **Accessibility:** Free on-site parking. Wheelchair accessible. Self-guided. Museum store.

Site Info: The Hartwick Pines Logging Museum returns visitors to the state's 19th-century logging era, when Michigan led the nation in sawed lumber production. Indoor and outdoor exhibits, period rooms, and live interpreters tell the stories of loggers, river men, and entrepreneurs. Walking through one of Michigan's largest remaining stands of old-growth white pine, visitors can see the kinds of trees the loggers prized.

Lovells Historical Museums

Location: 8405 Twin Bridge Rd., Grayling, MI 49738 **Contact Info:** (989) 348-7173 • lovellsmuseums@gmail.com • www.lovellsmuseum.com **Hours:** End Apr-End Sep: Wed, Fri 1-4 p.m., Sat 11 a.m.-4 p.m., Sun 10 a.m.-1 p.m. Also by appointment. **Admission:** Donations accepted. **Accessibility:** Tour guide available.

Site Info: The Lovells Township Historical Society maintains two museum buildings. The 1907 Lone Pine School House shares Lovells' community history and the Lovells' Museum of Trout Fishing History tells the AuSable River's history.

Wellington Farm Park

Location: 6944 S. Military Rd., Grayling, MI 49738 **Contact Info:** (989) 348-5187 • welfar32@gmail.com • www.grayling-mi.com/attractions/wellington-farm-usa **Hours:** May-Jun: Fri, Sat, Sun 10 a.m.-5 p.m.; Jul-Aug 10

a.m.-5 p.m. daily; Sep-Oct: Wed-Sun 10 a.m.-5p.m. **Admission:** $8/adult, $6/senior and military, $5/students, children 4 and under free. **Accessibility:** Free on-site parking. Partially wheelchair accessible. Tour guide available. Museum store.

Site Info: Wellington Farm is a working farm that is set in the year 1932, the deepest year of the Great Depression. Visitors can view a working summer kitchen and grist mill, a livestock barn, and a functional sawmill powered by a 1914 steam engine. Crafters alley includes an operating basket shop, broom shop, loom house, rock shop, blacksmith shop, and carpenter shop. Nature trails are available with guided nature walks upon request.

GREENBUSH

Greenbush School
Location: Campbell Street west of US-23, Greenbush, MI 48738 **Contact Info:** (989) 739-3911 **Hours:** Call for current hours. **Admission:** Free.

Site Info: The Greenbush Historical Society preserved and now maintains the 1870 one-room Greenbush School and the oldest structure in the community, the 1867 Swart House. The society's collections include an 1898 Elmer Car, a 1929 Durant car, and a wooden smokehouse.

HARBOR SPRINGS

Harbor Springs History Museum

Location: 349 E. Main St., Harbor Springs, MI 49740 **Contact Info:** (231) 526-9771 • info@ harborspringshistory.org • www. harborspringshistory.org **Hours:** Exhibit Hours: Fri-Sat 11 a.m.-3 p.m. Business Hours: Tue-Fri 9 a.m.-5 p.m.

Admission: $5/adult, $3/senior and child, HSAHS members free. **Accessibility:** Free on-site and street parking. Wheelchair accessible. Self-guided. Museum store.

Site Info: The Harbor Springs History Museum is located in the former city hall building on Main Street. Leading a journey beginning with the first residents—the Odawa Indians—the exhibits escort visitors through time stopping to visit with missionaries, homesteaders, loggers, downtown merchants, and resorters. The museum offers not only family-friendly exhibits and displays but also a year-round calendar of events, a genealogy center, and a community space for lectures and programs on the history of Harbor Springs.

NORTHERN

HARRISVILLE

Sturgeon Point Lighthouse and Old Bailey School

Location: 6072 E. Point Rd., Harrisville, MI 48470
Contact Info: (989) 724-6297 • www.alconahistoricalsociety.com **Hours:** Jun-Sep: 11 a.m.-4 p.m. **Admission:** Free.
Accessibility: Free on-site parking. Partially wheelchair accessible. Self-guided. Museum store.

 Site Info: Members of the Alcona Historical Society provide educational tours and programs, including exciting opportunities for residents and visitors to explore and enjoy three museums: Sturgeon Point Lighthouse, Bailey School, and the Lincoln Train Depot. The Sturgeon Point Lighthouse features an authentic lens, keeper's home, and two boats used by the Coast Guard. Also on-site is the actual Alcona County one-room schoolhouse, completely restored and furnished with authentic collections.

HILLMAN

Brush Creek Mill

Location: 121 State St., Hillman, MI 49746 **Contact Info:** (989) 742-2527 • brushcreekmill@myfrontiermail.com • www.brushcreekmill.com **Hours:** Jan-Apr: Fri-Sat 12-4 p.m.; May-Dec: Tue-Sat 12-4 p.m. **Admission:** Free.
Accessibility: Free on-site parking. Wheelchair accessible. Tour guide available by appointment. Museum store.

 Site Info: The Brush Creek Mill is a history museum and area cultural center that celebrates history and promotes and provides a learning environment. It also features history about local families, as well as information pertaining to solar power, water power, wind turbines, and geothermal energy.

HONOR

Drake School

Location: Corner of County Highway 610 and County Highway 67, Honor, MI 49640 **Contact Info:** (231) 882-5539 • bmuseum@att.net • www.benziemuseum.org **Hours:** Jul-Aug: Sat-Sun 1-4 p.m. **Admission:** Free. **Accessibility:** Free parking. Self-guided.

 Site Info: The Drake School in Platte Township was built in 1891 and used until 1943. Sit at student desks to experience what school was like more than 100 years ago. Displays show what children learned at the school and discuss daily activities.

KALEVA

Bottle House Museum

Location: 14551 Wuoksi St., Kaleva, MI 49645 **Contact Info:** (231) 362-2080 • caasiala@jackpine.com • www.kalevami.com/The_Bottle_House_Museum.html **Hours:** Memorial Day-Labor Day: Sat-Sun 12-4 p.m.; Sep-Oct: Sat 12-4 p.m. **Admission:** $3/individual suggested donation. **Accessibility:** Free street and on-site parking. Not wheelchair accessible. Tour guide available.

Site Info: Built in the 1940s, the Bottle House was constructed by John Makinen, who used 60,000 chipped or flawed bottles from his local pop bottling factory. Makinen even incorporated different colored bottles to create artistic designs and words within the walls of his house. Inside the museum, exhibits relate to the early settlement of Kaleva, Finnish-American culture, and early 20th-century farm life, along with a special display highlighting the lures of the Makinen Tackle Company.

LAKE ANN

Almira Historical Museum

Location: 19440 Maple St., Lake Ann, MI 49650 **Contact Info:** (231) 275-7362 • info@almirahistoricalsociety.org • www.almirahistoricalsociety.org **Hours:** May-Sep: Tue, Sat 1-4 p.m. **Admission:** Free. Donations accepted. **Accessibility:** Free on-site parking. Wheelchair accessible. Tour guide available. Museum store.

Site Info: The museum has more than 1,300 artifacts and includes the Thompson-Kuemin House. The property also includes the Almira Fire Barn Museum, which houses a 1946 international fire truck. There is also a blacksmith shop and boathouse. The Babcock House is currently being restored. Exhibits include military uniforms and American flags, vintage switchboards, wooden and brass post office boxes, early logging and farming equipment, and a fire display.

LELAND

Historic Fishtown

Location: 203 E. Cedar St., Leland, MI 49654 **Contact Info:** (231) 256-8878 • info@fishtownmi.org • www.fishtownmi.org **Hours:** Office Mon-Fri 9 a.m.-4 p.m. year-round. Site is open year-round. Shops are seasonal and hours vary. **Admission:** Free. **Accessibility:** Free street parking. Partially wheelchair accessible. Group tours available by appointment.

NORTHERN

Site Info: Historic Fishtown's attractions include historic fishing shanties, regional foods, unique shops, and exhibits about Fishtown's past and present as a working waterfront. Historic Fishtown is located along the mouth of the Leland River in Leland. Some exhibits are viewable all year, others are seasonal.

Leelanau Historical Society Museum

Location: 203 E. Cedar Street, Leland, MI 49654 **Contact Info:** (231) 256-7475 • info@leelanauhistory.org • www.leelanauhistory.org **Hours:** Jun-Oct: Wed-Fri 10 a.m.-4 p.m., Sat 10 a.m.-2 p.m. Call for seasonal hours or appointment. **Admission:** $2/individual. **Accessibility:** Free on-site parking. Wheelchair accessible. Self-guided.

Site Info: The museum preserves and displays local history and also serves as a research center. Its exhibits include shipwrecks of the Manitou Passage, North Manitou Island, and the Native-American Anishnabek Arts Collection.

LODGING IN LELAND

Riverside Inn

Location: 302 River St., Leland, MI 49654 **Contact Info:** (231) 256-9971 • info@theriverside-inn.com • www.theriverside-inn.com **Property Info:** Hotel/Inn. Open year-round. Privately owned; no public tours; pre-booking required. Partially wheelchair accessible. Food available on-site. **Price:** $143-$193.

Site Info: The Riverside Inn was built in 1901 by Jacob Schwarz, a German immigrant to Leelanau County. He built the inn with indoor plumbing, hot water, heat, and electricity to entice wealthy visitors from Indianapolis, Chicago, Cincinnati, and Detroit. Visitors today can choose from four guest rooms that have the charm of days gone by. The inn is in an ideal location, close to the heart of downtown Leland and several Lake Michigan and Lake Leelanau beaches.

LEWISTON

Kneeland-Sachs Museum

Location: 4384 Michelson Ave., Lewiston, MI 49756 **Contact Info:** (989) 786-2451 • lewareahistsoc@gmail.com • www.lewistonhistoricalsociety.com **Hours:** Call for current hours. **Admission:** Donations accepted. **Accessibility:** Free on-site parking. Partially wheelchair accessible. Tour guide available.

Site Info: Built in 1892, the Kneeland-Sachs Museum was the home of David Kneeland, manager of the Michelson & Hanson Lumber Company. The house was then sold to George & Martha Sachs, whose family occupied the building for the next 85 years. The museum shares their histories. The site also features a fully furnished trapper's cabin as well as a barn.

LINCOLN

Lincoln Train Depot

Location: Intersection of Lake St. and Fisk St., Lincoln, MI 48742 **Contact Info:** (989) 724-6297 • www.alconahistoricalsociety.com **Hours:** Jun-Sep: 11 a.m.-4 p.m. **Admission:** Free. **Accessibility:** Free on-site parking. Partially wheelchair accessible. Self-guided. Museum store.

Site Info: The Lincoln Train Depot, a wood structure that has been standing since 1886, was built by the Detroit, Bay City, and Alpena Railroad. The depot is located on Lake Street in Lincoln and served the community and surrounding area until 1929. The first rail service to the area passed through Lincoln from the south and continued north through Ossineke and Alpena. The display includes a caboose and switching engine.

MACKINAW CITY

Colonial Michilimackinac

Location: 102 West Straits Avenue, Mackinaw City, MI 49701 **Contact Info:** (231) 436-4100 • mackinacparks@michigan.gov • www.mackinacparks.com **Hours:** Early-May-mid-Oct: 9:30 a.m.-5 p.m. (Peak summer season hours extended to 7 p.m.). **Admission:** $11/adult, $6.50/youth (5-12). **Accessibility:** Free on-site parking. Partially wheelchair accessible. Tour guide available. Museum store.

Site Info: French fur-trading village and military outpost Michilimackinac was founded in 1715. It was later occupied by the British, who abandoned it in 1780 to establish a new fort on Mackinac Island. Today, the site features a reconstructed, fortified village of 13 buildings as it appeared in the 1770s, based on evidence gathered during the nation's longest archaeological excavation.

Heritage Village

Location: 1425 West Central Avenue, Mackinaw City, MI 49701 **Contact Info:** (231) 373-9793 • mail@mackinawhistory.org • www.mackinawhistory.org **Hours:** Memorial Day-Labor Day: Daily. Guided tours Fri, Sat, Sun, Mon 1-5 p.m. **Admission:** Free. **Accessibility:** Free on-site parking. Partially wheelchair accessible. Tour guide available.

Site Info: The village includes Pestilence House, a church, the artifacts building, the sawmill that cut the timbers for the Soo Locks, a one-room schoolhouse, a log cabin, the Stimpson Homestead, a machine shed, a tar-paper shack, and wigwams.

Historic Mill Creek Discovery Park

Location: 9001 US-23, Mackinaw City, MI 49701 **Contact Info:** (231) 436-4100 • mackinacparks@michigan.gov • www.mackinacparks.com **Hours:** Early-May-mid-Oct: 9 a.m.- 4:30 p.m. (Peak summer season hours extended to 5:30 p.m.). **Admission:** $9/adult, $6/youth (5-12). **Accessibility:** Free on-site parking. Partially wheelchair accessible. Tour guide available. Museum store.

Site Info: The straits' first industrial complex, now the site of the Historic Mill Creek Discovery Park, provided lumber for the settlement of Mackinac Island in the 1790s. Attractions include demonstrations of hand-saw techniques and a reconstructed 18th-century water-driven sawmill. There are also natural history programs, nature trails, and daily "high ropes" adventure tours.

Icebreaker Mackinaw Maritime Museum

Location: 131 S. Huron Ave., Mackinaw City, MI 49701 **Contact Info:** (231) 436-9825 • contact@themackinaw.org • www.themackinaw.org **Hours:** Check website for hours. **Admission:** $11/adult, $6/children (6-17), $8/veteran, children 5 and under free, USCG personnel free. **Accessibility:** On-site parking. Not wheelchair accessible. Tour guide available. Museum store.

Site Info: The United States Coast Guard Icebreaker Mackinaw WAGB-83 is known as the "Queen of the Great Lakes" and "The Largest Icebreaker on the Great Lakes." She was built as part of the war effort during World War II to meet the heavy demands of war materials and transportation during the winter months. Decommissioned in 2006, she now resides at Mackinaw City and is open for public tours, educational tours, overnight encampments, and group events.

Old Mackinac Point Lighthouse

Location: 526 North Huron Avenue, Mackinaw City, MI 49701 **Contact Info:** (231) 436-4100 • mackinacparks@michigan.gov • www.mackinacparks.com **Hours:** Early-May-mid-Oct: 9 a.m.- 4:30 p.m. (Peak summer season hours extended to 5:30 p.m.). **Admission:** $7.50/adult, $4.50/youth (5-12). **Accessibility:** Free on-site parking. Partially wheelchair accessible. Tour guide available. Museum store.

Site Info: Erected in 1892, the Old Mackinac Point Lighthouse served more than 60 years. The castle-like structure has been restored to its 1910 appearance and features period settings and hands-on exhibits. Interpreters lead frequent tours up the tower and in its lantern room.

MANCELONA

Mancelona Historical Society Museum

Location: 9826 South Williams, Mancelona, MI 49659 **Contact Info:** (231) 587-9687 • www.ole.net/~maggie/antrim/mancy.htm **Hours:** Jun-Sep: Sat 1-4 p.m. **Admission:** Donations accepted. **Accessibility:** Free on-site parking. Wheelchair accessible. Tour guide available Sat, Jun-Sep. Museum store.

 Site Info: Visitors can explore historical pictures and information about early days in Antrim and Mancelona, including an Emil Johnson glass-plate negative collection that consists of 60 years of photos of people from the Mancelona area.

MANISTEE

Northwest Maritime Museum

Location: 99 Arthur St. (US 31), Manistee, MI 49660 **Contact Info:** (231) 723-3587 • linjoyspencer49@yahoo.com • www.carferry.com **Hours:** Call or visit website for current hours. **Admission:** Price varies by ship. Combo rates available. **Accessibility:** On-site parking. Partially wheelchair accessible. Tour guide available.

 Site Info: The museum features walking tours through the carferry S.S. City of Milwaukee, from its engine room to its pilot house. A walking tour of USCGC Acacia, "Last of the 180s," is also offered. The museum also holds artifacts, records, and archival collections focusing on Lake Michigan car ferries.

MANTON

Manton Area Historical Museum

Location: 102 Griswald St. (Old US-31), Manton, MI 49663 **Contact Info:** (231) 824-3208 **Hours:** May-Oct: Wed-Sat 12-5 p.m., Sun 1-4 p.m. **Admission:** Donations accepted. **Accessibility:** Free on-site parking. Partially wheelchair accessible. Tour guide available.
Site Info: The Manton Area Historical Museum's exhibits cover important Manton history, such as the logging industry and electrification. The museum also features an old-fashioned drug store, a horse-drawn hearse, artifacts from the area, and much more.

NORTHERN

MAPLE CITY

Charles and Hattie Olsen Farmhouse

Location: 3164 W. Harbor Hwy., Maple City, MI 49664 **Contact Info:** (231) 334-6103 • phsb@leelanau.com • www.phsb.org **Hours:** Call for current hours. **Admission:** A National Park Pass is required for admission. **Accessibility:** Free on-site parking. Wheelchair accessible. Tour guide available. Museum store.

Site Info: Housed in one of the original homes of the Port Oneida Rural Historic District, the Charles and Hattie Olsen Farmhouse features videos, displays, and maps relevant to the settlers who immigrated and homesteaded on the Manitou Islands and in the Port Oneida Historic District. The farmhouse also features exhibits focused on the lives of Native Americans and pioneer settlers from the late 1800s to the early 1900s.

MILLERSBURG

Millersburg Area Historical Society Museum

Location: 324 E. Luce St., Millersburg, MI 49759 **Contact Info:** (989) 733-8210 • www.millersburghistory.org **Hours:** By appointment. **Admission:** Free. **Accessibility:** Free on-site parking. Wheelchair accessible. Tour guides available.

Site Info: The museum showcases artifacts from the Millersburg area in the D&M Railroad Depot, the only depot remaining in Presque Isle County. Visitors can explore photos of past residents; a model of a 1910 kitchen; artifacts; the Plat Book of Michigan, circa 1909; railroad memorabilia; and a map of all railroads in Michigan.

NORTHPORT

Grand Traverse Lighthouse Museum

Location: 15550 N. Lighthouse Point Road, Northport, MI 49670 **Contact Info:** (231) 386-7195 • gtlthse@triton.net • www.grandtraverselighthouse.com **Hours:** May, Sep, Oct, Nov: 12-4 p.m.; Jun, Jul, Aug: 10 a.m.-5 p.m. **Admission:** $4/adult, $2/student (6-18). **Accessibility:** State Park Recreation Passport required. Partially wheelchair accessible. Museum store.

Site Info: Organized in 1985, the Grand Traverse Lighthouse Museum is located in a 162-year-old lighthouse that has been restored to resemble a keeper's home from the 1920s and 1930s. Exhibits look at area shipwrecks and local history. A restored air diaphone foghorn is demonstrated throughout the year. There is also a fog signal building and oil house on-site. Visitors can also climb the tower.

NORTHERN

OMENA

Putnam-Cloud Tower House

Location: 5045 N. West Bayshore Drive, Omena, MI 49674
Contact Info: (734) 657-1897 • dlystra@sbcglobal.net • www.
omenahistoricalsociety.com **Hours:** Jun-Aug: Sat-Sun 1- 4
p.m.; Sep-Oct: Sat 1- 4 p.m. **Admission:** Donations accepted.
Accessibility: Free street parking. Not wheelchair accessible.
Tour guide available.

 Site Info: The Putnam-Cloud Tower House has
been restored as a museum and community gathering
place. The museum includes models of the village's
buildings from 1910 to 1920, artifacts, Native-
American baskets, rotating special exhibits, and
books by Omena authors. Also featured are tapes, letters, articles,
photos, maps, books, and videos pertaining to the Omena area.

ONEKAMA

LODGING IN ONEKAMA

Portage Point Inn & Marina

Location: 8567 Portage Point Drive, Onekama, MI 49675
Contact Info: (231) 889-7500 • info@portagepointresort.com •
www.portagepointresort.com **Property Info:** Hotel/Inn, Cabin,
Condominium Rental. Open year-round. Free on-site parking.
Wheelchair accessible. **Price:** $75-$500.

 Site Info: This beachfront resort has catered to
families, couples, and groups since August 1902.
The inn is located on a narrow, wooded, sand dune
peninsula that separates Lake Michigan from
Portage Lake, and a connecting channel is a quarter
mile from the inn. Until the mid-1930s, steamships were the
primary mode of transportation to get to the resort. A variety of
lodging options are available. Listed on the National Register of
Historic Places.

PESHAWBESTOWN

Eyaawing Museum and Cultural Center

 **Location:** 2304 N. West Bayshore Dr.,
Peshawbestown, MI 49682 **Contact
Info:** (231) 534-7768 • museum@
gtbindians.com • www.gtbindians.org
Hours: Wed-Sat 10 a.m.-4 p.m.
Admission: Donations accepted.
Accessibility: Free on-site parking.
Wheelchair accessible. Self-guided. Museum store.

 Site Info: The Eyaawing Museum and Cultural
Center features artifacts from various Grand
Traverse Band tribal members, some of which are
as old as Michigan's last ice age. The museum
welcomes visitors of all ages and encourages

everyone to stop in and learn the true culture, heritage, and traditions of Grand Traverse Band Anishinaabek.

PETOSKEY

Bay View Historical Museum

Location: 1715 Encampment, Petoskey, MI 49770 **Contact Info:** (231) 347-6225 • mike@bayviewassociation.org • www.bayviewassociation.org **Hours:** Jun-Aug: Sun 11 a.m.-1 p.m., Mon, Wed 1-3 p.m. **Admission:** Free. **Accessibility:** Free street parking. Self-guided.

Site Info: Designated as a National Historic Landmark in 1987, the site has 444 cottages, two hotels, one bed and breakfast, and two auditoriums. The two oldest buildings on campus—the speaker's stand and the bookstore—were designated as the Bay View Historical Museum in 1964. A new exhibit is featured each summer.

LODGING IN PETOSKEY

Bay View Inn

Location: 2011 Woodland Ave., Petoskey, MI 49770 **Contact Info:** (231) 758-3545 • beckyb@staffords.com • www.staffords.com **Property Info:** Hotel/Inn. Open year-round. Privately owned; no public tours; pre-booking required. Free on-site parking. Partially wheelchair accessible. Food available on-site. Gift shop. **Price:** $99-$339.

Site Info: Built circa 1886, the inn offers guests the grace and romance of a bygone era, set against the views of Little Traverse Bay. For more than 55 years, Stafford Smith and his family have owned, operated, and lovingly restored this Victorian country inn on the shores of Lake Michigan's Little Traverse Bay. It is a place to pause, reflect, and unwind. Visitors are invited to experience the charm and hospitality of the Bay View Inn. Listed on the National Register of Historic Places.

Perry Hotel

Location: 100 Lewis St., Petoskey, MI 49770 **Contact Info:** (231) 758-3545 • beckyb@staffords.com • www.staffords.com **Property Info:** Hotel/Inn. Open year-round. Privately owned; no public tours; pre-booking required. Free on-site parking. Wheelchair accessible. Food available on-site. Gift shop. **Price:** $99-$329.

Site Info: Perched high on a bluff overlooking Lake Michigan, the Perry Hotel stands as a symbol of the early 1900s when Northern Michigan tourism was in its infancy. Built in 1899 as one of some 20 original luxury resort hotels, Stafford's Perry Hotel is the only one still in operation. Open year-round, our full-service hotel has 79 individually appointed guest rooms, many with private balconies overlooking the crystal clear waters of Little Traverse Bay. Listed on the National Register of Historic Places.

ROGERS CITY

40 Mile Point Lighthouse

Location: 7323 U.S. 23 N, Rogers City, MI 48779 **Contact Info:** (989) 734-4587 • barbara71@hughes.net • www.40milepointlighthouse.org **Hours:** Tue-Sat 10 a.m.-4 p.m.; Sun 12-4 p.m. **Admission:** Free. **Accessibility:** Free on-site parking. Partially wheelchair accessible. Tour guide available. Museum store.

Site Info: The museum, located inside the lighthouse, is furnished with period items pertaining to the years 1896 to 1943. The tower is accessible and houses a 4th-order Fresnel lens, which is still an active light. The gift shop is located in the former bunkhouse that was used to house the workers as they built the lighthouse. The Calcite Pilot House is from the 1912 Calcite, one of the first self-unloading vessels to sail the Great Lakes.

The Bradley House

Location: 176 W. Michigan Ave., Rogers City, MI 49779 **Contact Info:** (989) 734-4121 • bradleymuseum@ yahoo.com • www.thebradleyhouse.org **Hours:** May-Sep: Wed-Sun 12:30-4:30 p.m. **Admission:** Free. **Accessibility:** Free street parking. Partially wheelchair accessible. Tour guide available. Call for groups.

Site Info: The Bradley House is listed on the National Register of Historic Places. In addition to the Bradley living room and dining room, the building houses several permanent exhibits, including "those fabulous 50s & 60s," the Bertram Sisters' Millinery Shoppe, the Larke Bedroom, the Hoeft General Store, lumbering, and pioneering. In addition to the permanent exhibits, two revolving exhibits are also featured each season.

The Henry and Margaret Hoffman Annex

Location: 185 W. Michigan Ave., Rogers City, MI 49779 **Contact Info:** (989) 734-4121 • bradleymuseum@yahoo.com • www.thebradleyhouse.org **Hours:** May-Dec: Wed-Sun 12:30-4:30 p.m. **Admission:** Free. **Accessibility:** Free on-site and street parking. Wheelchair accessible. Tour guide available.

Site Info: Located across the street from the Bradley House, the Henry and Margaret Hoffman Annex houses the museum's offices, museum store, and numerous exhibits. Permanent exhibits include the John Bunton Collection of more than 1,000 cameras and projectors and other photographic equipment, the

Calcite room with photos and other materials related to the World's Largest Limestone Quarry, and the Bradley Boats with photos, models, and artifacts from the Bradley Transportation Fleet.

ROSCOMMON

Civilian Conservation Corps Museum

Location: 11747 North Higgins Lake Dr., Roscommon, MI 48653 **Contact Info:** (989) 348-2537 • museuminfo@ michigan.gov • www.michigan.gov/ cccmuseum **Hours:** May 27-Sep 5: Daily 10 a.m.-4:30 p.m.; Sep 10-Oct 23: Sat-Sun 10 a.m.-4:30 p.m.

Admission: Free. Michigan State Parks Recreation Passport is required for entry. **Accessibility:** Free on-site parking. Wheelchair accessible. Self-guided.

Site Info: More than 100,000 young men worked in Michigan's forests and parks during the Great Depression and lived in barracks like those on display at the Civilian Conservation Corps (CCC) Museum. See how "Roosevelt's Tree Army" served the state, creating a legacy that endures today. The museum's location on the site of the state's 1903 tree nursery emphasizes the CCC's role in replanting Michigan forests.

Roscommon Area Historical Society Museum

Location: 404 Lake Street, Roscommon, MI 48653 **Contact Info:** (989) 344-7386 **Hours:** Memorial Day-Sep: Fri-Sat 12-4 p.m. **Admission:** Free. **Accessibility:** Free street parking. Wheelchair accessible. Tour guide available.

Site Info: The Roscommon Area Historical Society's museum is located in the 1880s-built Gallimore Boarding House, which operated between 1904 and 1931. Rooms are furnished in period style, and local artifacts include a parlor organ and old phonograph player. The archives, which concentrate on the Higgins Lake and Roscommon areas, offer pictures, ledger books, maps, memoirs, and oral history tapes.

SUTTONS BAY

LODGING IN SUTTONS BAY

Hillside Homestead

Location: 3400 N. Setterbo Rd., Suttons Bay, MI 49682 **Contact Info:** (231) 271-1131 • susan@ hillsidehomestead.com • www. hillsidehomestead.com **Property Info:** Bed & Breakfast. Open year-round. Privately owned; no public tours; pre-booking required. Free on-site parking. Food available on-site. **Price:** $200-$230.

Site Info: The Hillside Homestead occupies a typical Leelanau County large farmhouse with features common to the area, such as a large kitchen and hallways and narrow staircases. The house has been refurbished back to how it might have looked circa 1910 when it was new. The bedrooms upstairs are outfitted for guests to spend the night. The kitchen has a Round Oak Cooking Range, a dry sink, and handsome built-ins.

THOMPSONVILLE

Michigan Legacy Art Park

 **Location:** 12500 Crystal Mountain Drive, Thompsonville, MI 49683 **Contact Info:** (231) 378-4963 • director@michlegacyartpark.org • www. michlegacyartpark.org **Hours:** Daily during daylight hours. **Admission:** $5/ adult. **Accessibility:** Free on-site and street parking. Partially wheelchair accessible; call ahead to reserve a golf cart tour. Self-guided.

 Site Info: The 30-acre sculpture park boasts a collection of 44 major works of art and 30 poetry stones. The sculptures and poems help express the Michigan experience, giving visitors a more personal connection to the people, events, and natural resources that continue to shape the Great Lakes State. At each sculpture, interpretive signs help visitors have a deeper understanding and appreciation for the art and the Michigan stories expressed.

TRAVERSE CITY

Dougherty Old Mission House

 **Location:** 18549 Mission Rd., Traverse City, MI 49686 **Contact Info:** (231) 947-0947 • dobrum@aol.com • www. oldmissionhouse.com **Hours:** Log Cabin Days. Exterior of house and grounds open dawn to dusk. **Admission:** Free. Donations accepted. **Accessibility:** Free on-site parking. Not wheelchair accessible. Self-guided.

 Site Info: This house is the first frame house in Northwest Lower Michigan, built for the Presbyterian missionary in 1842, under the terms of the Treaty of Washington of 1836. The house was built by Native Americans under the guidance of Reverend Peter Dougherty. The site is listed on the State and National Register of Historic Places. Original furniture from the relevant historical period of this home are located inside along with artifacts produced by an archaeological dig at the site.

NORTHERN

History Center of Traverse City

Location: 322 Sixth St., Traverse City, MI 49684 **Contact Info:** (231) 995-0313 • archives@traversehistory.org • www.traversehistory.org **Hours:** Summer: Mon-Sat 10 a.m.-5 p.m., Sun 12-5 p.m. **Admission:** $5/individual (4+). **Accessibility:** Free on-site parking. Wheelchair accessible. Self-guided.

 Site Info: The History Center of Traverse City includes a pre-written history wing, which features Native-American items, a Wigwam, and interactive glacier panels depicting the two glaciers that formed Michigan. Children can dig through 2,000 pounds of cherry pits to forge for a souvenir copper ingot, arrowhead, Petoskey stone, or beach stone.

Maritime Heritage Alliance

Location: 13268 S. West Bay Shore Dr., Traverse City, MI 49684 **Contact Info:** (231) 946-2647 • info@maritimeheritagealliance.org • www.maritimeheritagealliance.org **Hours:** Call or visit website for current hours. **Admission:** Free. **Accessibility:** Call ahead for tour guide availability.

 Site Info: The Maritime Heritage Alliance currently owns and maintains a replica of an1850s schooner, a cutter Champion, several other boats, and a boat restoration shop. A number of woodshops, including the Edwin & Mary Brown Restoration Boat Shop, are housed in two large buildings. There is also a collection of vintage canoes, as well as motors and an old Singer sewing machine.

WEST BRANCH

Ogemaw County Historical Museum

 **Location:** 135 South 2nd St., West Branch, MI 48661 **Contact Info:** (989) 701-2525 • oghs1978@gmail.com • www.westbranch.com/ogemaw_genealogical.htm **Hours:** Thu-Fri 10 a.m.-2 p.m. Also by appointment. **Admission:** Donations accepted. **Accessibility:** Street parking. Not wheelchair accessible.

 Site Info: The museum includes exhibits on Native Americans, parliament wedding apparel, historic hats, local trophies, and military uniforms from past wars. The Ogemaw County Historical Society, which operates the museum, offers walking tours of cities and cemeteries and driving tours of historic sites in the county.

WILLIAMSBURG

Music House Museum

Location: 7377 US 31 North, Williamsburg, MI 49690 **Contact Info:** (231) 938-9300 • marketing@ musichouse.org • www.musichouse.org **Hours:** May-Oct: Mon-Sat 10 a.m.-4 p.m., Sun 12-4 p.m.; Nov-Dec: Sat 10 a.m.-4 p.m., Sun 12-4 p.m.

Admission: $12/adult, $5/children, $26/family. **Accessibility:** Free on-site parking. Wheelchair accessible. Tour guide available. Museum store.

Site Info: Visitors experience the sounds and history of automated instruments from the simplest music boxes through phonographs and radios. A silent movie is accompanied by the museum's "mighty" Wurlitzer. Tours provide visitors with a musical journey through the sounds, artistry, history, and science of the early forerunners to our modern-day music sources. The museum also features a scale model of Traverse City.

NORTHERN

ALLOUEZ TOWNSHIP
LODGING IN ALLOUEZ TOWNSHIP
Sand Hills Lighthouse Inn
Location: 6029 Five Mile Point Rd., Allouez Township, MI 49805 **Contact Info:** (906) 337-1744 • sandhills@pasty.net • www.sandhillslighthouseinn.com **Property Info:** Bed & Breakfast. Open year-round. Privately owned; tour by appointment; pre-booking required. Free on-site parking. Not wheelchair accessible. Food available on-site. Gift shop. **Price:** $175-$239, tax included.

Site Info: Sand Hills Lighthouse was built in 1917 to house three lightkeepers and their families. It is the last and largest lighthouse to be built on the Great Lakes. During World War II, the Coast Guard used the property as a boot camp for 200 trainees. A major refurbishment of the building was started in 1992. In 1995, the Bed and Breakfast opened with eight Victorian guest rooms, each with a private bath. Listed on the National Register of Historic Places.

BARAGA
Baraga County Historical Museum

Location: 803 U.S. Hwy 41 South, Baraga, MI 49946 **Contact Info:** (906) 353-8444 • baragacountyhistory@gmail.com • www.baragacountyhistoricalmuseum. com **Hours:** Jun-Aug: Fri-Sat 11 a.m.-3 p.m.; Sep-May: Appointment only.
Admission: $2/adult, $1/teens, children 12 and under free. **Accessibility:** Free on-site parking. Wheelchair accessible. Tour guide available. Museum store.

Site Info: Located adjacent to beautiful Keweenaw Bay, the Baraga County Historical Museum offers a variety of exhibits highlighting significant events in local history as well as illustrating what life was like 50, 100, or 150 years ago. RV parking is available, and a picnic area between the museum and the lakeshore provides a place for visitors to relax before or after touring the museum itself.

BESSEMER
Bessemer Area Heritage Center

Location: 403 S Sophie St., Bessemer, MI 49911 **Contact Info:** info@ bessemerhistoricalsociety.com • www. bessemerhistoricalsociety.com **Hours:** Late May-mid Sep: Fri-Sat 1-4 p.m. **Admission:** Free. **Accessibility:** Free on-site and street parking. Wheelchair accessible. Tour guide available. Museum store.

U.P.

Site Info: The collections of the Bessemer Area Historical Society are housed in the Bessemer Area Heritage Center. Exhibits cover mining, logging, farming, education, government, veterans, clothing, and household items. Visitors can also view slideshows on mining and logging at the heritage center.

BIG BAY

LODGING IN BIG BAY

Thunder Bay Inn & Restaurant

Location: 400 Bensinger St. (Hwy 550), Big Bay, MI 49808 **Contact Info:** (906) 345-9220 • thunderbayinn@ironbay.net • www.thunderbayinn.net **Property Info:** Hotel/Inn. Open year-round. Privately owned; no public tours; pre-booking required. Free on-site parking. Food available on-site. **Price:** Seasonal rates. Call for pricing.

 **Site Info:** The inn was once the home-away-from-home for traveling Ford executives visiting the Big Bay automotive plant. It was also the setting for the James Stewart film "Anatomy of a Murder." Today, visitors can enjoy the beaches of Lake Superior and fishing on Lake Independence. The winter traveler can explore wilderness trails by snowmobile. The historic town of Big Bay is 20 miles from Marquette, a great town for shopping and Upper Peninsula culture.

BRIMLEY

Point Iroquois Lighthouse

Location: 12942 W Lakeshore Dr., Brimley, MI 49715 **Contact Info:** (906) 248-3665 • euprussell@yahoo.com • www.fs.usda.gov/attmain/hiawatha/specialplaces **Hours:** May 15-Oct 15: Daily 9 a.m.-5 p.m.; Oct 16-May 14: Sat, Sun 10 a.m.-3 p.m. **Admission:** Donations accepted. **Accessibility:** Free on-site parking. Partially wheelchair accessible. Tour guide by appointment. Museum store.

 Site Info: The lighthouse is owned and operated by the USDA Forest Service with the help of the Bay Mills-Brimley Historical Research Society. From birch-bark canoes to giant ore freighters, this unique point of land has influenced travel for centuries. The museum reveals the stories of the lighthouse keepers and their families through family album photographs, antiques, and artifacts. Climb the 72 steps to the top of the tower for a picturesque view of Lake Superior.

Wheels of History Train Museum

Location: 6749 S. M-221, Brimley, MI 49715 **Contact Info:** (906) 248-3665 • eurussell@yahoo.com • www.baymillsbrimleyhistory.org **Hours:** May 15-Jun 20: Sat-Sun 10 a.m.-4 p.m.; June 20-Labor Day: Wed-Sun 10 a.m.-4 p.m.; Labor Day-Oct 15: Sat-Sun 10 a.m.-4 p.m. **Admission:** Donations accepted. **Accessibility:** Free street parking. Partially wheelchair accessible. Tour guide available. Museum store.

Site Info: The 1897 Replica Depot offers changing exhibits. The main collections include exhibits of maps, photos, and artifacts of one-room schools, the lumber industry, railroad history, early life in the area, and veterans' memorabilia and uniforms.

BOIS BLANC ISLAND
Bois Blanc Island Historical Society Museum

Location: 1030 W. Huron Drive, Bois Blanc Island, MI 49775 **Contact Info:** (231) 634-7025 • www.facebook.com/bbihs **Hours:** Jul-Labor Day: Tue, Thu, Sat 10 a.m.-2 p.m. **Admission:** Donations accepted. **Accessibility:** On-site parking. Partially wheelchair accessible. Tour guide available.

Site Info: Visitors will find lumber industry tools, relics from the soldiers on Mackinac Island who used Bois Blanc Island as a woodlot, household items, books from the island school, and cassette tapes of oral history.

CALUMET
Calumet Visitor Center

Location: 98 Fifth St., Calumet, MI 49913 **Contact Info:** (906) 337-3168 • www.nps.gov/kewe **Hours:** Call for current hours. **Admission:** Free. **Accessibility:** Free on-site and street parking. Wheelchair accessible. Self-guided.

Site Info: The Calumet Visitor Center is located at the entrance to Historic Downtown Calumet in the Union Building, a former lodge hall for various fraternal organizations. Visitors are able to experience interactive exhibits on what life was like for people in the mining community from its establishment through the boom times to the closure of the Calumet & Hecla Mining Company in 1968.

U.P.

Copper Country Firefighters History Museum

Location: 327 Sixth St., Calumet, MI 49913 **Contact Info:** (906) 337-4579 • jshs907@yahoo.com • www.coppercountryfirefighters historymuseum.com **Hours:** Jun-Labor Day: Mon-Sat 1-4:30 p.m. **Admission:** $3/adult, $7/family.

Site Info: Completed in 1990, the Red Jacket Fire Station is now home to the Copper Country Firefighters History Museum. The museum features firefighting equipment dating as far back as 1919, including a horse-drawn fire wagon and sleigh, hand-pulled carts, fire trucks from 1919 to 1951, tools, uniforms, and personal gear. There is also a photograph collection.

Norwegian Lutheran Church

Location: 338 Seventh Street, Calumet, MI 49913 **Contact Info:** (906) 337-3731 • www.nlc-calumet.org **Hours:** Jun-Oct: Daily 9 a.m.-5 p.m. **Admission:** By donation. **Accessibility:** Free street parking. Not wheelchair accessible. Self-guided.

Site Info: The Norwegian Lutheran Church Historical Society was founded in 2000 to restore and maintain the historic Norwegian Lutheran Church building, which was originally constructed in 1898. The former church contains the original alter, pews, organ, chandelier, and tin ceiling. Storyboards in the entry share the church's history, a list of its ministers, and photos of the people who were instrumental in the building and maintaining of the church and attached parsonage.

CASPIAN

Iron County Historical Museum

Location: 100 Brady Ave., Caspian, MI 49915 **Contact Info:** (906) 265-2617 • info@ironcountyhistoricalmuseum.org • www. ironcountyhistoricalmuseum.org **Hours:** Jun-Sep: Mon-Sat 10 a.m.-4 p.m., Sun 1-4 p.m. **Admission:** $8/adult, $7/senior, $3/ youth (5-18), children 5 and under free. **Accessibility:** Free on-site parking. Partially wheelchair accessible. Self-guided.

Site Info: The Iron County Historical Museum is located on nearly 10 acres of land and a former mine site. The site has 26 buildings and includes a log cabin home, a lumber camp, a mine site, a Victorian area with the Carrie Jacobs-Bond Home, a cultural center, and two galleries: the LeBlanc Wildlife Art Gallery and the Giovanelli Home and Gallery. The museum's 100-plus displays include mining, lumbering, shops, pioneer home, and the mining memorial room.

CEDARVILLE

Les Cheneaux Historical Museum

Location: 105 S. Meridian Rd., Cedarville, MI 49719 **Contact Info:** (906) 484-2821 • lcha@lchistorical.org • www.lchistorical.org **Hours:** Memorial Day-Labor Day: Tue-Sat 10:30 a.m.-4:30 p.m. **Admission:** Donations accepted. **Accessibility:** Free on-site parking. Wheelchair accessible. Tour guide available. Museum store.

Site Info: The Les Cheneaux Historical Museum displays artifacts showing many details from the past, including Native-American crafts, tools from the logging era, a model of a lumber camp, and photos from frontier life. The museum is in a log cabin depicting the early days of settlement in the area when lumbering and fishing were important industries. Attached to the log cabin is a modern building depicting changes in the life of the community over the years.

Les Cheneaux Maritime Museum

Location: 602 E M-134, Cedarville, MI 49719 **Contact Info:** (906) 484-2821 • lciboatshow@gmail.com • www.lchistorical.org **Hours:** Memorial Day-Labor Day: Tue-Sat 10:30 a.m.-4:30 p.m. **Admission:** Donations accepted. **Accessibility:** Free on-site parking. Partially wheelchair accessible. Tour guide available. Museum store.

Site Info: The Les Cheneaux Maritime Museum includes the O.M. Reif Boathouse, circa 1920, and is home to displays of vintage boats, marine artifacts, antique outboard motors, historic photos of area boating, and a museum store. Visit the boatbuilding workshop to view reconstruction projects and learn about boatbuilding.

CHASSELL

Chassell Heritage Center

Location: 42373 Hancock St., Chassell, MI 49916 **Contact Info:** (906) 523-1155 • info@chassellhistory.org • www.chassellhistory.org **Hours:** Jul-Aug: Tue 1-4 p.m.,Thu 4-9 p.m., Sat 1-4 p.m. **Admission:** Donations accepted. **Accessibility:** Free on-site parking. Not wheelchair accessible. Tour guides available.

Site Info: The Chassell Historical Organization maintains the township museum in a former elementary school. Exhibits include local strawberry farming, the old school, vintage clothing, a

U.P.

township time line, three consecutive boys basketball state championships from 1956 to 1958, and Chassell Lions Club. There are also exhibits of Finnish and French-Canadian immigrants and settlers. In addition, the museum is home of the Friends of Fashion Vintage Clothing Collection.

COPPER HARBOR

Copper Harbor Lighthouse

Location: 14447 Hwy M-28, Copper Harbor, MI 49918 **Contact Info:** (517) 373-3559 • museuminfo@ michigan.gov • www.michigan.gov/ michiganhistory **Hours:** Memorial Day-Labor Day: 10 a.m.-6 p.m. **Admission:** Free. Charge for boat transportation to and from the lighthouse. **Accessibility:** Free on-site parking. Partially wheelchair accessible. Self-guided.

Site Info: A 15-minute boat ride from the Copper Harbor Marina brings visitors to the lighthouse site. The original 1848 lightkeeper dwelling offers interpretive exhibits, and the 1866 lighthouse, the second on the site, features period rooms. A lakeside interpretive trail includes views of Lake Superior.

Fort Wilkins Historic Complex

Location: 15223 U.S. 41, Copper Harbor, MI 49918 **Contact Info:** (906) 289-4215 • museuminfo@ michigan.gov • www.michigan.gov/ michiganhistory **Hours:** Mid-May-mid-Oct: Daily 8:30 a.m.-dusk. **Admission:** Free. Michigan State Parks Recreation Passport required for entry. **Accessibility:** Free on-site parking. Partially wheelchair accessible. Self-guided.

Site Info: Built in 1844 on the rugged shoreline of Lake Superior, Fort Wilkins is a well-preserved example of mid-19th-century army life. It features hands-on exhibits, interpretive signs, and a historical video titled "Beyond the Wilderness: The Fort Wilkins Story." Re-enactors bring the fort to life each summer from mid-June to mid-August. The complex includes 19 buildings, 12 of which are original structures dating to the 1840s.

COVINGTON

Covington Township Historical Museum

Location: Elm Street, Covington, MI 49919 **Contact Info:** (330) 322-9215 • dhassler@kent.edu • www.covingtonmichigan. org/covington-historical-society **Hours:** Fri-Sat 11 a.m.-4 p.m. **Admission:** Donations accepted. **Accessibility:** Free street parking. Wheelchair accessible. Tour guide available; reservations can be made for after-hours.

Site Info: The Covington Township Historical Society maintains a museum in the former township hall. Exhibits include the first fire truck, a horse-drawn cutter, a military display, and a jail cell used to house only one prisoner.

CRYSTAL FALLS

Harbour House Museum

Location: 17 N. 4th St., Crystal Falls, MI 49920 **Contact Info:** (906) 875-4341 • harbourhousemuseum@up.net • www.facebook. com/HarbourHouseMuseum **Hours:** Jun-Aug: Thu-Sat 10 a.m.-2 p.m. **Admission:** $2/individual, $5/family. **Accessibility:** Free street parking. Wheelchair accessible. Tour guide available.

 Site Info: Built in 1900 by master mason and bricklayer Fred Floodstrand, the Harbour House Museum was constructed with cement blocks and designed in the "steamboat" style of architecture with wraparound twin porches. The first floor has been restored to a turn-of-the-century setting, including a kitchen, dining room, parlor, and library. Many of the rooms in the museum have a theme and include items from that topic or area.

CURTIS

Curtis Historical Society Museum

 **Location:** N9224 Portage Ave., Curtis, MI 49820 **Contact Info:** (906) 586-3382 • genilady@hughes.net **Hours:** Jun-Labor Day: Wed-Fri 1-4 p.m. **Admission:** Donations accepted. **Accessibility:** Free on-site and street parking. Wheelchair accessible. Self-guided.

Site Info: The Curtis Historical Society Museum houses artifacts from early logging and settlers. Exhibits include displays on school, military, and Native Americans. Also featured are scrapbooks, photographs, logging items, war memorabilia, obituary files, and an old school desk.

LODGING IN CURTIS

Chamberlins Ole Forest Inn

 **Location:** N9450 Manistique Lakes Road, Curtis, MI 49820 **Contact Info:** (906) 586-6000 • info@chamberlinsinn. com • www.chamberlinsinn.com **Property Info:** Hotel/Inn. Seasonal: Closed the month of April. Privately owned; no public tours; pre-booking required. Free on-site parking. Partially wheelchair accessible. Food available on-site. Gift shop. **Price:** $89-$130.

U.P.

Site Info: This dwelling was built circa 1890 by a railroad company to serve as a passenger hotel near the Curtis train station. In 1924, after the lumber boom, the building was moved to its present location, where it sits high on a bluff overlooking Big Manistique Lake. Today, this lakeside country inn with its beautiful 10-foot stone fireplace, open stairway, and rich woodwork continues to embrace travelers with warmth, comfortable lodging, casual fine dining, and stunning views.

DETOUR VILLAGE

DeTour Passage Historical Museum

Location: 104 Elizabeth St., DeTour Village, MI 49725 **Contact Info:** (906) 297-2081 • myreoffice@yahoo.com • www.facebook.com/DeTour-Passage-Historical-Society-189855464411087 **Hours:** May-Oct: Mon-Sat 11 a.m.-3 p.m., Sun 12 p.m.-4 p.m. **Admission:** Free. **Accessibility:** Free street parking. Wheelchair accessible. Tour guide available. Museum store.

Site Info: On display is one of the few rare 3rd-order Fresnel lenses. Also featured are many photos and displays depicting local lighthouses, ferries, early ship refueling docks, the history of local fishing and sawmills, early settlers, and Native Americans. There is also information on military, early schools to present, and the five cemeteries in the area.

DRUMMOND ISLAND

DeTour Reef Light

Location: Mouth of the St. Mary's River, Between DeTour Village and Drummond Island **Contact Info:** (906) 493-6609 • drlps@drlps.com • www.drlps.com **Hours:** Summer: By appointment. **Admission:** $95/tour ($75 to DRLPS members). Children accompanied by parent or guardian receive 50 percent discount. **Accessibility:** Free on-site parking. Not wheelchair accessible. Guided tours.

Site Info: The DeTour Reef Light exemplifies the distinctive architectural characteristics of an early 20th-century Great Lakes crib foundation lighthouse. Located where the St. Mary's River joins Lake Huron at the south end of DeTour Passage, the lighthouse has been an important aid to navigation throughout its existence for both commercial and pleasure ship traffic.

EAGLE HARBOR

Bammert Blacksmith Shop

Location: 670 Lighthouse Rd., Eagle Harbor, MI 49950

Contact Info: (906) 289-4990 • vjamison@pasty.com • www.keweenawhistory.org **Hours:** Mid-May-early Oct. **Admission:** Free. Donations accepted.

Site Info: The blacksmith shop of Amos Bammert was donated to the Keweenaw County Historical Society in 1998. The interior and exterior have been restored and now displays items and the equipment as they were at the end of the 19th century, including the forge. Visitors can see what the shop looked like when Amos built buggies, sleighs, and wagon wheels. The shop was first opened in the 1880s and was operated by Amos until his death in 1940.

Eagle Harbor Lighthouse Complex
Location: 670 Lighthouse Rd., Eagle Harbor, MI 49950
Contact Info: (906) 289-4990 • vjamison@pasty.com • www.keweenawhistory.org **Hours:** Mid-Jun-early Oct.
Admission: $5/adult, children are free. **Accessibility:** Free on-site parking. Partially wheelchair accessible (exterior). Tour guide available. Self-guided.

Site Info: The Eagle Harbor Lighthouse Complex includes an 1871 light station and museums depicting the history of maritime, mining, life-saving, and commercial fishing. It is a heritage site of Keweenaw National Historical Park.

Rathbone School
Location: 200 Center St., Eagle Harbor, MI 49950 **Contact Info:** (9060 289-4990 • vjamison@pasty.com • www.keweenawhistory.org **Hours:** Mid-Jun-early Oct. **Admission:** Free. Donations accepted.

Site Info: This restored one-room school served the community from 1853 to 1872. The school is named for Justus H. Rathbone, who began teaching at the school in 1860. While working at the school, Rathbone created the Knights of Pythias, a secret fraternal order. The museum is furnished as a school and includes Knights of Pythias exhibits.

EAGLE RIVER

Eagle River Museum
Location: M-26 and Fourth St, Eagle River, MI 49950
Contact Info: (906) 289-4990 • vjamison@pasty.com • www.keweenawhistory.org **Hours:** Mid-May-early Oct: Wed, Fri-Sat 12-4 p.m. **Admission:** Free. Donations accepted.

Site Info: The four major themes covered in the museum are the Cliff Mine, the town of Eagle River, the town and mine of Phoenix, and the amusement area known as Crestview. The museum is located in the old Eagle River School House. The Keweenaw County Historical Society has worked with the community and the Keweenaw National Historical Park to restore the building and create exhibits.

U.P.

ENGADINE

Engadine Historical Museum

Location: 14075 W Melville St., Engadine, MI 49827 **Contact Info:** (906) 477-6908 • deekaydee2000@yahoo.com **Hours:** Tue, Sat 10 a.m.-2 p.m. **Admission:** Free. **Accessibility:** Free street parking. Partially wheelchair accessible. Tour guide available. Call for other tours. Museum store.

Site Info: The Engadine Historical Museum, located in the former Hastings House, contains exhibits featuring artifacts that highlight local history. Each room in the museum has a dedicated theme. Examples include an old schoolhouse room, children's room, reading room, and workshop. There is also a historic log home on-site.

ESCANABA

Delta County Historical Society & Museum

Location: 16 Beaumier Way, Escanaba, MI 49829 **Contact Info:** (906) 789-6790 • arch@deltahistorical.org • www.deltahistorical.org **Hours:** Museum and lighthouse: Memorial Day-Labor Day: Daily 11 a.m.-4 p.m. Archives: Jun-Aug: Mon-Fri 1-4 p.m.; Sep-May: Mon 1-4 p.m. **Admission:** $3/adult, $1/child, $5/family, $50-75/bus tours. **Accessibility:** Free parking. Partially wheelchair accessible. Self-guided.

Site Info: Exhibits at the Delta County Historical Museum portray many aspects of the area's history, including logging, shipping, the railroad industry, military, Native-American culture, surveying, sports, fishing, local businesses, and much more. A new building now contains the museum and the archives. The society also maintains Sand Point Lighthouse. The lighthouse home, tower, and boathouse are open to visitors.

GARDEN

Fayette Historic Townsite

Location: 4785 II Rd., Garden, MI 49835 **Contact Info:** (906) 644-2603 • museuminfo@michigan.gov • www.michigan.gov/fayettetownsite **Hours:** May-Oct: See website or call for hours. **Admission:** Free. Michigan State Park Recreation Passport is required for entry. **Accessibility:** Free on-site parking. Partially wheelchair accessible. Self-guided. Museum store.

Site Info: Once a bustling industrial community, Fayette manufactured charcoal pig iron from 1867 to 1891. This well-preserved museum village recalls a time when it was a noisy, bustling iron-smelting town with an immigrant population that shared daily hardships, joys, and sorrows. The village includes 19 historic structures and a modern visitor center. Visitors can also enjoy the serenity of a Lake Michigan harbor, white dolomite bluffs, and verdant forests.

Garden Peninsula Historical Society Museum

Location: 6347 State St. Garden, MI 49835 **Hours:** Wed-Sat 11 a.m.-3 p.m. **Admission:** Free. **Accessibility:** Free street parking. Wheelchair accessible. Self-guided.

Site Info: The Garden Peninsula Historical Society Museum is located in a former schoolhouse that had an addition created to accommodate more artifacts. The museum considers local history and includes a genealogy department.

GRAND MARAIS

Gitche Gumee Agate and History Museum

Location: E. 21739 Braziel St., Grand Marais, MI 49839 **Contact Info:** (906) 494-3000 • karen@agatelady.com • www.agatelady.com **Hours:** Sun of Memorial Day Weekend-Jun: 2-5 p.m. daily; Sep: 2-5 p.m. daily, Sat 12-5 p.m.; Jul-Aug: 11 a.m.-5 p.m. daily, Sun 2-5 p.m. **Admission:** $1/adult, children 16 and under free. **Accessibility:** Free on-site parking. Not wheelchair accessible. Self-guided. Museum store.

Site Info: The museum features numerous agate and mineral displays as well as exhibits about local history. Rock-hounding and other classes can be arranged in advance. The museum store features books, hand-crafted agate art, jewelry, raw and polished agates, and other rocks and minerals.

The Lightkeeper's House Museum

Location: Coast Guard Point Rd., Grand Marais, MI 49839 **Contact Info:** (906) 494-2570 • gmhistoricalsociety@gmail.com • www.historicalsociety.grandmaraismichigan.com **Hours:** Jun & Sep: Sat-Sun 1-4 p.m.; Jul- Aug: Daily 1-4 p.m. **Admission:** Donations accepted. **Accessibility:** Free on-site parking. Not wheelchair accessible. Tour guide available. Museum store.

Site Info: The Grand Marais Lightkeeper's House dates to 1906 and has been restored to its original appearance as the lightkeeper's home of the early

1900s. Period furniture and artifacts are on display. Museum T-shirts, sweatshirts, mugs, historical society publications, and historic prints and postcards are available.

The Old Post Office Museum

Location: N 14252 Lake Ave., Grand Marais, MI 49839 **Contact Info:** (906) 494-2570 • gmhistoricalsociety@gmail.com • www.historicalsociety.grandmaraismichigan.com **Hours:** Jun & Sep: Sat-Sun 1-4 p.m.; Jul- Aug: Daily 1-4 p.m. **Admission:** Donations accepted. **Accessibility:** Free street parking. Wheelchair accessible. Self-guided.

Site Info: The Old Post Office Museum features exhibits that tell the story of Grand Marais from the earliest inhabitants to the present day. Local artifacts from railroads, lumbering, fishing, and shipwrecks are on display. The building is the original Grand Marais Post Office.

The Pickle Barrel House Museum

Location: N 14272 Lake Ave., Grand Marais, MI 49839 **Contact Info:** (906) 494-2570 • gmhistoricalsociety@gmail.com • www.historicalsociety.grandmaraismichigan.com **Hours:** Jun & Sep: Sat-Sun 1-4 p.m.; Jul-Aug: Daily 1-4 p.m. **Admission:** Donations accepted. **Accessibility:** Free street parking. Not wheelchair accessible. Tour guide available. Museum store.

Site Info: Originally constructed as a summer cottage for cartoonist William Donahey, creator of the "Teenie Weenies," it has been restored to its 1920s appearance. The two-story main barrel contains living space and a bedroom upstairs, and a one-story kitchen barrel is attached. A 25-stop walking tour takes visitors to historic sites around Grand Marais, beginning at the Pickle Barrel House Museum. The cost of that tour is $1.00.

GULLIVER

Seul Choix Point Lighthouse

Location: 905 S Seul Choix Rd., Gulliver, MI 49840 **Contact Info:** (906) 283-3183 • msfischer@hughes.net • www.greatlakelighthouse.com **Hours:** Memorial Day-mid Oct: 10 a.m.-6 p.m. **Admission:** $4/adult, $1/children (0-16). **Accessibility:** Free on-site parking. Partially wheelchair accessible. Tour guide available. Museum store.

U.P.

Site Info: Built in 1895, the Seul Choix Point Lighthouse has been fully restored to reflect the 1900 to 1920 period. The lighthouse is located in a public park, along with state of Michigan public boat access, and is fully operational. The complex has a Boat House Maritime Museum, a Fog Signal Area History Museum, a large gift shop, a 30-seat theater, a research/genealogy library, and the Lighthouse Museum with tower tours.

GWINN

Forsyth Township Historical Society Museum

Location: 186 W. Flint St., Gwinn, MI 49841 **Contact Info:** (906) 346-5413 • rpwills@yahoo.com **Hours:** Call for current hours. **Admission:** Free. **Accessibility:** Street parking. Not wheelchair accessible.

Site Info: The museum showcases the history of the township's small mining and railroad villages from 1860s as well as the history of K.I. Sawyer Air Force Base. There's a special emphasis on the unique "model town" of Gwinn, built in 1908 by Cleveland-Cliffs Iron Company President William Gwinn Mather. The museum is located above Forsyth Township Hall.

HANCOCK

Quincy Mine Hoist Association, Inc.

 **Location:** 49750 US Highway 41, Hancock, MI 49930 **Contact Info:** (906) 482-3101 • glenda@quincymine. com • www.quincymine.com **Hours:** End of Apr-end of May: Fri-Sun 9:30 a.m.-5 p.m. Daily early Jun to mid-Oct. **Admission:** Surface: $12/adult, $11/ senior, $5/youth. Full Tour: $20/adult, $19/senior, $10/youth. **Accessibility:** On-site parking. Partially wheelchair accessible. Guided tours. Museum store.

 Site Info: Although tour options vary, all tours include a museum visit, video tour of the No. 2 Shaft-Rock House, and a guided tour of the Nordberg steam-powered hoist engine—which is the largest one in the world—and the building that houses it. The museum has mineralogical exhibits and items such as a 17-ton copper boulder from Lake Superior.

HERMANSVILLE

IXL Historical Museum

Location: W5561 River St., Hermansville, MI 49847 **Contact Info:** (906) 498-2181 • wgdaniels@hughes.net • www.ixlmuseum.com **Hours:** Jun-Aug: Thu-Sun 12:30-4 p.m. **Admission:** Free. Donations accepted. **Accessibility:** Free on-site parking. Partially wheelchair accessible, outer buildings only. Tour guide available. Museum store.

U.P.

Site Info: The IXL Historical Museum consists of the original 1881 to 1882 office building of the Wisconsin Land and Lumber Company and IXL Flooring Company of Hermansville. The main building contains four floors of lumber and hardwood flooring artifacts as well as estate furnishings. Surrounding the main office building is a complex of outer buildings: the original Hermansville Produce Warehouse, the IXL Carriage House, a company house, a train depot, and a caboose.

HOUGHTON

Carnegie Museum of the Keweenaw

Location: 105 Huron St., Houghton, MI 49931 **Contact Info:** (906) 482-7140 • history@cityofhoughton.com • www.carnegiekeweenaw.org **Hours:** Tue, Thu 12-5 p.m.; Sat 12-4 p.m. **Admission:** Free. **Accessibility:** Free on-site and street parking. Self-guided.

Site Info: Opened in 2007, the Carnegie Museum of the Keweenaw is a reuse of Houghton's Carnegie Library, circa 1910. The museum features changing interactive exhibits on the main floor that uncover the region's cultural and natural history.

HULBERT

LODGING IN HULBERT

Tahquamenon Hotel

Location: 10429 S. Maple St., Hulbert, MI 49748 **Contact Info:** (906) 876-2388 • grantinhulbert@yahoo.com • www.facebook.com/tahquamenonhotelhulbert **Property Info:** Hotel/Inn. Open year-round. Privately owned; no public tours; pre-booking required. Free on-site parking. Food available on-site. **Price:** $40-$75.

Site Info: The hotel was originally built in 1919 as a bunkhouse and company store for the Parrish Wooden Bowl Factory. Visitors can enjoy outdoor recreation and several interesting attractions, including the Toonerville Trolley and Riverboat Tour to Tahquamenon Falls, the Crisp Point Lighthouse, and fishing on the east branch of the Tahquamenon River. Surrounded by the Hiawatha National Forest and the Lake Superior State Forest, there are hundreds of acres of public land for hiking, ATVing, and snowmobiling.

IRON MOUNTAIN

Cornish Pumping Engine & Mining Museum

Location: 300 Kent St., Iron Mountain, MI 49801 **Contact Info:** (906) 774-4276 • mrh-museum@sbcglobal.net • www.menomineemuseum.com **Hours:** Jun-Aug: Mon-Sat 9 a.m.-5 p.m., Sun 12-4 p.m.; Sep: Mon-Sat 10 a.m.-4 p.m., Sun 12-4 p.m.; Call for Oct hours. **Admission:** $5/adult, $4.50/senior, $3/

student, children 9 and under free. **Accessibility:** Free on-site and street parking. Wheelchair accessible. Self-guided. Museum store.

 Site Info: The Cornish Pumping Engine & Mining Museum features the largest steam-driven pumping engine ever built in the United States. Additionally, the museum also features an extensive collection of rare equipment used to mine iron ore in the region including tuggers, ore cars, drilling equipment, a dynamite car, and much more.

Menominee Range Historical Museum

 **Location:** 300 E. Ludington St., Iron Mountain, MI 49801 **Contact Info:** (906) 774-4276 • mrh-museum@sbcglobal.net • www.menomineemuseum.com **Hours:** May-Aug: Tue-Fri 11 a.m.-3 p.m. **Admission:** $5/adult, $4.50/senior, $3/student, children under 10 free. **Accessibility:** Free on-site parking. Not wheelchair accessible. Self-guided. Museum store.

 Site Info: Housed in the former Carnegie Public Library, the Menominee Range Historical Museum features more than 100 exhibits representing life on the Menominee Iron Range between the nineteenth and twentieth centuries. Exhibits include a country store, a birch-bark canoe, a schoolroom, a Victorian kitchen and parlor, and various early-American artifacts.

World War II Glider and Military Museum

Location: 302 Kent St., Iron Mountain, MI 49801 **Contact Info:** (906) 774-4276 • mrh-museum@sbcglobal.net • www.menomineemuseum.com **Hours:** Jun-Aug: Mon-Sat 9 a.m.-5 p.m., Sun 12-4 p.m.; Sep: Mon-Sat 10 a.m.-4 p.m., Sun 12-4 p.m.; Call for Oct hours. **Admission:** $8/adult, $7/senior, $4/student, children 9 and under free. **Accessibility:** Free on-site and street parking. Wheelchair accessible. Self-guided.

 Site Info: The World War II Glider and Military Museum features one of only seven completely restored CG-4A gliders in existence, a "Heiserman" aircraft, and a 3/4-scale replica of a Piper Club aircraft. Also featured is a comprehensive collection of military uniforms ranging from the Civil War to the wars in Iraq and Afghanistan. Various other military artifacts are also featured.

IRON RIVER

Beechwood Hall

 **Location:** 178 Beechwood Store Road, Iron River, MI 49935 **Contact Info:** (906) 367-5652 • beechwoodhistoricalsociety@gmail.com • www.beechwoodhistoricalsociety.org **Hours:** Tue 8 a.m.-12 p.m. **Admission:** Free. **Accessibility:** Free

on-site parking. Wheelchair accessible. Tour guide available.

Site Info: The former Beechwood School Hall still maintains the features of a rural one-room schoolhouse. It houses temporary historical exhibits and a growing collection of art and photographs depicting life in rural Beechwood. A museum will open in the adjacent Bethany Church in the near future.

IRONWOOD

Historic Ironwood Depot

Location: 150 N. Lowell, Ironwood, MI 49938 **Contact Info:** (906) 932-0287 • ironwoodhistoricalsociety@gmail.com • www.ironwoodareahistoricalsociety.com **Hours:** May-Oct: Mon-Sat 12-4 p.m. **Admission:** Donations accepted. **Accessibility:** Free on-site parking. Wheelchair accessible. Tour guide available. Museum store.

Site Info: Headquartered in the Historic Ironwood Depot, which is on the National Historic Register, the Ironwood Area Historical Society maintains a small informational and gift shop, as well as exhibits focused on the mining and railroading past. Exhibits include mining history and its significance to the area, as well as a replica of an early general store as stocked in early days of Ironwood.

Ironwood Memorial Building

Location: 213 South Marquette St., Ironwood, MI 49938 **Contact Info:** (906) 932-0287 • ironwoodhistoricalsociety@gmail.com • www.ironwoodareahistoricalsociety.com **Hours:** Mon-Fri 8 a.m.-5 p.m. **Admission:** Free. **Accessibility:** Free street parking. Wheelchair accessible. Self-guided.

Site Info: The Ironwood Memorial Building houses a self-guided tour of Ironwood history. See early mining and logging exhibits and artifacts. The structure was built in 1922 and is listed on the National Register of Historic Places. A brochure is available to help visitors explore two floors of displays and historic photo exhibits.

ISHPEMING

Cliffs Shaft Mining Museum

Location: 501 W. Euclid St., Ishpeming, MI 49849 **Contact Info:** (906) 485-1882 • steelworkers1@aol.com • www.gincc.org/business/index.php?q=&c=176 **Hours:** Tue-Sat 10 a.m.-4 p.m. **Admission:** $10/adult, $5/student (13-17), children 12 and under free. **Accessibility:** Free on-site parking. Partially wheelchair accessible. Tour guide available. Museum store.

Site Info: Cliffs Shaft Mining Museum is known for having a well-preserved example of underground iron mining in Michigan. Other items to explore include mining artifacts, railroad artifacts, Ishpeming rock, and more than 700 mineral specimens. In addition, visitors can view historical displays of miners and mines.

Ishpeming Area Historical Society Museum

Location: 308 Cleveland Avenue, Ishpeming, MI 49849 **Contact Info:** (906) 360-3970 • ishphistoricalsociety@gmail.com • www.facebook.com/Ishpeming-Area-Historical-Society-139057219479529 **Hours:** Nov-Apr: Mon 10 a.m.-4 p.m.; May-Oct: Mon, Thu 10 a.m.-4 p.m. Also by appointment. **Admission:** Donations accepted. **Accessibility:** Free street parking. Wheelchair accessible. Self-guided. Call for groups.

Site Info: Discover some of Ishpeming's legends—like John Voelker, Kelly Johnson, and Glenn Seaborg—at the Ishpeming Area Historical Society Museum. It features early city documents, "Anatomy of a Murder" and historic Gossard building artifacts, and military uniforms. Blue Notes Drum and Bugle Corp; Ishpeming High School yearbooks, city directories, 1911 Sanborn maps, and other materials are available for research. The museum also offers a treasure hunt for children.

LAKE LINDEN

Houghton County Historical Museum

Location: 53150 Highway M-26, Lake Linden, MI 49945 **Contact Info:** (906) 296-4121 • info@houghtonhistory.org • www.houghtonhistory.org **Hours:** Call ahead for current hours. **Admission:** Call for prices. **Accessibility:** Free on-site parking. Partially wheelchair accessible. Self-guided. Call for group tours.

Site Info: Exhibits include Lake Linden & Torch Lake Railroad as well as a steam locomotive and a three-foot-gauge track to support tours interpreting the former Calumet and Hecla Mill. Trains run during weekends. The site also houses a general history museum, a 1940s log cabin, a schoolhouse, and the former First Congressional Church of Lake Linden with a restored pipe organ.

L'ANSE

Shrine of the Snowshoe Priest

Location: Lambert Road, L'Anse, MI 49946 **Contact Info:** (906) 353-7779 • kvizina@up.net **Hours:** Open year-round, 24 hours a day. Access restricted by snow in winter. **Admission:** Donations accepted. **Accessibility:** On-site parking. Wheelchair accessible. Self-guided.

U.P.

Site Info: Located one mile west of L'Anse next to US-41 and rising six stories above the Red Rocks Bluff near L'Anse, this historic shrine commands a breathtaking view of Michigan's Keweenaw Bay. Holding a 7-foot-high cross and snowshoes 26 feet long, this handwrought brass sculpture of Bishop Baraga is 35-five feet tall and weighs four tons. It floats on a cloud of stainless steel supported by five laminated wooden beams, which represent Bishop Baraga's five major missions.

MACKINAC ISLAND

Fort Mackinac

Location: 7127 Huron Rd., Mackinac Island, MI 49757 **Contact Info:** (231) 436-4100 • mackinacparks@michigan. gov • www.mackinacparks.com **Hours:** Early-May to Mid-October: 9:30 a.m.-5:00 p.m. (Peak summer season hours extended to 6:00 p.m.)

Admission: $11.00/adult, $6.50/children (5-12). Fort Mackinac ticket allows entrance to downtown historic buildings during main season. **Accessibility:** Tour guide available.

Site Info: Fort Mackinac includes 14 original buildings, including one of Michigan's oldest buildings: the officers' stone quarters, which dates back to 1780. Through exhibits, visitors learn about life at the fort, including military training, battles, medical treatments, and family life.

Richard and Jane Manoogian Mackinac Art Museum

Location: 7070 Main Street, Mackinac Island, MI 49757 **Contact Info:** (231) 436-4100 • mackinacparks@michigan. gov • www.mackinacparks.com **Hours:** Early-May-mid-Oct: 10 a.m.-4:30 p.m. (Peak summer season hours extended to 6 p.m.). **Admission:** $5.50/adult, $4/youth (5-12). **Accessibility:** Free on-site parking. Partially wheelchair accessible. Tour guide available. Museum store.

Site Info: The Richard and Jane Manoogian Mackinac Art Museum showcases the historic artwork in Mackinac State Historic Parks' collection. Exhibits include views of Mackinac from the early 19th to late 20th century, historic maps, decorative and Native-American art, and Mackinac photography.

LODGING ON MACKINAC ISLAND

Grand Hotel

Location: 286 Grand Ave., Mackinac Island, MI 49757 **Contact Info:** (800) 334-7263 • jrogers@grandhotel.com • www.grandhotel.com **Property Info:** Hotel/Inn. Seasonal: May-Oct. Privately owned; no public tours; pre-booking

required. Wheelchair accessible. Gift shop. Food available on-site.
Price: Accommodations start at $304 per person, per night and children 11 and under stay and eat for free.

Site Info: Third-generation family-owned by the Musser family, this National Historic Landmark has been a place where time moves at the pace of horse-drawn carriages and bicycles since 1887. Experience the spectacular views from a rocking chair on the porch overlooking the Straits of Mackinac and traditions such as a five-course dinner, afternoon tea, and nightly dancing. Each guest room is uniquely decorated. Listed on the State and National Register of Historic Places.

Mission Point Resort

Location: 6633 Main St., Mackinac Island, MI 49757 **Contact Info:** (906) 847-3000 • info@missionpoint.com • www.missionpoint.com **Property Info:** Hotel/Inn. Seasonal: May-Oct. Privately owned; no public tours; pre-booking required. Wheelchair accessible. Food available on-site. Gift shop.

Site Info: Located on the sunrise side of Mackinac Island with 18-plus acres of lakefront property, Mission Point is a resort unlike any other. Enjoy a diverse set of amenities at this resort that was built circa 1954, including a full-service spa and movie theater. With more than 38,000 square feet of event space across the resort, the property is also ideal for weddings, meetings, and events of all sizes.

MANISTIQUE

Schoolcraft County Historical Park

Location: 100 Deer St., Manistique, MI 49854 **Contact Info:** (906) 341-5045 • m085@centurytel.net • www.schs.cityofmanistique.org **Hours:** Jun-Labor Day: Wed-Sat 1-4 p.m. **Admission:** $1/individual donation. **Accessibility:** Free on-site parking. Partially wheelchair accessible. Tour guide available.

Site Info: The museum is located in a small 1910 house. The log cabin has exhibits from the 1890s. The fire engine building contains a hook and ladder truck from the 1800s as well as a 1950 La France Firetruck. The Manistique Water Tower, circa 1923, is open and contains special exhibits.

U.P.

MARQUETTE

Beaumier U.P. Heritage Center

Location: Northern Michigan University/Gries Hall, 1401 Presque Isle Ave., Marquette, MI 49855 **Contact Info:** (906) 227-3212 • dtruckey@nmu.edu • www.nmu.edu/beaumier **Hours:** Sep-Apr: Mon-Wed 8 a.m.-5 p.m., Thu 8 a.m.-8 p.m., Sat 10 a.m.-3 p.m.; May-Aug: Mon-Fri 7:30 a.m.-4 p.m., Sat 10 a.m.-3 p.m. **Admission:** Free. **Accessibility:** Free on-site and street parking. Wheelchair accessible. Self-guided.

Site Info: The Beaumier U.P. Heritage Center maintains a schedule of rotating exhibits on the history and culture of the Upper Peninsula. There are also displays on the history of Northern Michigan University. Special collections include artifacts related to the lives of scientist Glenn Seaborg, author/judge John Voelker, politician Dominic J. Jacobetti, and businessman Sam Cohodas.

Marquette Regional History Center

Location: 145 W. Spring St., Marquette, MI 49855 **Contact Info:** (906) 226-3571 • mrhc@marquettehistory.org • www.marquettehistory.org **Hours:** Mon, Tue, Thu, Fri 10 a.m.-5 p.m., Wed 10 a.m.-8 p.m., Sat 10 a.m.-3 p.m. **Admission:** $7/adult, $6/senior, $3/student, $2/children 12 and under. **Accessibility:** Free on-site parking. Wheelchair accessible. Self-guided. Museum store.

Site Info: The Marquette Regional History Center is a jewel in the crown of the Queen City. It offers two exhibit galleries: a special exhibit gallery that has rotating exhibits throughout the year and a permanent exhibit gallery that highlights the natural, Native-American, industrial, transportation, and sports history of the region.

The Baraga House

Location: 615 S. Fourth St., Marquette, MI 49855 **Contact Info:** (906) 227-9117 • lmckeen@dioceseofmarquette.org • www.bishopbaraga.org **Hours:** Mon, Sat: 8 a.m.-1 p.m., Thu: 3-7 p.m. Also by appointment. **Admission:** Free. **Accessibility:** Free on-site parking. Wheelchair accessible. Tours available by appointment. Museum store.

Site Info: Baraga House visitors will find 800 letters written by Frederic Baraga and more than 1,000 letters to him from various people, such as Henry Schoolcraft, Mary Penny, and Ramsey Cooks. There are also materials and artifacts relating to the life of Bishop Baraga, the Chippewa, the Ottawa, and the American Fur Company.

MENOMINEE

Heritage Museum and M.J. Anuta Research Center

Location: 904 11th Ave., Menominee, MI 49858 **Contact Info:** (906) 863-9000 • jcallow1@new.rr.com • www.menomineehistoricalsociety.org/history.htm **Hours:** Memorial Day-Labor Day: Mon-Sat 10 a.m.-4 p.m. **Admission:** Donations accepted.

Accessibility: Free on-site and street parking. Partially wheelchair accessible. Tour guide available; call ahead to schedule a group tour.

Site Info: Located in a former church, the Heritage Museum focuses on the area's early history. Artifacts relate to Native Americans, early settlers, and the development of industry in the county from 1863. The Anuta Research Center is located in the rear of the museum.

MICHIGAMME

Michigamme Museum

Location: 110 Main St., Michigamme, MI 49861 **Contact Info:** (906) 323-9016 • michigammetownship@gmail.com • www.michigammetownship.com/michigamme-museum **Hours:** Memorial Day-Labor Day: 12-5 p.m. **Admission:** Donations accepted.

Accessibility: Free street parking. Wheelchair accessible. Tour guide available.

Site Info: Exhibits at the Michigamme Museum include logging, mining, "Anatomy of a Murder," a log house, and a 1900 American LaFrance Steam Fire Engine.

MUNISING

Alger County Historical Society's Heritage Center

Location: 1496 Washington Street, Munising, MI 49862 **Contact Info:** (906) 387-4308 • algerchs@jamadots.com • www.algerhistoricalsociety.org **Hours:** Mon-Thu 1-4:30 p.m., Fri 2:30-8 p.m., Sat 9 a.m.-5 p.m. **Admission:** Donations accepted.

Accessibility: On-site parking. Wheelchair accessible.

Site Info: In 1993, the Alger County Historical Society opened its heritage center in the former Washington Grade School. Exhibits cover history of historic Grand Island and the Grand Island

Recreation Area, Munising Woodenware Company, barn-building, homemaking, Native Americans, and sauna. There is also a fur trader's cabin and blacksmith shop on-site.

NAUBINWAY

Top of the Lake Snowmobile Museum

Location: W11660 US-2, Naubinway, MI 49762 **Contact Info:** (906) 477-6298 • info@snowmobilemuseum.com • www.snowmobilemuseum.com **Hours:** Open daily 9 a.m.-5 p.m. **Admission:** $5/adult, children 16 and under free. **Accessibility:** Free on-site parking. Wheelchair accessible. Museum store.

Site Info: "Where the history of snowmobiling comes to life." The museum instantly transforms visitors back in time to the era of snowmobiling when it first began, to the era of the sport machine when there were more than 200 manufacturers, and also to the racing era. Visitors will see snowmobile memorabilia and its history; dealer signs hanging from the ceiling; and helmets, suits, and gloves that "grandpa" wore. There are 130-plue machines on display.

NEGAUNEE

Michigan Iron Industry Museum

Location: 73 Forge Rd., Negaunee, MI 49866 **Contact Info:** (906) 475-7857 • webspinners@michigan.gov • www.michigan.gov/ironindustrymuseum **Hours:** Jun-Sep: Daily 9:30 a.m.-4:30 p.m.; May-Oct: Daily 9:30 a.m.-4 p.m.; Apr-Nov: Mon-Fri 9:30 a.m.-4 p.m. Call for winter hours. **Admission:** Free. Donations accepted. **Accessibility:** Free on-site parking. Wheelchair accessible. Self-guided. Museum store.

Site Info: In the forest ravines of the Marquette Iron Range, the Michigan Iron Industry Museum overlooks the Carp River and the site of the first iron forge in the Lake Superior region. Museum exhibits, audiovisual programs, and outdoor interpretive trails depict the large-scale capital and human investment that made Michigan an industrial leader. The museum serves as trailhead #7 along the 48-mile Iron Ore Heritage Trail. The museum is part of the Michigan Historical Center.

NEWBERRY

Luce County Historical Museum

Location: 411 W. Harrie St., Newberry, MI 49868 **Contact**

Info: (906) 293-8417 • www.exploringthenorth.com/newberry/histmuseum.html **Hours:** Jun-Labor Day: Wed-Fri 1-4 p.m. Also by appointment. **Admission:** Donations accepted. **Accessibility:** Free parking. Wheelchair accessible. Tour guide available.

Site Info: The Luce County Historical Museum is located in the former sheriff's residence and jail, circa 1894. The brownstone Queen Anne-style residence with an attached jail features the original kitchen, dining room, parlor, and bedrooms with related artifacts. Public areas contain the men's and women's jail cells, the sheriff's office, and an 1890 judge's bench with a witness stand and jury chairs.

Tahquamenon Logging Museum

Location: 9651 N M-123, Newberry, MI 49868 **Contact Info:** (906) 293-3700 • www.tahquamenonloggingmuseum.org **Hours:** Memorial Day-Sep 30: daily 10 a.m.-5 p.m. **Admission:** $5/adult, $2/children (6-12), children 5 and under free. Veterans and members of the Recreation Passport Perks receive 10 percent off admission. **Accessibility:** Free on-site parking. Wheelchair accessible. Tour guide available. Museum store.

Site Info: The Tahquamenon Logging Museum provides information and artifacts depicting the early logging days. Attractions include an authentic log cook shack, the original Camp Germfask CCC building, a bronze CCC statue, Port Huron steam engine #6854, the original Williams Family log home, the original one-room Pratt Schoolhouse, a Goldthorpe logging truck, and a nature trail. A campground with electric and water is also available.

PAINESDALE

Champion #4 Shafthouse

Location: 42631 Shafthouse Road, Painesdale, MI 49955 **Contact Info:** (9060 231-5542 • painesdalemineshaft@yahoo.com • www.painesdalemineshaft.com **Hours:** By appointment. **Admission:** Free. **Accessibility:** Free street parking. Partially wheelchair accessible. Self-guided.

Site Info: Painesdale Mine Shaft, Inc., offers tours of the Champion #4 Shafthouse, hoist house, and mining captain's office. Copper Range Mining Company records, family histories, mining history of Painesdale, photos, and tour maps of Painesdale are also available.

PARADISE

Great Lakes Shipwreck Museum

Location: 18335 N. Whitefish Point Rd., Paradise, MI 49768 **Contact Info:** (906) 635-1742 • glshs@shipwreckmuseum.com • www.shipwreckmuseum.com **Hours:** May-Oct: Daily 10 a.m.-6 p.m. Business office Mon-Fri 8 a.m.-5 p.m. **Admission:** $13/adult, $9/child, $40/family, children 5 and under are free. **Accessibility:** Free parking. Wheelchair accessible. Self-guided. Group tours for 20 or more, call in advance.

Site Info: Visitors to the Great Lakes Shipwreck Museum at Whitefish Point will experience numerous shipwreck exhibits, including a permanent exhibit dedicated to the 1975 wreck of the Edmund Fitzgerald. The Fitzgerald's bell has been made a part of this exhibit and a memorial to her 29-man crew. A restored lighthouse keeper's quarters, a USCG rescue station surfboat house, and a 1920s U.S. Navy radio station, now a video theater, all feature historical interpreters and a variety of thoughtful exhibits.

PHOENIX

Central Mine Village

Location: 5 miles northeast of Phoenix, US-41 and Central-Gratiot Lake Roads intersection, Phoenix, MI 49918 **Contact Info:** (906) 289-4990 • vjamison@pasty.com • www.keweenawhistory.org **Hours:** Mid-Jun-early Oct. **Admission:** Free. Donations accepted.

Site Info: In 1996, the Keweenaw County Historical Society acquired the old Central Mine and Village site, including several of the miners' homes and buildings. Some of the residences are being restored. The visitors center includes exhibits about the mine, miners' families, homes, schools, and churches. Two hiking trails provide views of several house foundations, a glimpse at the site of the schoolhouse, and a view of the valley from the top of the upper rock pile.

Phoenix Church & Museum

Location: Junction of US-41 and MI-26, Phoenix, MI 49950 **Contact Info:** (906) 289-4990 • vjamison@pasty.com • www.keweenawhistory.org **Hours:** Mid-May-early Oct. **Admission:** Free. Donations accepted.

Site Info: The Keweenaw County Historical Society has completed extensive repair and restoration work to the church since it took over the property in 1985. Artifacts in the church have come from many different Catholic churches in the area. Visitors can see how the church appeared when it was first built in 1858 to serve the Catholic residents of nearby mining communities. The final service was held in the church in 1957.

PICKFORD

Pickford Historical Museum

Location: 175 E. Main St., Pickford, MI 49774 **Contact Info:** (906) 647-1372 • kdschmitigal@centurylink.net • www.pickfordmuseum.org **Hours:** Jun-Aug: Mon-Sat 10 a.m.-3 p.m.; Aug-Oct: Fri-Sat 10 a.m.-3 p.m. **Admission:** Donations accepted.

Accessibility: Free street parking. Wheelchair accessible. Self-guided. Museum store.

Site Info: A National Register of Historic Places site, the museum constantly changes the exhibits while showcasing life in the area since 1877. Included in the collection are exhibits dealing with logging, farming, music, churches, schools, outdoor sports, military, and more. Guests are invited to peruse the large genealogy section and the children's interactive hands-on area.

ROCKLAND

Rockland Township Historical Museum

Location: 40 National Ave., Rockland, MI 49960 **Contact Info:** (906) 886-2821 **Hours:** Memorial Day-Sep: Daily 11:30 a.m.-4:30 p.m. Also by appointment. **Admission:** Free. **Accessibility:** Wheelchair accessible. Museum store.

Site Info: The Rockland Township Historical Museum is dedicated to the history of Rockland Township's people, copper mines, and businesses, along with the first telephone system in the state of Michigan. Home settings include kitchen, dining room, parlor, and bedroom. Mining, farming, school, and military displays are also available.

SAULT STE. MARIE

Chippewa County Historical Society History Center

Location: 115 Ashmun St., Sault Ste. Marie, MI 49783 **Contact Info:** (906) 635-7082 • cchs@sault.com • www.cchsmi.com **Hours:** May-Dec: Mon-Fri 1-4 p.m. **Admission:** Donations accepted. **Accessibility:** Free on-site and street parking. Partially wheelchair accessible. Self-guided. Museum store.

Site Info: The Chippewa County Historical Society is located in the 1889 building that originally housed the "Sault Ste. Marie News," owned by Chase S. Osborn, the only governor to come from the Upper Peninsula. Attractions include an American cafe, railroads, Chase Osborn, Native Americans, and telephone displays.

U.P.

Museum Ship Valley Camp

Location: 501 E. Water St., Sault Ste. Marie, MI 49783
Contact Info: (906) 632-3658 • admin@saulthistoricsites.com •
www.saulthistoricsites.com **Hours:** Mid-May-late-Jun: Mon-Sat
10 a.m.-5 p.m., Sun 11 a.m.-5 p.m.; Late Jun-Labor Day: Mon-
Sat 9 a.m.-6 p.m., Sun 10 a.m.-5 p.m.; Labor Day-Oct: Mon-Sat
10 a.m-5 p.m., Sun 11 a.m.-5 p.m. **Admission:** $13.50/adult,
$7/children (5-17). **Accessibility:** Free on-site parking. Partially
wheelchair accessible. Tour guide available.

Site Info: This 550-foot bulk carrier was built in
1917, sailed until 1966, and was converted into a
maritime museum in 1968. Visitors view all parts
of the Valley Camp to see how a 29-person crew
lived and worked. The cargo hold has displays of
artifacts, paintings, shipwreck items, models, and exhibits related
to maritime history.

Ojibwe Learning Center and Library

Location: 523 Ashmun St., Sault Ste.
Marie, MI 49783 **Contact Info:** (906)
635-6050 • cstonge@saulttribe.net •
www.saulttribe.com **Hours:** Mon-Fri 8
a.m.-5 p.m. **Admission:** Free.
Accessibility: Free street parking.
Street parking available for a fee.
Wheelchair accessible. Self-guided.

Site Info: The Sault Ste. Marie Tribe of Chippewa
Indians operates a small library that has mainly
Native-American subject resources and displays
museum items that are authentic Native-
American-made pieces. The library also provides
Anishinaabemowin language classes in the library two days per
week. The Ojibwe Learning Center and Library is committed to
the preservation and protection of Anishinaabe culture,
traditions, and language.

Tower of History

Location: 326 East Portage Street, Sault Ste. Marie, MI 49783
Contact Info: (906) 632-3658 • admin@saulthistoricsites.com •
www.saulthistoricsites.com **Hours:** Mid-May-late-Jun: Mon-Sat
10 a.m.-5 p.m., Sun 11 a.m.-5 p.m.; Late Jun-Labor Day: Mon-
Sat 9 a.m.-6 p.m., Sun 10 a.m.-5 p.m.; Labor Day-Oct: Mon-Sat
10 a.m-5 p.m., Sun 11 a.m.-5 p.m. **Admission:** $7/adult, $3.50/
children (5-17). **Accessibility:** On-site and street parking.
Wheelchair accessible.

Site Info: In addition to the story of the early
missionaries, this 210-foot tower includes local and
Native-American history, exhibits, and a video
presentation. The upper level features a 360-degree
view of the Sault Locks and the surrounding area.

Water Street Historic Block

Location: 405 East Water Street, Sault Ste. Marie, MI 49783
Contact Info: (906) 632-3658 • admin@saulthistoricsites.com •

www.saulthistoricsites.com/water-street-historic-bloc **Hours:** Jun-Sep: 12-5 p.m. **Admission:** Donations accepted. **Accessibility:** Street parking. Wheelchair accessible. Tour guide available.

 Site Info: Visitors can explore the 1793 home of early fur trader John Johnston; the Henry Rowe Schoolcraft Office, the first Native-American agent in the United States; and the Kemp Industrial Museum, a museum of local industries in the former Kemp Coal Company office. These buildings are available through a cooperative effort between the Chippewa County Historical Society, Sault Historic Sites, and the city of Sault Ste. Marie.

SOUTH RANGE

Copper Range Historical Museum

 **Location:** 44 Trimountain Ave., South Range, MI 49963 **Contact Info:** (906) 482-6125 • johnandjeanp@chartermi.net • www.pasty.com/crhm **Hours:** Jun & Sep: Tue-Fri 12-3 p.m.; Jul & Aug: Mon-Fri 12-3 p.m. **Admission:** $1 donation, CRHS members and children 12 and under free. **Accessibility:** Free street parking. Not wheelchair accessible. Tour guide available.

 Site Info: The Copper Range Historical Society's museum features copper samples, a "cooper" and his tools, stereoscopes, photos of area mining-related sites, and mining memorabilia. Other items on display include photos of local music hall-of-fame winners, items from the logging era, artifacts from the Copper Range Railroad and Bus Line, a loom, items from Copper Range Mining Company Doctor Hillmer's office, the former Busch Brewery, South Range Baseball team memorabilia, and an old Victrola record player.

SOUTH REPUBLIC

Pascoe House Museum

 **Location:** 183 Cedar St., South Republic, MI 49879 **Contact Info:** (906) 376-2258 • lavantl@aol.com • www.republicmichigan.com/historical-society **Hours:** Memorial Day-Labor Day: Sat-Sun 1-3 p.m. Also by appointment. **Admission:** Donations accepted. **Accessibility:** Free street parking. Partially wheelchair accessible, downstairs only. Call for tours.

 Site Info: The Pascoe House, an 1800s house operated by the Republic Area Historical Society, displays changing exhibits that uncover the occupational, economic, social, and cultural history of the city of Republic.

U.P.

ST. HELENA ISLAND
St. Helena Island Light Station
Location: SE Corner, St. Helena Island, MI **Contact Info:**
(231) 436-5580 • info@gllka.com • www.gllka.com **Hours:**
Visitors with their own boat can visit anytime. **Admission:**
Donations requested. **Accessibility:** Boat access only. Not
wheelchair accessible. Tour guides available mid-Jun to mid-Aug.

 Site Info: St. Helena Island Light Station is a fully
restored light station with live-in volunteer keeper
program. The Great Lakes Lighthouse Keepers
Association offers workshops in residence at St.
Helena Island Light Station in Northern
Michigan's Straits of Mackinac.

ST. IGNACE
Father Marquette National Memorial
 **Location:** 720 Church St., St. Ignace,
MI 49781 **Contact Info:** (906)
643-8620 • burnettw@michigan.gov •
www.michigan.gov/marquettememorial
Hours: May-Nov: Daily 8 a.m.-10
p.m. **Admission:** Free. **Accessibility:**
Free on-site parking. Wheelchair
accessible. Self-guided.

 Site Info: The Father Marquette National
Memorial tells the story of the French missionary-
explorer who founded Sault Ste. Marie in 1668 and
St. Ignace in 1671 and explored the Mississippi
River with Louis Jolliet in 1673. In addition to the
memorial itself, the site features a short interpretive trail and views
of the Mackinac Bridge. Picnic facilities and modern restrooms
provide travelers with a spot to rest.

Fort de Buade Museum
Location: 334 N. State St., Saint Ignace, MI 49781 **Contact
Info:** (906) 643-6627 • fortdebuademuseum@gmail.com •
www.michilimackinachistoricalsociety.com **Hours:** Tue-
Thu, Sat 10 a.m.-6 p.m., Fri 10 a.m.-9 p.m. **Admission:**
Donations accepted. **Accessibility:** Street parking available for
a fee. Partially wheelchair accessible. Tour guides available by
appointment for a fee.

 Site Info: The Fort de Buade Museum advances
the understanding of the area's cultural heritage
through research, collection, interpretation, and
exhibition of objects of historical significance. On
display are the Newberry Tablets. Other exhibits
include a Native-American collection, which includes stone tools,
everyday objects, baskets, ceremonial artifacts, headdresses, and
regalia; dioramas depicting a voyageur with trade goods; a trading
post; and a representation of Chief Satigo's lodge.

U.P.

VULCAN

Iron Mountain Iron Mine

Location: W4852 US-2, Vulcan, MI 49892 **Contact Info:** (906) 563-8077 • ironmine@uplogon.com • www. ironmountainironmine.com **Hours:** Memorial Day-Oct 15: Daily 9 a.m.-5 p.m. **Admission:** $14/adult, $10/ children (6-12), children 5 and under are free. **Accessibility:** Free on-site parking. Wheelchair accessible. Guided tours included in admission. Museum store.

Site Info: Located nine miles east of Iron Mountain, the Iron Mountain Iron Mine keeps alive the heritage of the area's underground mining ancestors. The site provides guided underground mine tours by a train of the former east Vulcan mine, which produced more than 22 million tons of iron ore from 1870 to 1945.

WAKEFIELD

Wakefield Museum

Location: 306 Sunday Lake Street, Wakefield, MI 49968 **Contact Info:** (906) 224-1045 • djferson@att.net **Hours:** Jun-Sep: Tue-Sat 1-4 p.m. **Admission:** Donations accepted. **Accessibility:** Free street parking. Not wheelchair accessible. Tour guide available.

Site Info: With artifacts dating from 1884, the Wakefield Historical Society's museum features displays that include a mining room; a general store; a classroom; a doctor's office; "Esther's closet," an exhibit of period women's clothing; and an area dedicated to the military service of the city's residents.

Index

1838 Old Village Cemetery—87
1845 Eaton County Courthouse—50
1885 Lyon One-Room Schoolhouse—86
40 Mile Point Lighthouse—157
Ada—9
Adrian—79
Albert L. Lorenzo Cultural Center—91
Albion—45
Alden B. Dow Home & Studio—68
Alfred P. Sloan Museum—101
Alger County Historical Society's Heritage Center—183
Algoma Township Historical Society Displays—36
Algonac—79
Algonac-Clay Historical Society Museum—79
Allegan Old Jail Museum—9
Allegan—9
Allen House Museum—84
Allendale Historical Museum Complex—10
Allendale—10
Allouez Township—163
Almira Historical Museum—149
Alpena—137
Alpine Township Historical Museum—15
Alto—10
Ann Arbor—80
Antique Toy & Firetruck Museum—46
Applewood Estate—101
Arab American National Museum—92
Argus Museum—83
Atlanta—137
Augusta—45
Averill Historical Museum of Ada—9
Bad Axe—84
Baldwin—10
Bammert Blacksmith Shop—170
Bancroft-Stranahan Museum—125

Banner Oak School—130
Baraga County Historical Museum—163
Baraga House—182
Baraga—163
Barnes Street Bed & Breakfast—67
Barryton Area Historical Museum—46
Barryton—46
Battle Creek—46
Bay City—46
Bay View Historical Museum—156
Bay View Inn—156
Beaumier U.P. Heritage Center—182
Beaver Island Marine Museum—138
Beaver Island—138
Beechwood Hall—177
Belding Museum at the Historic Belrockton—48
Belding—48
Belleville Area Museum—84
Belleville—84
Bellevue Area Historical Museum—48
Bellevue—48
Belmont—11
Bentley Historical Library—80
Benton Harbor—11
Bergelin House Museum—48
Berkley Historical Museum—85
Berkley—85
Berrien Springs—11
Bessemer Area Heritage Center—163
Bessemer—163
Besser Museum for Northeast Michigan—137
Big Bay—164
Big Rapids—48
Big Sable Point Lighthouse—27
Birmingham Museum—85
Birmingham—85
Blair Historical Farm—60
Bloomfield Hills—86
Bloomingdale Depot Museum—12
Bloomingdale—12
Bohannon Schoolhouse—69

Bois Blanc Island Historical
    Society Museum—165
Bois Blanc Island—165
Bonine House—40
Bonnie's Parsonage 1908 Bed
    & Breakfast—25
Bottle House Museum—149
Bowne Township Historical
    Museum and Bowne
    Center School—10
Bradley House—157
Breckenridge—49
Brethren Heritage
    Museum—138
Brethren—138
Bridgeport Historic Village &
    Museum—49
Bridgeport—49
Brighton—86
Brimley—164
Brooklyn—87
Brush Creek Mill—148
Buick Automotive Gallery and
    Research Center—102
Byron Area Historical
    Museum—12
Byron Center—12
Caledonia Historical
    Museum—12
Caledonia—12
Calumet Visitor Center—165
Calumet—165
Cannon Township Historical
    Museum—13
Cannonsburg—13
Canton Historical
    Museum—87
Canton—87
Capac Community Historical
    Museum—88
Capac—88
Capitol Hill School—65
Cappon House & Settler's
    House—23
Caretaker House at Cranberry
    Lake Historic District
    Park—118
Carnegie Center
    Museum—121
Carnegie Museum of the
    Keweenaw—176
Cartier Mansion—29
Caseville—88
Caspian—166
Cass City—88
Cass County Pioneer Log
    Cabin Museum—13

Cassopolis—13
Castle Farms—139
Castle Museum of Saginaw
    County History—72
Catholic Heritage
    Museum—72
Cedar Springs—14
Cedarville—167
Ceder Springs Museum—14
Cell Block 7—62
Central Lake—139
Central Mine Village—186
Chadwick-Munger House—21
Chaldean Cultural
    Center—134
Chamberlins Ole Forest
    Inn—169
Champion #4
    Shafthouse—185
Chapin Home—34
Charles and Hattie Olsen
    Farmhouse—154
Charles H. Wright Museum
    of African American
    History—94
Charles W. Liken
    Museum—126
Charlevoix Railroad
    Depot—139
Charlevoix South Pier
    Lighthouse—140
Charlevoix—139
Charlotte—50
Chassell Heritage Center—167
Chassell—167
Cheboygan River Front Range
    Lighthouse—140
Cheboygan—140
Chelsea Area Historical
    Museum—89
Chelsea—89
Chesaning Historical
    Museum—50
Chesaning—50
Chesterfield Historical
    Village—89
Chesterfield—89
Chippewa County Historical
    Society History
    Center—187
Chippewa Nature Center—68
City of Brighton Arts, Culture,
    and History (CoBACH)
    Center—86
Civilian Conservation Corps
    Museum—158

Clare County Museum
　　Complex—51
Clare—51
Clarke Historical Library—69
Clarkston Heritage
　　Museum—90
Clarkston—90
Clarksville—14
Clawson Historical
　　Museum—90
Clawson—90
Clay Township—90
Cliffs Shaft Mining
　　Museum—178
Clinton Township—91
Clinton—91
Clyde Craig Blacksmith Shop
　　Museum—125
Coe House Museum—58
Coldwater—51
Coloma—14
Colon—15
Colonial
　　Michilimackinac—151
Columbiaville Historical
　　Society Museum—91
Columbiaville—91
Commandant's Quarters—93
Community Historical
　　Museum of Colon—15
Community Pride & Heritage
　　Museum—112
Comstock Park—15
Concord—52
Conklin Reed Organ and
　　History Museum—59
Coopersville Area Historical
　　Society Museum—15
Coopersville—15
Copemish—141
Copper Country Firefighters
　　History Museum—166
Copper Harbor
　　Lighthouse—168
Copper Harbor—168
Copper Range Historical
　　Museum—189
Cornish Pumping Engine &
　　Mining Museum—176
Covington Township Historical
　　Museum—168
Covington—168
Cranberry Lake Farm Historic
　　District—118
Cranbrook Archives—86

Crawford County Historical
　　Society & Museum
　　Complex—145
Crocker House Museum—116
Crystal Falls—169
Crystal Township Historical
　　Society Building—52
Crystal—52
Curtis Historical Society
　　Museum—169
Curtis—169
Davis Brothers Farm Shop
　　Museum—110
Davison Area Historical
　　Museum—92
Davison—92
Dearborn—92
Dekker-Huis and Zeeland
　　Museum—43
Delta County Historical Society
　　& Museum—172
Depot Museum of
　　Transportation—18
Depot Museum—61
DeTour Passage Historical
　　Museum—170
DeTour Reef Light—170
DeTour Village—170
Detroit Historical
　　Museum—95
Detroit Observatory—80
Detroit—94
Dewey School Museum—58
Dewitt School House—38
Dexter Area Historical
　　Museum—97
Dexter—97
Doan Midland County History
　　Center—68
Dossin Great Lakes
　　Museum—95
Dougherty Old Mission
　　House—159
Douglas—16
Dowagiac Area History
　　Museum—16
Dowagiac—16
Drake School—148
Drummond Island—170
Dryden Historical Depot—98
Dryden—98
Dundee—98
Durand—52
Durant-Dort Carriage
　　Company
　　Headquarters—102

Eagle Harbor Lighthouse
    Complex—171
Eagle Harbor—170
Eagle River Museum—171
Eagle River—171
East Grand Rapids History
    Room—17
East Grand Rapids—17
East Jordan City Hall—141
East Jordan Portside Art
    & Historical Society
    Museum—142
East Jordan—141
East Lansing—53
East Tawas—142
Eastpointe—98
Eaton County's Museum at
    Courthouse Square—50
Eaton Rapids—54
Edmore—54
Edsel & Eleanor Ford
    House—106
Edward Lowe Information and
    Legacy Center—13
Edwardsburg Area Historical
    Museum—17
Edwardsburg—17
Elk Rapids Area Historical
    Museum—143
Elk Rapids—143
Ella Sharp Museum of Art &
    History—63
Empire Area Museum
    Complex—144
Empire—144
Engadine Historical
    Museum—172
Engadine—172
Escanaba—172
Essexville—55
Evart Public Library
    Museum—55
Evart—55
Eyaawing Museum and
    Cultural Center—155
Fairview—144
Farmall Acres Farm
    Museum—14
Farmington Hills—99
Farmington—99
Farwell Area Historical
    Museum—55
Farwell—55
Father Marquette National
    Memorial—190
Fayette Historic
    Townsite—172

Ferndale Historical
    Museum—100
Ferndale—100
Fife Lake Historical
    Museum—144
Fife Lake—144
Fighting Falcon Military
    Museum—59
Fire Barn Museum—31
Flat River Historical
    Museum—59
Flat Rock—101
Flint—101
Flushing Area Museum and
    Cultural Center—103
Flushing—103
Ford Piquette Avenue
    Plant—96
Ford Rouge Factory Tour—93
Ford-MacNichol Home—135
Forsyth Township Historical
    Society Museum—175
Fort Custer Museum—45
Fort de Buade Museum—190
Fort Gratiot Light
    Station—122
Fort Mackinac—180
Fort St. Joseph Museum—35
Fort Wilkins Historic
    Complex—168
Fowlerville—55
Frankenmuth Historical
    Museum—56
Frankenmuth—56
Frankfort—145
Friend-Hack House
    Museum—113
Friends of Point Betsie
    Lighthouse, Inc.—145
Gagetown—104
Galesburg Historical
    Museum—18
Galesburg—18
GAR Memorial Hall and
    Museum—54
Garden City—104
Garden Peninsula Historical
    Society Museum—173
Garden—172
Gardner House Museum—45
Gerald R. Ford Presidential
    Library—80
Gerald R. Ford Presidential
    Museum—19
Gilmore Car Museum—23
Gitche Gumee Agate and
    History Museum—173

Gladwin County Historical Museum—57
Gladwin County Historical Village—57
Gladwin—57
Goodells—104
Gordon Hall—97
Governor Warner Mansion—99
Grand Blanc Heritage Museum—105
Grand Blanc—105
Grand Haven—18
Grand Hotel—180
Grand Ledge Area Historical Society Museum—57
Grand Ledge—57
Grand Marais—173
Grand Pacific House Museum—117
Grand Rapids Public Museum—19
Grand Rapids—19
Grand Traverse Lighthouse Museum—154
Grandville Museum—20
Grandville—20
Grass Lake—58
Gratiot County Historical Museum—62
Grayling—145
Great Lakes Maritime Heritage Center—137
Great Lakes Shipwreck Museum—186
Green Oak Township Historical Society Heritage Museum—127
Greenbush School—147
Greenbush—147
Greenfield Village—93
Greenmead Historical Park—111
Greenville—21, 59
Grice House Museum—108
Gross Ile North Channel Light—105
Grosse Ile—105
Grosse Pointe Farms—106
Grosse Pointe Shores—106
Gulliver—174
Gwinn—175
Hackley & Hume Historic Site—31
Hadley Hill Museum—107
Hadley House Museum—109
Hadley—107

Halfway Schoolhouse—98
Hamburg Township Historical Museum—107
Hamburg—107
Hammond House Museum—76
Hamtramck Historical Museum—108
Hamtramck—108
Hancock—175
Hanover—59
Hanover-Horton Heritage Park—60
Harbor Beach—108
Harbor Springs History Museum—147
Harbor Springs—147
Harbour House Museum—169
Harrisville—148
Harsens Island St. Clair Flats Historical Society Museum—108
Harsens Island—108
Harsha House Museum—140
Hart Historic District—22
Hart—21
Hartford—22
Hartman School—37
Hartwick Pines Logging Museum—146
Hastings—22
Heddon Museum—17
Henry and Margaret Hoffman Annex—157
Henry Ford Museum—94
Heritage & History Center of Farmington Hills—100
Heritage Hill Historic District—19
Heritage House Farm Museum—55
Heritage Museum and M.J. Anuta Research Center—183
Heritage Park—69
Heritage Room at the Richard L. Root Branch Library—26
Heritage Village—151
Hermansville—175
Hickory Corners—23
Hillman—148
Hillsdale—60
Hillside Homestead—158
Historic Adventist Village—46
Historic Charlton Park—22
Historic Fishtown—149

Historic Fort Wayne—96
Historic Ironwood Depot—178
Historic Michigan Theater—81
Historic Mill Creek Discovery Park—152
Historic Village at Goodells County Park—104
Historic Waterford Village—133
Historic White Pine Village—27
Historical Museum of Bay County—47
History Center at Courthouse Square—11
History Center of Traverse City—160
Holland Museum—24
Holland—23
Holly—109
Holocaust Memorial Center—99
Homer—60
Honolulu House Museum—66
Honor—148
Hotel Frankfort—145
Houghton County Historical Museum—179
Houghton—176
Howell—61
Hubbardston Area Historical Society Museum—61
Hubbardston—61
Hudson—109
Hulbert—176
Huron Lightship—122
Hyser Rivers Museum—11
Icebreaker Mackinaw Maritime Museum, Inc.—152
Imlay City Historical Museum—110
Imlay City—110
Inn at Ludington—29
Ionia—62
Iosco County Historical Society & Museum—142
Iron County Historical Museum—166
Iron Mountain Iron Mine—191
Iron Mountain—176
Iron River—177
Ironwood Memorial Building—178
Ironwood—178

Ishpeming Area Historical Society Museum—179
Ishpeming—178
Ithaca—62
IXL Historical Museum—175
Jackson—62
Jarvis Stone School Local Historic District—120
Jenison Museum—25
Jenison—25
John C. Blanchard House—62
John C. Pahl Historical Village—9
John Schneider Blacksmith Shop—112
Joint Archives of Holland—24
Kalamazoo Valley Museum—26
Kalamazoo—26
Kaleva—149
Kempf House Museum—81
Kentwood—26
Kitchen School—92
Kneeland-Sachs Museum—150
Knowles Historical Museum—139
Knowlton's Ice Museum of North America—122
L'Anse—179
Lager Mill Brewing Museum—56
Lake Ann—149
Lake Linden—179
Lakeshore Museum Center—31
Lakeview Area Museum—63
Lakeview—63
Lansing—63
Lapeer County Heritage Museum—110
Lapeer—110
Leelanau Historical Society Museum—150
Leland—149
Lenawee County Historical Museum—79
Leon Buyse Memorial Library and Museum—125
Les Cheneaux Historical Museum—167
Les Cheneaux Maritime Museum—167
Lewis House Bed & Breakfast—42
Lewiston—150

Liberty Hyde Bailey Museum—37
Library of Michigan—63
Lightkeeper's House Museum—173
Lincoln Park Historical Museum—111
Lincoln Park—111
Lincoln Train Depot—151
Lincoln—151
Linden Mills Historical Society & Museum—111
Linden—111
Little Red School House—51
Little Sable Point Lighthouse—29
Livingston Centre Historical Village—55
Livonia—111
Log Cabin and Detroit Urban Railway Wait Station and Annex—90
Longway Planetarium—102
Loren Andrus Octagon House—132
Lovells Historical Museums—146
Lowell Area Historical Museum—27
Lowell—27
Luce County Historical Museum—184
Ludington North Breakwater Light—28
Ludington—27
Maccabees Hall Museum—88
Mackinac Island—180
Mackinaw City—151
Madden Hall Historical Area—79
Mancelona Historical Society Museum—153
Mancelona—153
Manchester—112
Manistee—153
Manistique—181
Mann House—52
Manton Area Historical Museum—153
Manton—153
Maple City—154
Marilla Museum & Pioneer Place—141
Marine City—112
Maritime Heritage Alliance—160
Maritime Museum—80

Marlette—112
Marquette Regional History Center—182
Marquette—182
Marshall Historical Museum at the G.A.R. Hall—66
Marshall—65
Mary Jackson's Childhood Home—113
Mary Myers Museum—71
Mary Thompson Farmhouse—127
Mary's City of David—11
Mason Historical Museum—67
Mason—67
McFadden-Ross House & Gardner House—94
McKenzie One-Room School—137
Mears—29
Mecosta County Historical Society & Museum—49
Mecosta County Old Jail—49
Memory Lane Village—101
Menominee Range Historical Museum—177
Menominee—183
Meridian Historical Village—71
Michigamme Museum—183
Michigamme—183
Michigan Central Railroad Depot Museum & Customs House—106
Michigan Flywheelers Museum—37
Michigan Historical Center—64
Michigan Iron Industry Museum—184
Michigan Legacy Art Park—159
Michigan Maritime Museum—38
Michigan Masonic Museum & Library—20
Michigan Military Technical & Historical Society Museum—99
Michigan Railroad History Museum—52
Michigan State Capitol—64
Michigan State University Archives & Historical Collection—53
Michigan State University Museum—53

Michigan Transit Museum—117
Michigan Women's Historical Center & Hall of Fame—64
Michigan's Heritage Park—41
Michigan's Military & Space Heroes Museum—56
Midland—68
Midwest Miniatures Museum—23
Milan—113
Milford Historical Museum—114
Milford—113
Mill Race Historical Village—117
Millersburg Area Historical Society Museum—154
Millersburg—154
Millington—114
Millington-Arbela Historical Society & Museum—114
Mission Point Resort—181
Monroe County Museum—114
Monroe—114
Montague Museum—30
Montague—30
Montcalm Heritage Village—74
Montrose Historical & Telephone Pioneer Museum—116
Montrose—116
Mormon Print Shop Museum—138
Motown Museum—96
Mount Clemens—116
Mount Pleasant—69
Munising—183
Museum of Cultural and Natural History—70
Museum on Main Street—81
Museum Ship Valley Camp—188
Music House Museum—161
Muskegon Heritage Museum—32
Muskegon Museum of Art—32
Muskegon—31
National House Inn—67
Naubinway—184
Naval Air Station GI Museum—106
Negaunee—184

New Baltimore—117
New Boston—117
New Groningen Schoolhouse—43
Newaygo County Museum and Heritage Center—34
Newaygo—34
Newberry—184
Niles—34
No. 10 Schoolhouse—21
North Berrien Historical Society and Museum—14
Northport—154
Northville—117
Northwest Maritime Museum—153
Norwegian Lutheran Church—166
Norwood Schoolhouse—140
Oakfield Museum—21
Oakland—118
Oceana Historical Park & Museum—30
Ogemaw County Historical Museum—160
Ojibwe Learning Center and Library—188
Okemos—71
Old Fence Rider Historical Center—54
Old Fire Barn—113
Old Mackinac Point Lighthouse—152
Old Mill Museum—119
Old Mill Museum—98
Old Post Office Museum—174
Old School House History Center and Garden—16
Old Sebewaing Township Hall—127
Old Town Hall—30
Olive Township Historical Society & Museum—24
Omena—155
Onekama—155
Orchard Lake Museum—134
Ortonville—119
Otisville Area Museum—119
Otisville—119
Otsego Area Historical Museum—35
Otsego—35
Ovid—71
Owosso—71
Packard Proving Grounds Historic Site—127

Paine-Gillam-Scott
 Museum—75
Painesdale—185
Palmer House Inn Bed &
 Breakfast—45
Paradise—186
Pascoe House Museum—189
Pentwater Historical
 Museum—35
Pentwater—35
Perry Hotel—156
Peshawbestown—155
Petoskey—156
Phoenix Church &
 Museum—186
Phoenix—186
Pickford Historical
 Museum—187
Pickford—187
Pickle Barrel House
 Museum—174
Pigeon Historical Depot
 Museum—119
Pigeon—119
Pine Forest Historical
 Museum—54
Pine Grove Museum/Governor
 Moses Wisner Home—
 120
Pink School—67
Pioneer Log Cabin Village—84
Plank Road Museum—49
Plymouth Historical
 Museum—120
Plymouth—120
Point Iroquois
 Lighthouse—164
Pointe aux Barques Lighthouse
 Museum—121
Pontiac—120
Port Austin History
 Center—121
Port Austin—121
Port City Victorian Inn Bed
 and Breakfast—33
Port Hope—121
Port Huron & Detroit Railroad
 Historical Society
 Museum—123
Port Huron—121
Port of Ludington Maritime
 Museum—28
Port Sanilac—123
Portage Point Inn &
 Marina—155
Priscilla U. Byrns Heritage
 Center—38

Provencal-Weir House—106
Putnam-Cloud Tower
 House—155
Quincy Mine Hoist
 Association, Inc.—175
R.E. Olds Transportation
 Museum—65
Rathbone School—171
Raven Hill Discovery
 Center—142
Remus Area Historical
 Museum—72
Remus—72
Rentschler Farm
 Museum—126
Richard and Jane Manoogian
 Mackinac Art
 Museum—180
Richmond Historic
 Village—124
Richmond—124
River Raisin National
 Battlefield Park—115
River Raisin Territorial
 Park—115
Riverside Inn—150
Rives Junction—124
Rochester Hills Museum at Van
 Hoosen Farm—124
Rochester Hills—124
Rockford Area Historical
 Museum—36
Rockford—36
Rockland Township Historical
 Museum—187
Rockland—187
Rogers City—157
Romeo Arts & Archives
 Center—125
Romeo—125
Roscommon Area Historical
 Society Museum—158
Roscommon—158
Roseville—125
Royal Oak Historical Society
 Museum—126
Royal Oak—126
S.S. Badger—28
Saginaw Railway Museum—73
Saginaw—72
Saline—126
Samuel Adams Historical
 Museum—117
Sand Hills Lighthouse
 Inn—163
Sanford Centennial
 Museum—73

Sanford—73
Sanilac County Historic Village and Museum—123
Sanilac Petroglyphs Historic Site—88
Saranac Depot—73
Saranac—73
Saugatuck—36
Saugatuck-Douglas Museum—36
Sault Ste. Marie—187
Schoolcraft County Historical Park—181
Scolnik House of the Depression Era—32
Sebewaing—126
Selinsky-Green Farmhouse Museum—129
Seul Choix Point Lighthouse—174
Shelby Township—127
Shepherd Powerhouse Museum—74
Shepherd—74
Sheridan Stewart Museum—124
Shiawassee County Historical Society Archives and Museum—71
Shrine of the Pines—10
Shrine of the Snowshoe Priest—179
Sidney—74
Silver Beach Carousel—39
Sindecuse Museum of Dentistry—82
South Haven—37
South Lyon—127
South Range—189
South Republic—189
Southern Michigan Railroad Museum—91
Southfield—127
Spies Heritage Hall—141
Spring Lake—38
St. Charles Area Museum—75
St. Charles—75
St. Clair County Farm Museum—105
St. Clair Historical Museum and Research Center—128
St. Clair Shores—129
St. Helena Island Light Station—190
St. Helena Island—190
St. Ignace—190

St. John the Baptist Catholic Church Complex—61
St. Johns—75
St. Joseph—38
St. Louis Historic Park—75
St. Louis—75
St.Clair—128
Stahls Automotive Museum—89
Steiner Logging and Pioneer Museum—144
Sterling Heights—129
Stockton Center at Spring Grove—103
Stone Chalet Bed & Breakfast Inn and Event Center—83
Straight Farmhouse—104
Sturgeon Point Lighthouse and Old Bailey School—148
Sturgis Museum—39
Sturgis—39
Sue Silliman House & Blacksmith Shop—39
Sunfield—76
Sutherland-Wilson Farm Museum—82
Suttons Bay—158
Tahquamenon Hotel—176
Tahquamenon Logging Museum—185
Tawas Point Lighthouse—143
Taylor Historical Museum—129
Taylor—129
Tecumseh Historical Museum—130
Tecumseh—130
Tekonsha Historical Museum—76
Tekonsha—76
Temperance—130
Temple Emanuel of Grand Rapids Archives—20
Ten Cent Barn—131
Thomas Edison Depot Museum—123
Thompson House Museum—109
Thompsonville—159
Three Rivers—39
Thumb Agricultural Museum—104
Thunder Bay Inn & Restaurant—164
Top of the Lake Snowmobile Museum—184

Tower of History—188
Town Hall Museum—128
Train Depot Museum—112
Traverse City—159
Trenton Historical
    Museum—130
Trenton—130
Tri-Cities Historical
    Museum—18
Trombley-Centre House—47
Troy Historic Village—131
Troy—131
Turner-Dodge House—65
U.S. Land Office Museum—41
Ubly—131
Union City—76
USS Edson DD-946—47
USS LST 393 Veterans
    Museum—33
USS Silversides Submarine
    Museum—33
Van Buren County Historical
    Museum—22
Vandalia—40
Vassar—131
Vicksburg Historic Village—40
Vicksburg—40
Vietnam Veterans Memorial
    and Museum—115
Voyager's Inn Bed &
    Breakfast—40
Vulcan—191
Wahbememe Memorial
    Park—41
Wakefield Museum—191
Wakefield—191
Wales Township Hall—132
Wales—132
Walker Tavern Historic
    Complex—87
Walters Gasoline and
    Interurban Railroad
    Museum—66
Warren Historical &
    Geneological Society
    Historical Gallery—132
Warren—132
Washington Historical Society
    Museum—133
Washington—132
Water Street Historic
    Block—188
Waterford—133
Waterloo Farm Museum—58
Watrousville Museum—131
Wayne Historical
    Museum—133

Wayne—133
Webster Corners—97
Welch Museum—76
Wellington Farm Park—146
West Bloomfield—134
West Branch—160
Whaley Historic House
    Museum—103
Wheels of History Train
    Museum—165
White Pigeon—41
White River Light Station and
    Museum—42
White Swan Inn Bed &
    Breakfast—42
Whitehall—41
Will Carleton Poorhouse—60
William L. Clements
    Library—83
William Upton House—129
Williamsburg—161
Williamston Depot
    Museum—77
Williamston—77
Windmill Island Gardens—25
Wing House Museum—51
Wixom—134
Wixom-Wire Museum—134
World War II Glider and
    Military Museum—177
Wyandotte—135
Yankee Air Museum—85
Ypsilanti Automotive Heritage
    Museum—135
Ypsilanti Historical
    Society, Museum, &
    Archives—135
Ypsilanti—135
Zeeland—43
Ziibiwing Center of Anishinabe
    Culture & Lifeways—70

About HSM

Keeping Michigan's history at everyone's fingertips.

As the state's official historical society and Michigan's oldest cultural institution, the Historical Society of Michigan (HSM) has told the stories of the Great Lakes State since 1828, when we were founded by territorial governor Lewis Cass and explorer Henry Schoolcraft. Those efforts to keep Michigan's history at everyone's fingertips are accomplished through HSM's five mission areas: publications, educational programs, conferences, awards and recognition, and assistance for local organizations.

As a 501(c)(3) nonprofit educational organization that receives no state funding, we rely on our members and subscribers to support our programming, which includes the publication of this guide. You can learn more about HSM, its work to keep Michigan history-related activities going and growing, and its mission points through the following pages and by visiting hsmichigan.org.

To become a member or subscribe...
hsmichigan.org • (800) 692-1828

Publications

Award-winning *Michigan History* magazine provides history enthusiasts with exciting stories about Michigan.

Published quarterly, *Chronicle* magazine is the membership publication of the Historical Society of Michigan.

Written for third and fourth graders, *Michigan History for Kids* magazine goes beyond the textbooks, exploring the history and heritage of all Michigan's peoples.

The *Historic Michigan Travel Guide* is a pocket-size publication that lists more than 600 historical "tourist attractions" in Michigan.

The *Michigan History Directory* keeps Michigan's history at everyone's fingertips by listing more than 1,000 historical locations statewide.

hsmichigan.org

Educational Programs

Michigan History Day, an affiliate of National History Day, is a yearlong educational program that encourages students to explore local, state, national, and world history.

Michigan History Day

Written for third and fourth graders, *Michigan History for Kids* magazine goes beyond the textbooks, exploring the history and heritage of all Michigan's peoples.

History Skills Workshops offer a continued learning experience for local historical organizations and history enthusiasts.

The "Michigan History Educator" section of *Chronicle* magazine provides historical organizations and classrooms with ideas for bringing history to life for communities and youth.

Conferences

hsmichigan.org

Michigan in Perspective: The Local History Conference is held annually in the Wayne/Oakland/Macomb tri-county area and is open to anyone interested in state or regional history.

The Annual Meeting and State History Conference moves to a different location every year to highlight that region's history. The State History Awards are also presented during this conference.

The Upper Peninsula History Conference pays particular attention to Upper Peninsula history topics and themes. The Upper Peninsula History Awards are also presented at this conference.

211

Awards and Recognition

HISTORICAL SOCIETY OF MICHIGAN · 1828

hsmichigan.org

The Centennial Farm Program recognizes farms that have remained in the same family for 100 years or more.

MICHIGAN CENTENNIAL FARM

OWNED BY THE SAME FAMILY OVER ONE HUNDRED YEARS

THE HISTORICAL SOCIETY OF MICHIGAN

Sponsored By: Your Power Co.

MICHIGAN CENTENNIAL BUSINESS

THIS PLAQUE IS ISSUED BY THE HISTORICAL SOCIETY OF MICHIGAN IN RECOGNITION OF

ABC COMPANY, INC.

FOUNDED IN 1903 FOR MORE THAN 100 YEARS OF CONTINUOUS OPERATION IN SERVICE TO THE PEOPLE OF MICHIGAN AND FOR CONTRIBUTING TO THE ECONOMIC GROWTH AND VITALITY OF OUR STATE.

The Michigan Milestone Awards celebrate the 50th, 100th, or 150th anniversary of an organization, a business, or a municipality.

100 years MILESTONE

HSMICHIGAN.ORG

State History Awards are presented annually to individuals and organizations that have made outstanding contributions to the appreciation and understanding of Michigan history.

The Upper Peninsula History Awards annually honor an individual and a historical organization that have worked to preserve and promote the history of Michigan's Upper Peninsula.

Assistance for Local Historical Organizations

The Historical Society of Michigan partners with media groups and statewide PR organizations and uses social media to help promote local organizations and their missions.

Print and online calendars list events and special exhibits, and sections of *Michigan History, Chronicle,* and a digital newsletter are devoted to sharing news items from organizations.

The *Michigan History Directory* and *Historic Michigan Travel Guide* have detailed listings that include contact and location specifics and information on exhibits, collections, visitor accessibility, and more.

History Skills Workshops and other educational materials give local historical organizations skills and ideas that they can use at their museums or sites.